Mrs. Mai...

Mrs. Mark Twain

The Life of
Olivia Langdon Clemens,
1845–1904

MARTIN NAPARSTECK
with MICHELLE CARDULLA

McFarland & Company, Inc., Publishers
Jefferson, North Carolina

ALSO OF INTEREST

Sex and Manifest Destiny: The Urge That Drove Americans Westward, by Martin Naparsteck (McFarland, 2012)

Richard Yates Up Close: The Writer and His Works, by Martin Naparsteck (McFarland, 2012)

ISBN 978-0-7864-7261-1
softcover : acid free paper ∞

LIBRARY OF CONGRESS CATALOGUING DATA ARE AVAILABLE

BRITISH LIBRARY CATALOGUING DATA ARE AVAILABLE

On the cover: Olivia Langdon Clemens as a young wife, c. 1872 (Mark Twain House, Hartford, Connecticut); artwork Light at the End of Day (iStockphoto/Thinkstock)

Manufactured in the United States of America

McFarland & Company, Inc., Publishers
Box 611, Jefferson, North Carolina 28640
www.mcfarlandpub.com

For all the women who,
like Livy Langdon Clemens,
do not receive the
recognition they deserve

Acknowledgments

Thank you to Barbara Snedecor, director, Center for Mark Twain Studies, Elmira College, for permitting a useful and informative stay at Quarry Farm; to Tim Morgan, Quarry Farm caretaker, for hosting that stay and answering so many questions; to the helpful staff in the Grosvenor Room of the Buffalo and Erie County Public Library, which houses the original manuscript of *The Adventures of Huckleberry Finn*; to the friendly staff at the Chemung Valley History Museum in Elmira; and to all those, far too numerous to list, who offered words of encouragement.

Table of Contents

Preface

Olivia Langdon grew up in the richest family in Elmira, New York, the daughter of loving, compassionate parents, with a devoted older sister and an admiring younger brother, and she married a man just beginning to become the best-known, and probably the best-loved, American in the world. Her husband loved her and was always kind to her. As a child and as an adult her needs were met by capable and considerate servants. She was intelligent and gifted. She loved literature and met and befriended many of the major literary luminaries of her era. She traveled around the world and lived a decade in European countries; also in a mansion she helped to design in Connecticut. Everyone who knew her and left a written record of what she was like praised her. They praised her beauty, her intelligence, her charm, her basic decency.

Yet there can be no doubt that her life was a tragic one. She was bedridden for years at a time with various ailments. Her son, born prematurely, lived only a year and a half. Her oldest daughter died at 24. Her youngest daughter was epileptic. Her husband invested foolishly and drove the family into bankruptcy.

This is the story of her life. It is not a biography of her husband, Mark Twain. Anyone looking for a biography of Twain will be disappointed. Most of what happened in his life is omitted from this volume. That is a deliberate choice. He was and remains such an imposing figure, he could only obscure the woman he cared about so much. Yet it's obvious that no one today would have any interest in Olivia Langdon if she had married, say, a wealthy Elmira businessman. Or if she had never married. Our interest in her today derives entirely from her marriage to the man whose towering fame still threatens to make impossible any attempt to see her as an individual. The only book previously written about her was actually a dual biography about both her and her husband.[1] Much of the rest that has been written about her has been in passing references, often in scholarly articles, suggesting or stating directly that she had an inhibiting effect on her husband's writing. And much of what has been written emanates from the character named Mrs. Clemens that Mr. Clemens created, just as he created the character named Mark Twain. He created her in conversations with his friends, in letters to friends and in-laws and relatives, and in his autobiography. And that character is — and this is always presented in obvious jest — someone to be feared. Why, an editor, wanted to know, did you take out the profanity? Because Mrs. Clemens made me. Why did you do that? Because Mrs. Clemens told me to. Why did you not do this? Because Mrs. Clemens forbade me. Mrs. Clemens, Livy, indeed was able to get him to behave himself. When she heard him once on the telephone yelling at the person on the other end, she put her finger to her lips and he immediately became calm. When he yelled at the maid, Katy Leary, Livy defended her and calmed him. And when his bad investments drove the family into bankruptcy, Livy never scolded him but insisted that they pay back every penny. And they did.

But we approached this biography with a prejudice, one useful, we think, to any biographer. We assumed there was an Olivia Langdon Clemens who was an individual, who, while forever in the public mind a part of her husband's identity, was also a person with her own thoughts and attitudes and personality. And we found her.

Katy Leary, their maid for 30 years, told us who she was. William Dean Howells, their friend, told us about her. So did two of their daughters, Susy and Clara. And so, too, did Mark Twain. He told us in those same letters and that same autobiography in which he presented Mrs. Clemens to the world as another woman, a woman named Livy, a woman who called him "Youth," who shared some traits with Mrs. Clemens but who had a distinct, recognizable personality.

We sensed who she was when we walked around Elmira, around the same neighborhoods she grew up in. During a stay at Quarry Farm, where she spent 20 summers. By going page by page —1,400 pages in all — through the digital copy of the original manuscript of *The Adventures of Huckleberry Finn* at the Buffalo and Erie County Public Library, looking for evidence that she may have influenced the writing of her husband's most famous book. By standing next to the bed she slept in as a child, now on display on the Elmira College campus. By searching through hundreds of books and articles about her husband, about Victorian America, about the places she had lived and visited, about the diseases that afflicted her and her children.

She was a Victorian woman. Or, more precisely, an American woman of the American Victorian age. She was, by the standards of her time, very well educated, having been sent to an expensive private school and being among the first few hundred women in the country to attend college. Her wealthy father, in fact, helped to fund the college. He and his wife were leaders in Elmira's anti-slavery movement and in believing females had as much right to be educated as men. And they hired private tutors for her. But beyond that, much of her education came from the extensive reading she did, as did everyone in the Langdon family. And from meeting the cultural and political leaders who visited her parents' home, including Frederick Douglass, William Lloyd Garrison, and Gerrit Smith, perhaps the three most important leaders of the abolitionist movement. After she was married she continued to meet famous people, including Ulysses S. Grant, Charles Dickens, Lewis Carroll, Ivan Turgenev, and kings and queens. She became so accustomed to meeting important and famous people that she was surprised when she missed an opportunity to have an audience with Pope Leo XIII.

Her husband spent far less time in classrooms than she did and never had a private tutor. He did not meet anyone famous until his mid-twenties, yet he read so widely, traveled so extensively, and was such a careful observer of humanity that he may have been as well educated as anyone in his era. And he undertook to continue Livy's education, often advising her on what books to read carefully, which ones to merely scan, and which to avoid totally. Sometimes he told her not to read certain books, including works by Shakespeare, because they were not fit for a proper young lady.

Sometimes she heeded his guidance, sometimes she did not, just as sometimes he obeyed her instructions and often did not. Tellingly, about both of them, he did not omit things from *Huckleberry Finn* that she wanted omitted but approached the writing of the *Personal Recollections of Joan of Arc* with attitudes she fostered.

We don't know what she wanted omitted from *Huck Finn*, only that Susy said he kept some material out because of her objections and his comment that his daughter was mistaken, he did not remove anything because of Livy. That's what we searched for in the *Huck Finn* manuscript, some indication, perhaps by a note she wrote in the margins, that this or that needed to be changed. We found no such proof. We did find dozens of pages with tiny — about an eighth of an inch each — folded corners, always in the lower left. Susy told us to look for those folds. She said that's how her mother told her father there was something on a page that needed attention. But most of those pages had no marginalia on them, and most of the marginalia that was there seemed to be clearly made by Mark Twain, not Livy. And what was not Mark Twain's was not clearly Livy's. We can't be certain who made some of it. But nothing, nothing, on the manuscript provided even a hint that Mark Twain censored his writing because of his wife's objections.

Joan of Arc is different. It's not the manuscript. It's the style, so unlike anything else Twain wrote, so openly flowery, so transparently arty, so non–Mark Twain. Someone must have influenced him, and Livy is the one candidate who had the most access to the writer. A small point worth considering, perhaps, about the Joan of Arc book is its title: *Personal Recollections of Joan of Arc*. Another book associated with Twain has a similar-sounding title, the *Personal Memoirs of Ulysses S. Grant*. It was the first book published by Webster & Co. that was not written by Twain. Webster was a company created by Twain to publish his own books. Sue Crane, Livy's older sister, wrote a letter to her little sister saying that Grant had much in common with their father, Jervis Langdon. Livy admired her father, and she admired Grant, and she admired Joan of Arc. Tributes seldom make good literature, and that is the basic fault, as some critics have noted, with *Joan of Arc*. Admiration always gets in the way of honesty.

If Livy did not influence Twain's best book and did influence his worst, are we to conclude that when she did have influence on his writing it was always bad? That's not the conclusion we reached. What we concluded is more complicated. *Huckleberry Finn* was written when they were wealthy and healthy. *Joan of Arc* was written when they were struggling with bankruptcy and when Livy's health was clearly deteriorating. He knew that he, not her, was responsible for their financial problems. And her illness, clearly leading to her early death, pained him. The faults of *Joan of Arc* are the faults of a man under immense pressure, of a man in love with his wife.

There is an irregularity to her life, as there is to everyone's. Her influence on his writing was inconsistent, as was his willingness to allow her to influence him. This irregularity was reflected in her admiration of the picturesque, an architectural and decorating style popular in post–Civil War America. That style is very notable in Quarry Farm, the home on East Hill, just outside of Elmira, that Livy's father left to Livy's older, adopted sister, Susan. Unlike, say, the Greek and Roman models so admired by Thomas Jefferson, Quarry Farm seems to have a gable poking out here, an extension tacked on there, one chimney aligned here, the other seemingly out of place on the other side. The interior of the home is similar. The room Livy and Mark slept in has a sloping ceiling on one side, a corner where you don't expect one, a sense of non-uniformity that is very natural. When you look closely, you realize it's all designed, but that is an impression that comes from reflection, not initial reaction. It's much like one of Frederick Law Olmstead's principles in designing parks: the hand of man may be present, but it must not be visible. Both of the Langdon sisters, Sue Crane and Livy Clemens, admired the picturesque and read several books about the style.[2]

We've designed this book with a similar approach. Lives are lived chronologically, but that is seldom the most effective way to reveal patterns and influences and results of those lives. So we have arranged our seven chapters in chronological order, but within each we move around in a manner that has a purpose. We hope that purpose is hidden, by which we mean we hope the result is a feel for the life lived by Livy Clemens, not for the one we've written down. If you come away from this book liking or disliking Livy Clemens, admiring her, believing she was a good person or a bad person, reacting to her the way you react to anyone you meet and get to know well enough to feel confident about your judgments, then we have succeeded.

Introduction:
Olivia Langdon, Livy
and Mrs. Clemens

Olivia Langdon Clemens was, all the available evidence suggests, a good mother, a good wife, a good conversationalist. She was well read, widely traveled, generous to the poor, kindhearted to those she knew and loved and often to strangers. She was also frail, prone to illness, and lived a life filled with tragedy. All of that should make her interesting enough to write a book about, but the reality is, sadly, that few people would be interested in her as a subject for those reasons alone. The interest almost anyone is likely to have in this 19th-century woman is based entirely on whom she married. Mark Twain.

And that is unfair. She lived a life of her own, the majority of it in companionship with Twain but still as an individual. And every person has a right to be seen as an individual, not just as the companion of someone else. This book seeks to grant her that right.

She didn't even like the name Mark Twain. To her it conjured up a humorist, and she wanted her husband to be seen as a great American writer, not just a funny one. Nor did she like his given name, Samuel. Just didn't sound right to her. So she called him "Youth." He was ten years older than her, and the nickname could have been a way of narrowing the gap. But also it was a nickname she had for him; no one else used it. Once he became famous, which happened just about the time they married, his closest friends called him Mark. His children would call him Papa. Only she called him Youth. It was a way of individualizing herself.

We've arranged this book with an overriding chronological arc, but we've often digressed from that arc, put irregularities in it, to capture the ways lives are actually lived, with emotional connections between points past, current, and anticipated. It's the way Livy Clemens lived her life, the way we all live our lives.

Her father was an example of a peculiarly American type, too often portrayed as merely a cliché or stereotype, the self-made man. He was born into what was not quite poverty, worked himself up in the management of several different stores, purchased an interest in a timber business in Elmira, used the money he made there to invest in an anthracite mine, and when the Civil War started and anthracite, which produces more energy than other types of coal, was in demand became a wealthy man, the wealthiest man in Elmira. He and his wife, Olivia, were devout Congregationalists, active in the abolitionist movement, and avid readers. The sentiments that led them to be abolitionists also contributed to a broader social consciousness, one that embraced sympathy for the poor, better opportunities for women, and a general commitment to the improvement of their community.

They wanted children, and when they thought that one or the other was not able to produce one they adopted a little girl, Susan. Nine years later, Livy was born.

Livy was thus born into a home with anti-slavery, pro-equality, love-of-literature sentiments. Those sentiments would be instilled in her and stay with her the rest of her life. They meshed well with those of the man she would marry. The family she was born into believed in a benevolent God, one who watched over the world carefully and who rewarded those who did his bidding with eternal salvation. Although during their courtship and the early years of their marriage her future husband tried hard to adapt to her religious beliefs, his inborn skepticism about all institutions, including churches, would not permit him to sustain those views, and she found herself, as their marriage stretched from years into decades, moving closer and closer to his religious outlook. But when later in life his view of the world seemed filled with bitterness, she would not, or perhaps could not, make the full conversion to his near nihilism. And late in life, although she never stopped loving him, when he made it a habit of denouncing the damned human race she was happy for opportunities to spend time away from him. And while she never fully returned to the religious devoutness of her youth, as she approached death, like so many people, she sought solace in beliefs that once seemed indisputable to her.

Her love of literature, by contrast, did not ebb and flow in the years of marriage to a writer who, in his own lifetime, was recognized as one of America's greatest. Because of his fame she dined and chatted with Rudyard Kipling, Henry Wadsworth Longfellow, William Dean Howells, Lewis Carroll, Robert Browning, Bret Harte, Harriet Beecher Stowe, Ivan Turgenev, Anthony Trollope, and a list of others too long to enumerate. They visited her homes; she visited theirs. But she never became nearly as liberated when judging literature as she was when judging humanity. She did not like profanity in writing or in speech and often sought to censor her husband's use of any words stronger than *darn* and *gee whiz*. She was usually unsuccessful, but not always. Her best-known attempt to censor him, when she repeated almost word for word profanity he had uttered without realizing she could hear him, was so comical that even she laughed. Her voice was, as Twain said, so "absurdly weak and unsuited to the great language" of profanity that he promised, if he really sounded like that, to never swear again.[1] It was a promise made in jest, one he never intended to keep, one she never expected him to keep. Of more importance is the fact that great writers cannot create great writing unless they can overcome any inhibitions that block the truth from being told, and Livy's objections to her husband's profanity were indicative of an attitude that said propriety is more important than truth telling. To whatever extent she encouraged his inhibitions to flourish, his writing was damaged; to whatever extent he was able to overcome her objections, his writing flourished. The older she grew, the sicker she grew, the closer she approached death, the more he was willing, as an act of loving-kindness, to accede to her wishes in how and what he wrote. Which is why most of his best writing was done when she was younger and healthier.

Livy had met Frederick Douglass when she was a young girl. Douglass, an escaped slave and the best-known African American in the country, sometimes visited her parents' home in Elmira. She grew up in a household where slavery was considered the great evil of the day, where blacks were considered to be entitled to the same rights as whites, where the Civil War was seen as a moral crusade. Samuel Clemens grew up the son of a father who at one time owned a slave but who later said slavery was wrong. It's sometimes said that young Sam Clemens fought for the Confederate Army, but that is a distorted simplification of a complicated truth. He was 25 years old when Fort Sumter was fired upon and living in a slave state, Missouri. Some of his young male friends, sympathetic to the South, formed a militia with the idea that they would eventually join the Confederate Army. But Missouri was one of four slave states that did not secede (the others were Kentucky, Maryland and Delaware), and young Sam's commitment was far more to his friends than it was to any cause, noble or otherwise. In any case, the "militia" had weapons no more deadly than broomsticks, and whatever commitment or bravery they possessed evaporated when a rumor reached Hannibal that the Union Army was approaching. They fled into the hills.

Meanwhile, his older brother, Orion, editor of a newspaper that backed Lincoln for president, was rewarded with the political position of secretary

to the governor of the Territory of Nevada, and young Sam found it more pru-
dent to travel with his brother than to fight for a cause he just didn't care
about.[2] Young Sam Clemens, thus, was never truly a supporter of the Confederacy or of slavery. Yet as a young man he may have been a borderline racist
in that he both used the word *nigger* in his journalism and speech and thought
of blacks as intellectually inferior to whites. But Livy's influence changed that.
Her view that a black person should be treated as the equal of a white unless
proven unworthy of that equality became Twain's standard. When Livy tried
to fire their black servant, George Griffin, it was her husband who protected
the butler's job.[3] Not firing George Griffin may be the only time Mark Twain
made an important decision regarding servants, a power he otherwise always
left to Livy. And from the earliest days of his marriage to Livy, when he wrote
about slaves and ex-slaves, his writing shows sympathy, understanding, and,
often, admiration. The most likely explanation for this change is a new understanding of slavery and its legacy as a result of conversations with Livy.

The shared love of literature, the accommodations on religion, her
influence on his views of blacks, all this shaped their relationship. But nothing
shaped it, and nothing shaped her, as much as the seemingly endless string of
tragedies that afflicted their lives. Shortly after her wedding and setting up
home in a new, large house in Buffalo, a home that was a gift from her father,
a time that should have been the happiest in her life, the first tragedy struck.

Her father, to whom she was very close, was diagnosed with stomach
cancer. And he died within months.

A close friend of Livy's, Emma Nye, came to visit in Buffalo and contracted typhoid fever and died in the Clemenses' home.

Their son was born one month prematurely and was constantly sick, frequently coughing throughout the night, clearly never comfortable. At 19
months of age he died.

In two years, Livy's father died, a close friend visiting her died, her son
was born prematurely, suffered and died. Instead of a honeymoon period,
death, death, and death.

Then there was an extended period when their lives progressed smoothly.
Twain became more and more famous, becoming eventually the best-known
American in the world. He earned hundreds of thousands of dollars through
his writings, which, combined with her inheritance from her father, valued at
a quarter of a million dollars, made him and Livy very wealthy. They built a
mansion in Hartford, Connecticut, traveled throughout Europe, and clearly
enjoyed life. Livy gave birth to three daughters, Susy, Clara, and Jean, and they
all seemed happy and healthy. Even Livy's always frail health seemed at times
more a nuisance than a real handicap.

Then the pattern of tragedy returned. Twain was addicted to investments. Bad investments. He started a publishing company that made money for a while but then published one unsuccessful book after another. For example, an authorized biography of Pope Leo XIII, which Twain naively believed would be purchased by every Catholic in America. When it wasn't, the publishing company commenced a downward spiral. He invested and invested again in a typesetting machine, the Paige Compositor. And invested again. It had thousands and thousands of moving parts, but Twain was convinced it would make him a fabulously rich man. Livy didn't interfere with his investments, even though much of the money he invested was hers. And there were dozens of other investments, which Twain, like so many addicted gamblers, said involved only money he could afford to lose. What they lost was their fortune. They were forced into bankruptcy.

They went on a world lecture tour, Mark, Livy, and Clara, and he earned enough money to pay off their debts. Every penny, something Livy insisted upon. And when they completed the tour, expecting Susy and Jean, who had stayed in Elmira, to join them in England, where they planned to then live, they received word that Susy was sick. She was very sick: spinal meningitis. She died while Livy and Clara were on a ship sailing back home to take care of her.

Then Jean was diagnosed with epilepsy. And Livy's health became worse.

Their marriage was always filled with tenderness, but it was never more tender than in Livy's final years when doctors, first in New York and then in Florence, Italy, forbade Twain from spending more than a few minutes each day with his dying wife. He was just too excitable, they said, and she needed rest and quiet. The same prohibition applied to Jean, for the same reason. Only Clara, among family members, could spend extended periods with Livy. Katy Leary, their longtime and devoted maid, could see her, and so could hired nurses. So Youth had to find another method of communicating with her. His solution was to send little notes, loving notes, often written on scraps of paper, reporting the day's activities outside her bedroom. Two or three times a day he could enter the room to see her for five or ten minutes, and they would hug and kiss and say how much they loved each other. And his notes always, always, professed that same love.

When Susy, at age 13, started to write a biography of her father, her mother told her that the love letters he had sent to her over the years were "the loveliest love-letters that ever were written ... that Hawthorne's love-letters to Mrs. Hawthorne are far inferior." But Livy would not let Susy read them, saying she was too young.[4] Many of those letters have been collected and printed, as have many of the notes,[5] and most readers are likely to conclude that those final notes, while lacking the details and information and most of the loving teasing so frequent in the letters of their courtship, are, as pure love letters, more lovely. More tender, more heartfelt, more instilled with the gentle love that, as we age, replaces the passion of youth.

The final days of her life were heartbreaking. At times she had so much difficulty breathing she feared she would die of strangulation. When the end did arrive, however, it was mercifully peaceful, in Florence, Italy, where doctors had advised her to move believing the mild climate might help her. Death came on June 5, 1904.

The tragedies so common in her life, sadly, did not end with her death. Her death caused a nervous breakdown in Clara, and she needed to be admitted to a sanitarium. And on Christmas Eve, 1909, Jean, age 29, suffered an epileptic seizure while taking a bath and drowned in the bathtub. And Livy's only grandchild, Nina, Clara's daughter, became an alcoholic and drug addict and died a suicide in 1966. Livy and Mark have no living descendants.

Also sad is the fact that most of the time Livy is mentioned in scholarly articles about her husband it is in the context that she damaged his writing, that she censored it, or more accurately, that she successfully encouraged him to censor himself. But she deserves better than that simplistic analysis. She deserves, as we all do, to be seen as a complete person who had a range of influences, good and bad, on those whose lives she shared. She was, as those who knew her best recorded, an intelligent, caring, generous, loving mother, wife, and daughter. Person. That is whom we have tried to portray in this volume. Not just Olivia Langdon the daughter, or Mrs. Clemens the wife and mother, but Livy, the complete human being. Youth's Livy.

CHAPTER ONE

Ice

Eighteen thousand years ago, the last of the great ice ages, known as the Wisconsin Glacial Episode, extended just south of what is now the New York–Pennsylvania line. As the glaciers retreated over thousands of years they shaped the landscape, carving long, narrow chasms in the earth that would later fill with water to form the Finger Lakes and leaving accumulated debris of soil and rock that form today's moraines, or rolling hills, typical of upstate New York. The ice formed a bridge connecting Siberia with Alaska, allowing humans to migrate from Asia to North America and to spread across the continent, some of their descendants ending up, thousands of years later, in southern New York. The hills in and around Elmira, New York, and the earliest human residents of the area would not have existed except for ice.

In late 1861 or early 1862, Livy Langdon, a pretty 16-year-old girl from a wealthy family in Elmira, slipped on a patch of ice. The exact date isn't known, nor the exact location. Nor the exact nature of the fall. Did she hit her head? Or fall flat on her back? Or did she, perhaps, bounce, resulting in several different parts of her body making contact with the ground? What is known is that she spent the next two years of her life bedridden, unable to walk, and was made nauseous just by the act of sitting up. All that lasted until she was cured by a quack.[1] Maybe.

Livy was the lifelong nickname of Olivia Louise Langdon, who was born November 27, 1845, in a home in Elmira, New York, on the corner of Main and West Second (or West Third) streets. She had an older sister, Susan, who had been adopted by the Langdons nine years earlier. Jervis and Olivia Lewis Langdon (Livy was named for her mother) had believed that after four years of marriage they would not have any children. It wasn't until the 13th year of their marriage that Livy was born. Later, a son, Charles would be born, in 1849. Susan, Livy, and Charles, would remain close their entire lives. And all three would have close, loving relationships with their parents.[2]

The earliest known incident documented in Livy's life occurred in the home at Main and West Second (although it may, in fact, have been on Third Street). A letter written in 1908 from Livy's older sister, Sue, to Mark Twain says she, Sue, visited the old family home in Elmira where she lived during 1846 or 1847 on Third Street and was shown a "little window cut under eaves" at her request to let light into her attic bedroom. She wrote, "A large part of the joy of the small window was the light, a still larger joy was in the fact that I was allowed to take the baby Livy up to that room. Seat her on a chair on the inside, next to the window while I sat outside with a chair in front as a horse. In this way we took long journeys to Ithaca and other points of interest, while you and Huck Finn and others were having some of your fun. To have that dear little girl to myself, near that window was joy enough, making me very rich, she too was happy in the play." The same letter says that Livy was born in parlor of the Third Street house.[3]

Livy's father came from a family of successful men. One member, John Langdon, fought in the American Revolution, served as a delegate to the Continental Congress, was President Pro Tempore of the U.S. Senate while George Washington was president, and held the office of governor of New Hampshire four times (1785–1786, 1788–1789, 1805–1809, and 1810–1812). In 1812, when Vice President George Clinton died of a heart attack, President James Madison asked Langdon to fill the office, but he declined the offer. (The office remained unfilled for the rest of Madison's first term.)[4] Another ancestor, Samuel Langdon, served as president of Harvard University from 1774 to 1780.

Jervis Langdon was born in Vernon, about 15 miles east of Syracuse, New York, on January 9, 1809, the son of Andrew Langdon and Eunice King Langdon, both children of farmers. Andrew died when Jervis was three, but Eunice survived two more husbands and, in fact, Jervis. She died in 1873 at age 90. Jervis took a job in a country store when he was 16 years old and later moved about 60 miles southwest to work at a store in Ithaca. His employer, a Mr. Stevens, in 1827 put Jervis in charge of a second store he opened in nearby Enfield, just west of Ithaca, and later of a third store in Salina, just to the northwest of Syracuse. Over the next decade, Jervis moved back and forth, from one store to another, and in 1832 felt financially secure enough to marry Olivia Lewis, whose father was a farmer in Lenox, which is near Jervis's hometown of Vernon. He was 23 and she was one year younger. Their future looked happy.[5]

Then the national economy turned sour. America's first great depression hit the country and ruined thousands of lives. President Andrew Jackson's hostility to the Bank of the United States is often blamed for the panic. Jackson removed federal deposits from the bank, the bank stopped giving loans, credit all but disappeared in the country, and the economy sickened. Cotton prices dropped, land values plummeted, and nearly everyone suffered.[6] For Jervis Langdon, it meant finding a new profession. If people did have not money they did not shop in stores beyond purchasing minimum necessities. So, he became an agent for T.S. Williams in 1838, and later became his partner. They sold lumber, particularly pine. In 1845 he and Olivia moved from Ithaca to Elmira, where he started his own lumber firm, Andrus and Langdon. The new Chemung Canal connected what had been a rather remote community to Seneca Lake and, eventually, to the Erie Canal, making Elmira one of numerous canal towns that prospered because of one of America's first great public works projects. The firm did well enough to purchase parts of pine forests in Allegany County a few hundred miles to the west. That land had coal beneath it, and it was coal, more than managing stores or selling lumber, that would make Jervis Langdon the wealthiest man in Elmira.[7] Coal and the Civil War.

Elmira had been founded in 1792 as Newtown, the earliest white settlers being Revolutionary War veterans. In 1808 the name was changed to Elmira for reasons that are historically unclear, although a popular local legend says the name came from a mother who so frequently called in a high-pitched voice for her young daughter to come home that the daughter's name became synonymous with the area. Over the first half of the 19th century the city grew steadily from a few hundred to more than 10,000. By the end of the Civil War there were more than 12,000 residents, but it seemed larger, with a thriving downtown that provided retail and government services for thousands living beyond the city's limits.[8]

The Civil War was not the first war to help shape Elmira. Even before Elmira existed, war came to the area. In 1778, during the Revolution, British and Iroquois, mostly Seneca, attacked settlements at Cherry Valley in eastern New York and Wyoming Valley, just north of Wilkes-Barre, Pennsylvania, massacring hundreds of civilian and militiamen. Dozens of children were among the victims. The primary purpose of the attacks remains unclear, although it seems to have been to force George Washington to divert soldiers to protect outlying communities and to discourage men in those areas from joining Washington's army. Washington responded by dispatching Major General John Sullivan to lead a punishing expedition through Iroquois country. Sullivan marched north from Pennsylvania and was intercepted by a force of British soldiers and Iroquois, again mostly Seneca, at a hill about five and a half miles from today's downtown Elmira. The Battle of Newtown on August 29, 1779, was a decisive victory for the American army. Sullivan's March, as it became known, then proceeded unhindered, destroying about 40 Seneca villages and burning more than 160,000 bushels of corn, effectively driving the

Seneca into near starvation. Most, but not all, historians believe Sullivan's March ended useful aid to the British by any Iroquois nations.[9]

The Civil War also came to Elmira, but not as a battle. For several years a 30- to 40-acre plot of land along the Chemung River was used as a training ground for soldiers, mostly because two major railroads passed through the city, making it easy to send soldiers there for instruction and then send them south to fight. But in mid–1864, because of crowding elsewhere, Confederate prisoners of war began to arrive. The camp was outfitted to hold 5,000 prisoners, but 10,000 were sent. The sanitation was inadequate. There wasn't enough food or medical supplies. And as rumors filtered north about the horrible conditions endured by Union prisoners of war in the South, especially at Andersonville in Georgia, Elmira Prison Camp officials vindictively withheld some food from their prisoners. About 3,000 prisoners of war died at Elmira in the 13 months it was open. (By comparison, nearly 13,000 Union soldiers died at Andersonville.)[10]

Shortly before the war began Jervis bought a coal mine in Shamokin, Pennsylvania, and one in Nova Scotia. It was the anthracite from Pennsylvania that made him rich. Anthracite, or hard coal, burns cleaner and produces more energy than bituminous coal. And sold for more than twice what bituminous and lignite, the other two major types of coal, could bring. The anthracite fields of northeastern Pennsylvania, where Jervis Langdon's Shamokin mine was located, were and remain the largest anthracite fields in the country. Anthracite was particularly useful for railroads. (In the 20th century, the Lackawanna Railroad advertised that it burned only anthracite in its engines, because anthracite is smokeless and thus made for a more pleasant trip; during the Civil War, those Confederate blockade runners who used steam to power their ships used anthracite if they could get it, because, being smokeless, their ships were harder to detect.) The fact that the North had more anthracite than the South to power its battleships, locomotives, and factories contributed to the North's eventual victory.[11] In a real sense, Jervis, who strongly opposed slavery and saw the Civil War as necessary to bring it to an end, became wealthy as a result of the death and destruction created by the war.

The family's wealth grew along with Livy. And Jervis used his wealth to play a role in the great issues of the day. None, of course, was greater than slavery. Both of the Langdons believed slavery was a great moral wrong and needed to be opposed. Both were also regular churchgoers, so when their church, the Presbyterian church in Elmira, refused to condemn slavery they had a personal crisis to deal with. In the mid–19th century, many American churches were split over the issue and some denominations, including Presbyterians, Baptists, and Methodists, split in two, usually along North/South lines. Many Southern preachers, although certainly not all, found verses in the Bible to defend slavery, while many Northern preachers found in the same book passages to prove that God did not approve of human bondage.[12] As Abraham Lincoln would later say of the two warring armies, "Both read the same Bible, and pray to the same God; and each invokes his aid against the other. It may seem strange that any men should dare to ask a just God's assistance in wringing their bread from the sweat of other men's faces; but let us judge not, that we be not judged."[13] But Lincoln, of course, was making a judgment, as even a casual reading of the excerpt or the full speech makes clear. Slavery, he believed, was wrong, and as he said earlier in the speech, "Both parties deprecated war; but one of them would make war rather than let the nation survive; and the other would accept war rather than let it perish. And the war came."[14] The Langdons faced a similar, if lesser, choice two decades before Lincoln delivered that speech, his second most famous speech. And they decided they would accept the breakup of their church, Elmira's Presbyterian church, rather than be part of any institution that supported what they were convinced was a great moral wrong. They were among 42 congregants who left the Presbyterian church in Elmira and started the First Independent Congregational Church in the same city. Their new church had a constitution that said "no person shall be admitted to the church, or allowed to remain in it, who practices or approves of buying or selling human beings, or holding them in slavery." The same constitution also forbade consumption of alcohol, theater attendance, and parties.[15] But everyone understood that for the Langdons, and probably the other 40 men and women who joined them, the real issue was slavery.

The Langdons' opposition to slavery did not stop with helping to form a new church, which later became known as the Park Church. A tunnel ran underground from the church to the Langdon home to allow runaway slaves to move between the two buildings in case they were pursued by slave catchers. It was unusual only in that it was one of the few cases where a part of the Underground Railroad was actually underground. The Langdons' role in the Underground Railroad was also unusual in that it included transporting runaway slaves on a railroad, the line that carried Langdon coal into Canada. William Lloyd Garrison, among the country's best-known abolitionists, founder and editor of *The Liberator*, the country's best-known abolitionist newspaper, was a guest at the Langdon home when Livy was a young girl. Garrison was among the least compromising of abolitionists, insisting on complete and immediate freedom for all slaves. Livy's father, a man by temperament willing to listen to opposing views, agreed with the less flexible Garrison.[16]

Gerrit Smith also visited the home. Smith's father had been a business

partner of John Jacob Astor, one of the richest men in the world. When his
father died, Smith took over management of the family fortunes and much of
that money went to the same types of causes both Garrison and the Langdons
could support, including temperance, women's rights, and, most of all, abolition of slavery. Smith provided most of the money to build and support North
Elba, a community of freed slaves in the northern part of New York's Adiron-
dack Mountains. (Present-day Lake Placid, twice host to the Winter
Olympics—1932 and 1980—is within the town of North Elba.) Among the
people attracted to this experimental community was John Brown, and Smith
was attracted enough to the fire-and-brimstone personality of Brown that he
provided much of the money Brown needed to mount his unsuccessful raid
on Harpers Ferry in Virginia (now in West Virginia) in 1859. Brown intended
to capture the store of weapons at the federal armory there and to use those
arms to lead an insurrection of slaves. Brown went to the gallows for his role.
Mississippi senator Jefferson Davis, among others, wanted Smith arrested,
tried, and executed, but no charges were ever brought against him. Smith
claimed he provided funds to Brown with the understanding that they would
be used to arm former slaves who needed weapons for self-protection and he
did not know where Brown intended to obtain the weapons.[17]

Among the most illustrious visitors to the Langdon home was Frederick
Douglass, the best-known escaped slave in the world. He was born a slave in
Maryland in 1818, taught himself to read and write, escaped to the North in
1838, and settled for a decade in Rochester, New York. He was a powerful
speaker and widely read author. Livy grew up in a home of readers, and she
was expected to be one. As a young girl she was familiar with, even if she was
too young to read it, his autobiography, *Narrative of the Life of Frederick Douglass, an American Slave*. It was, at the time, the most famous book written by
an African American.[18]

For the anti-slavery movement no book was more influential except one,
Uncle Tom's Cabin by Harriet Beecher Stowe, published in 1852, and that
book, too, would be part of Livy's childhood. The author's half brother,
Thomas K. Beecher, was the minister at the Park Church that her parents
helped to establish. The new Congregational church had four pastors in its
first four years, but then the church, in 1854, recruited Beecher, a member of
one of the best-known religious families in the country, all of them staunchly
anti-slavery. Unlike his four predecessors, Beecher's sermons filled the church.
Overfilled it. To accommodate everyone who wanted to hear, sermons were
moved to the downtown opera house and, sometimes, when the weather was
warm and pleasant, to Eldridge Park. And when he asked the congregation
for $50,000 to build a new, larger church, the members pledged $80,000. He

would become a frequent visitor at the Langdon home, particularly for Sunday, after-sermon meals.[19]

William Lloyd Garrison, Gerrit Smith, Frederick Douglass, and Thomas K. Beecher all played prominent roles in the anti-slavery movement, and all also supported increased women's rights, aid for the poor, and other social issues. As did Jervis and Olivia Langdon. And their children. Young Livy Langdon grew up in a home that did not separate religion and social causes. Ending slavery, winning rights for women and the poor, all this, for adolescent and teenage Livy, was God's work.

Slavery had, in fact, existed in Elmira less than two decades before Jervis and Olivia moved there. The legal process to end slavery in New York State began in 1799, but it provided for gradual abolition and the last slaves were not freed until 1827. A section of Elmira known as Slabtown became home to former slaves freed under state law and runaway slaves arriving from the South. With the passage of the 1850 Fugitive Slave Act, Northern states were supposed to cooperate with Southern slave catchers, but seldom did. What became known as Jury Nullification was common in New York; juries routinely refused to convict anyone helping a slave to flee to Canada.[20] And in 1851 in Syracuse, less than 90 miles to the north of Elmira, a group of several hundred abolitionists broke into a jail to free William "Jerry" Henry, an escaped slave, and arranged for him to flee to Canada. The case became known as the Jerry Rescue and inflamed Northern abolitionists and Southern slave owners alike.[21]

And one of the most important "agents" on the Underground Railroad was John W. Jones, an escaped slave who helped more than 800 that other escaped slaves find their way into northern New York and Canada. During the Civil War, with the influx of escaped slaves reduced to near zero, Jones devoted himself to seeing that Confederate soldiers who died at the Elmira POW camp received proper burials. He helped to dig graves for about 2,900 of those who perished and kept such careful records that eventually all but seven would have markers with names above their final resting place. The federal government paid him $2.50 for each burial. And when he died in 1900, the day after Christmas, at the age of 83, he was buried in the same place, Woodlawn Cemetery.[22]

His grave is close to that of Livy Clemens and her husband, Mark Twain, and their four children and their one grandchild and Livy's parents and sister and brother.

The wealthy Jervis told Beecher he would give him whatever money he needed because "you can do more good with it than I can."[23] Beecher said he was not so much a minister as a teacher, and he usually dressed in workingmen's clothing, often helping out with painting, carpentry, and other manual labor.

And his wife, Julia Ward Beecher, wore her hair in a bob to make it easier to care for and wore comfortable flat, unfashionable shoes. Practicality was more important than fashion. And she taught the poetry of Walt Whitman and the essays of Ralph Waldo Emerson in Sunday-school classes. Emerson, who in his famous 1837 essay "The American Scholar" had urged Americans to develop their own way of writing, to break free of European traditions, and Whitman, who created an American poetry with American rhythms and American idioms and extolling American equalitarianism.[24] And Livy, who went to some of those Sunday-school classes, must have wondered why there was no mention of an American novelist who wrote independently of European ways of writing.

As the Langdons prospered, they were able to live better. They moved from the comfortable but modest home at Main and West Second (or maybe it was on Third) into a larger home on East Union Street, with an assessed value of $2,500. Livy was two at the time. During the Civil War, when she was 16, they moved into a large downtown mansion worth $25,000, more than a lifetime's income for many Americans at the time. It was a three-story house, with a basement and topped by a cupola, and stood on a lot that occupied an entire city block. The lot contained dozens of trees that towered over the house and a well-manicured lawn. Except for the buildings on it, it looked much like a public park. There were servants to cook, clean, run errands, do whatever the Langdons did not want to do. And that left time for them to do what they wanted, and much of that time was spent reading. Olivia tended to her children's education throughout their earliest years. Susan and Livy, and Charles, born in 1849 and four years younger than Livy, all had instilled in them a love of reading. Novels and poetry and history, mostly, but sometimes mathematics and science. Learning was largely achieved by reading books, they believed, and most evenings books were read aloud by one or another family member with the rest serving as the audience.

The Langdons' concern with social issues included a belief that women should receive educations equal to those offered to men, and they were thus instrumental in establishing what would eventually become Elmira Female College, and Livy would briefly attend classes there. Some sources cite Elmira Female College as the first women's college in the country to offer a curriculum on par with those offered at men's colleges, but that's not quite accurate. Tennessee and Alabama Female Institute, in Winchester, Tennessee, was founded in 1851 and modeled its course offerings after those common at men's colleges. It later changed its name to Mary Sharp College and closed its doors in 1896 because of financial difficulties. And Vassar College, in Poughkeepsie, New York, 130 miles to the east of Elmira, became, in the early 1860s, the first fully functioning women's college in the country, largely because it was much better funded than either Elmira or Tennessee and Alabama, being the beneficiary of a $408,000 gift from Matthew Vassar, a wealthy brewer. (In 2013 dollars, the gift would be worth about $10,000,000.)[25]

Elmira Female College actually got its start in Albany, the state capital, when a group of six men decided to establish a women's college equal to those that existed for men. After considering the New York towns of Carmel and Auburn as possible locations, they finally settled on Elmira, largely because local leaders promised financial support. One, Simeon Benjamin, who had made a fortune in local land sales, gave $5,000. Jervis Langdon, as a member of the college's founding board of trustees, was among local civic leaders who urged the Albany group to locate their women's college in his city.

Both of the Langdon daughters had already been enrolled at the Elmira Ladies' Seminary, which was run by Clarissa Thurston. When Livy enrolled in 1855 at age nine in what was known as Miss Thurston's, Sue had already graduated from the same school two years earlier. Students in the seminary studied reading, arithmetic (both mental and written versions were in the curriculum), geography, American history. And grammar. And orthography, which is the system of rules that govern a written language. The first part of the word *orthography* comes from a Greek word that means "correct." Orthography includes a study of "correct" spelling. It is a subject that Livy, intelligent and a good student, had a lifelong problem with.

Miss Thurston's, at 413 Main Street, was a one-room school in a much larger, mostly residential building. The other rooms housed 12 boarding students and six teachers.[26]

Livy went to Miss Thurston's for five years.[27] The institution's literature from the period provides some insight into what type of education a young woman could expect to receive there. (Actually, many, like Livy, were still young enough to accurately be referred to as girls — Livy was, after all, just nine when she enrolled.) That literature said, among other things, that the education of a female student there "shall compare favorably with the best institutions for the other sex." It was "for the purpose of affording a thorough and extensive education for Ladies, with the special reference to the best practical preparation for the duties of life, and at the lowest cost." And the education should be "a thorough scientific as well as ornamental education." It said a "lady" should have "genuine courtesy which flows from a desire to render others happy, and which is the result of esteeming others better than ourselves." And, pointedly, a young woman's education was "by no means intended to serve as an incentive to a professional career." That is, the young women at Miss Thurston's were being trained to be aides and ornaments for their future husbands.[28]

The texts Livy was required to read at Miss Thurston's were the normal fare for schools of the time. They stressed learning by rote and were dictatorial in their pronouncements. They tended not to present opposing views on a subject and were not merely unimaginative but actually anti-imagination. Students were discouraged from seeking their own solutions to problems presented at the end of a chapter. There was only one way and only one way to spell a word, one way and only way to think about a subject. It was an approach that dominated American education, and much of world education, well beyond the midpoint of the 20th century. The texts included *A Third Book of Reading and Spelling* by Samuel Worcester, *Grammar School Reader* by Salem Town, *Spelling Book* by Charles Sander, *Manual for Spelling* by James Napoleon McElligott, *First Lessons in Arithmetic* by George R. Perkins, *Treatise on the Structure of the English Language* by Samuel Green (used in 1854–1855), *A System of Modern Geography* by Augustus Mitchell, *Geography* by D.M. Warren (used in 1857), and *A History of the United States of America* by Egbert Gurnsey. These were books that trained more than educated.[29]

The full course of study at the school was six years long, but more than 90 percent of the 250 or so students there at any one time were not seniors, indicating that few of them completed the entire program.

When she was 13 Livy moved into the dormitory at Elmira Female College, even though she lived only about a mile away. Admission required that she take an exam that covered geography, spelling, grammar, reading, arithmetic, and other subjects. The $95 fee paid by her father covered tuition, room, and meals. The college at the time had only one building, housing students, offices, and classrooms. That building, "Cowles Hall [was] originally the college's entire physical plant, ... a five-story Romanesque octagonal structure based on the octagonal concept originated by Orson Fowler. A chapel was including in the building."[30] Fowler, who lived from 1809 to 1897, was not an architect, but his basic design for octagonal buildings was widely copied in the mid- and late 19th century. He argued that the design wasted less space because it didn't have sharp corners, reduced heat loss because it had less external surface space than a four-sided figure, and was cheaper to build. The ideal shape, he believed, would be a circle, but that was too difficult to build. The octagon best approximated the circular design. Fowler was actually best known as a phrenologist (that is, he practiced the pseudoscience that claimed the contour of a person's head determined personality characteristics, including intellect and character).[31] The octagonal shape would, famously, be the basic design for the study where Mark Twain would do much of his writing in later decades.

The octagonal part of Cowles Hall was in the center and was four stories high, topped by a cupola. Two three-story extensions stretched from the octagon to the east and west. The $80,000 building included a wide central staircase (to accommodate the wide skirts sometimes worn by young women). Student rooms were furnished, carpeted, lit with gas lamps, and heated with hot air from a central furnace. Students were encouraged to take a half-hour walk each day on college grounds, but they were not permitted to leave the campus without a chaperone. Rooms were inspected every day, and students were expected to devote up to an hour, and no more than an hour, each day working on the general upkeep of the building and grounds. Such labor built character, they were told. Other labor, like cooking and heavy cleaning, was done by servants. In fact, the storerooms and kitchen were off-limits to students. Livy and the other young women at Elmira College almost always came from homes that included maids, butlers, and other hired help. Whether it was intended as part of the lessons or not, the arrangement at the college taught that there were classes of people and they, the young women, belonged to one class and the hired help belonged to another. Students had to provide their own bedding, towels, napkins, clothes, and also a dictionary, atlas, and Bible. And everything must have the young woman's name on it. Church attendance was required twice on Sundays, morning and evening. The college was non-denominational, but it was definitely Christian. Even visitors and visiting were prohibited on Sundays, including visiting one another's rooms.

Livy spent only one year on campus, and during that year the college opened an observatory with a telescope and graduated its first class, 17 young woman receiving bachelor of arts degrees. Livy would maintain long friendships with many of the women she met at Elmira College, including Ida Clark (who later married Livy's younger brother, Charles), Emma Nye, Alice Hooker, Clara Spaulding, and Emma Sayles. Livy lived on campus only for the Spring term in 1859. In the Fall of the same year she continued to attend classes, but she commuted from home. And that was her final term at Elmira College.

The texts Livy was required to read at Elmira College suggest that the level or learning was neither overly sophisticated nor particularly tolerant of challenging accepted ways of thinking about a subject. They included *Institutes of English Grammar* by Goold Brown, *A Grammar of the Latin Language* by Ethan Allen Andrew and Solomon Stoddard, *History of the United States, or Republic of America: With Chronological Table and Series of Progressive Maps* by Emma Hart Willard, and *Scripture Geography and History: Illustrating the Historical Portion of the Old and New Testaments* by Edward Hughes.[32]

When Livy left the college, she did not lose her interest in her studies, particularly in literature. She began to accumulate quotes and poems and excerpts from books in a journal, a widespread practice in the mid–19th century, especially for young women. The journals were known as commonplace books. Some commonplace books consisted of clippings from newspapers and magazines and handwritten copies of favorite passages from books. These journals were not diaries but rather accumulations of the writings of other, often-esteemed, authors. One of Livy's earliest entries was a portion of a poem written by 18th-century English poet John Byrom:

> In reading Authors, when you find
> Bright Passages that strike your Mind,
> And which perhaps you may have Reason
> To think on at another Season,
> Be not contented with the Sight,
> But take them down in *Black* and *White*;
> Such a Respect is wisely shown
> That makes another's Sense one's own.[33]

By the time Livy made this entry in her commonplace book, she was already an invalid, a result of her fall on the ice. Perhaps.

There are numerous indications that Livy continued her education even when bedridden. Mary Nye, sister of Livy's friend Emma, came over to give her a lesson in French. She read *Vicar of Wakefield* by Oliver Goldsmith (this novel, published in 1766, a riches-to-rags-to-riches story, was part of the unofficial canon that all well-bred upper-class men and women in England and America were expected to read). And Professor Darius R. Ford visited and gave her lessons in natural philosophy (which covered some of the same material now covered in a modern physics class). And she studied French with nuns teaching at a nearby parochial school. In a letter dated September 29, 1868, to Alice Hooker, Livy wrote, "I have commenced studying Natural Philosophy with Prof. Ford and French with the nuns. I enjoy both very much. Prof. Ford is as delightful a lecturer as ever. I expect to finish Nat. Phil. This winter. Sue and I go together to the nuns, we like it very much! I am sure they must be good teachers and they are exceedingly pleasant." The nuns were members of the Order of St. Mary, from Lockport, New York, near Buffalo, and taught at the Academy of Our Lady of Angels, about eight blocks from the Langdon home. The letter says Livy went to the nuns, so by September 1868 she was not always bedridden.[34]

Livy's parents' desire to see that their children were well educated sometimes ran into difficulties, especially with their youngest, Charles. In him his parents saw a son who was intelligent but not a good student. The sent him to Gunnery School in Washington, Connecticut, when he was 15.[35] Named for its founder, Frederick Gunn, an ardent abolitionist who is sometimes called the father of recreational camping, the school was located in northwestern

Connecticut, amid rolling hills and quiet surroundings.[36] It promised wealthy parents a well-rounded education for their sons, with emphasis on intellectual, physical, and spiritual development, although it was not associated with any denomination. But Charlie lasted there only one term.

The Langdons then decided Charlie might be better educated outside of a schoolroom, so in July 1865 Jervis and Olivia Langdon took their only son on a trip to Niagara Falls, the Thousand Islands, Montreal, Quebec City, Vermont, the White Mountains of New Hampshire, and Saratoga Springs, New York. A year and a half later, in February 1867, they sent him without other family members on a trip to the Middle East. He went on a cruise aboard the ship *Quaker City* that was organized in Brooklyn by Henry Ward Beecher, brother of their pastor at Elmira's Park Church. The cruise visited the Holy Land, the Crimea, and Greece. Charlie was 17 at the time.[37] Two years later, Livy wrote a letter to Alice Hooker commenting on Charlie's Holy Land trip. What Livy said revealed much about her brother's educational aptitude: "Father wanted to compensate Charlie as much as he could for his inability to study, he was obliged to gain in some way other than books — Father felt that if he could get Pro. [Darius R.] Ford to go as Charlie's companion, he would be just the right man. When they were on ship board Charlie would be able to study with him some and then traveling on land, Prof. Ford could give him all the history of the place also the geology and Botany of the country — they intend to take up astronomy while on the ocean."[38]

Two years earlier, Livy wrote another letter, also to Alice Hooker, about Charlie's then-upcoming trip on the *Quaker City*, saying "we are all glad to have him go hoping he will return improved in many ways. I told him I expected him to return a gentleman; he thought me rather uncomplimentary."[39] Her comment should be seen as friendly teasing between siblings who loved each other, not as mean-spirited criticism.

Although Livy did not accompany Charlie on his Holy Land excursion, it would prove to be an eventful trip for her, because her brother befriended an older fellow passenger and showed that passenger a picture of his older sister. Years later that passenger would say he was immediately smitten by the picture. He was a not-yet-famous writer by the name of Mark Twain.

Resa Willis in her dual biography of Mark Twain and Livy (*Mark and Livy*) explores the possibility that Livy suffered more or at least as much from a social ailment as from a physical one. Any diagnosis, even a speculative one, is hampered by the fact that so little is known about what happened. When did the fall on the ice occur? Where? What parts of her body made contact with the ground? The answers to none of these questions are known. Willis calls Livy's ailment "a prevalent malady" and goes on to explain, "It was known by many names: nervous prostration or exhaustion, hysteria, neurasthenia. Dr. George Miller Beard studied the disease and described it in his book *American Nervousness: Its Causes and Consequences*, published in 1881. Beard characterized it as a peculiarly American illness that resulted from the increasing pace of life in the nineteenth century. Some of its manifestations included a partial or complete paralysis, headaches, depression, anorexia nervosa, lethargy, insomnia. It was a frustrating malady, for the symptoms often 'simulate so perfectly other diseases to deceive for a time the best physician.'"[40]

Beard's mention of anorexia nervosa will, of course, lead many people to see a connection between social and environmental factors and the "frustrating malady." It's even possible that Livy's ailment was not actually caused by the fall on the ice but rather that the fall and the first manifestations of the illness were coincidental.

While Beard did not examine Livy, Willis offers a plausible explanation of what, if he had examined her, his diagnosis might be: "In men and women it struck those 'among the well-to-do and the intellectual.' In a society that encouraged hard work and being a success, it was an acceptable illness for men of the middle class struggling to get ahead. Beard, as well as many others in the nerve doctor business, had suffered from it himself. The majority who succumbed to the sickness were, like Livy, educated middle-to-upper-class women, who Beard and others felt used too much mental energy. Modern life was too demanding on delicate women."[41]

One physician who did examine Livy was Dr. Rachel Gleason. She was one of the first female doctors in the United States, earning her medical degree just two years after Elizabeth Blackwell became the country's first woman doctor. Rachel Gleason actually could not find a medical school that would admit her, so she studied with her husband, Silas, a doctor, and earned her legal right to practice medicine in what amounted to an apprenticeship.[42] Gleason and Silas ran a sanatorium in Elmira beginning in 1852 and specialized in treating the type of nervous disorder that Livy suffered from. Gleason sometimes lectured at Elmira Female College and wrote books that found their way into the Langdon home library. As Willis notes, "Gleason believed that 'the fast ways of the American people, with their hurried lives, late hours, and varied excesses, wear upon the nervous system of all, especially that of sensitive, impressible women. Those who are brilliant and fascinating early become frail, freaky, fidgety—a condition difficult to cure, but which could be prevented by leading a quiet life, with more of simple, useful work, of which the world furnishes an abundance.' The problems of Livy's social class were even compounded when 'anxiety as to dress, social position, calls and company, wears one more than needed work.'"[43]

Gleason also wrote, in *Talks to My Patients*, her best-known book, "Growing girls are proverbially weak and sensitive" and "mental application also, close and long-continued, results often in invalidism." Such activity, in some women, could result in "life-long dullness," but "[i]n others, the mental burns more and more brilliantly, and the body dies or falls into incurable invalidism. Our modern excellent educational advantages furnish specimens of both classes, but mostly of the latter." All this "proved fatal, simply because the long course of study had so enfeebled the system that it had little power to resist disease or sufficient recuperative force to rally even from slight sickness."[44] Willis cites all these quotes and observes, "The disease of frailty has always been with us, but it became a high art in Victorian times that saw women as weak, childlike, to be lifted onto a pedestal. Delicacy went with refinement."[45]

Dr. Gleason prescribed changes in diet, lots of rest, limiting physical and mental activities, and, later, a "water cure." Water cures of varying types were popular in the United States and Europe in the 19th century. In fact, in some forms they continue today. A water cure could consist of bathing in spa waters, seawater, water treated with some chemical, heated water, cold water, or whirling waters. Or of drinking large amounts of water so, presumably, a patient's system would be cleansed. By far the most common method, however, was immersion of most of the body in cold water. That was followed by immersion in mineral waters, preferably waters that contained minerals naturally rather than as additives. The Gleasons' Elmira Water Cure spa, near the bottom of East Hill, was among the best-known centers of its kind in the country. Other treatments by other physicians included electric shock, almost total isolation (often only a doctor or nurse being permitted to visit the patient), massage, and extreme limits on any intellectual activities. Commonly, patients were told to neither read nor write.[46]

Livy, in fact, was typical of most of those young women who did suffer from neurasthenia, the term most often applied by 19th-century doctors to the malady from which Willis thinks she suffered. Teenage, from a wealthy family, intellectually inclined, artistically sensitive, loving parents. Willis offers no argument to support the possibility that Livy might have had actual physical damage as a result of her fall on the ice. Willis writes, "Why did any intelligent young woman succumb to the mysterious malady? Livy may have been reacting to the growing pressures of her sexuality and ambivalence concerning her intelligence, her place in society, and the changing role of women."[47] And she adds, "Illness made Livy the center of the family's attention."[48]

The analysis of the class-related malady is at least mildly supported by an attitude that Livy possessed her entire life, namely that the burdens imposed upon an upper-class woman are varied and endless. When she had been married about a decade she wrote a revealing letter (dated November 30, 1879) to her mother that said, "I told Mr. Clemens the other day that in this day women must be everything. They must keep up with all the current literature, they must know all about art, they must help in one or two benevolent societies, they must be perfect mothers, they must be perfect housekeepers and gracious hostesses, they must know how to give perfect dinners, they must go and visit all the people in the town where they live, they must be ready to receive their acquaintances, they must dress themselves and their children becomingly and above all they must make their homes charming and so on without end — then if they are not studying something, their case is a hopeless one."[49]

A 21st-century reader, if unsympathetic and prone to sarcasm, is likely to think, *Poor little rich girl.*

Sympathizing with Livy's complaint would be easier if we were not aware that many poor women in her time, the second half of the 19th century, worked all day in filthy conditions in factories, or labored on farms or as domestics, and were still expected to raise children and cook meals. And without servants. And could not afford to dress themselves or their children "becomingly." Livy had a lifelong sympathy for the poor, but not empathy. Never having lived it, she never truly understood what poverty is. Observation is not enough.

Although Willis's conclusion is the way most biographers of Mark Twain, when writing about his wife, view Livy's teenage ailment, one important observer of her life had a very different view: Mark Twain himself. In his autobiography he writes, "She became an invalid at sixteen through a partial paralysis caused by falling on the ice and she was never strong again while her life lasted. After that fall she was not able to leave her bed during two years, nor was she able to lie in any position except upon her back. All the great physicians were brought to Elmira one after another during that time, but there was no helpful result."[50] His information about his wife's illness had to come from her and members of her immediate family, and there's nothing in his reporting of what he knows to indicate that he in any way doubted that she suffered from actual physical ailments. He was, of course, a loving, even doting husband, and no doubt he was not willing to admit to himself that she might have suffered something more psychosomatic than with actual physical cause.

Livy's parents were wealthy and they brought in many doctors from Elmira. Others from New York City. At one point they took her to Washington, D.C., for a treatment. The Gleason water cure was tried. Nothing worked.

As Twain reports, two years in bed, unable to sit up, made nauseous even by the attempt. The Langdons, even if they suspected that their daughter's problem was less physical than psychological, or a result of societal pressure, were desperate. Mark Twain explained what happened:

> In those days both worlds were well acquainted with the name of Doctor Newton, a man who was regarded in both worlds as a quack. He moved through the land in state; in magnificence, like a potentate; like a circus. Notice of his coming was spread upon the dead walls in vast colored posters, along with his formidable portrait, several weeks beforehand.[51]

Newton was James Rogers Newton, who publicly performed his healings in both the United States and England, the "both worlds" Twain refers to.[52] He was "a businessman from Newport, Rhode Island, [who] performed massively attended public 'healings.'... He was not well regarded by either the scientific or the religious community. He seems to have had no medical training, and attributed his powers variously to 'magnetic force,' 'controlling spirits,' and 'the Father that dwelleth in me.'" Usually he "laid on hands," but he sometimes used less familiar methods, such as the time he told a tuberculosis patient to cut off the head of a male chicken, split it open, and place it on his chest.[53]

Twain continues:

> One day Andrew Langdon, a relative of the Langdon family,[54] came to the house and said, "You have tried everybody else; now try Doctor Newton, the quack. He is down town at the Rathbun House practicing upon the well-to-do at war prices and upon the poor for nothing. *I saw him* wave his hands over Jake Brown's head and take his crutches away from him and send him about his business as good as new. *I saw him* do the like with some other cripples. *They* may have been 'temporaries' instituted for advertising purposes, and not genuine. But Jake is genuine. Send for Newton."[55]

How accurate, one should wonder, is Twain's memory on the details he presents? The portion of his autobiography containing the quotes was dictated in 1906, when he was 71 years old and probably four decades after he first heard them, since it's reasonable to assume he first became knowledgeable about Livy's teenage ailment not long after he first met her, when he was 32. He undoubtedly re-created what Andrew Langdon is reported to have said. It's not clear if Andrew said it to Livy or to her parents or to someone else or to multiple people. But while the exact wording may be in doubt because of the passage of time, one key word rings with authenticity: *quack*. Newton was viewed as a quack by the established medical profession, and much of the educated populace, and probably by the Langdons. The fact that they would consider using his services is a recognition of the desperation they must have felt, the desperation and sense of futility that any loving parents would have felt.

And they had enough money to not worry that spending it on a quack would in any way limit their spending on some other, more medically accepted, cure.

Jervis and Olivia listened to Andrew and sent for the quack. Twain continues,

> Newton came. He found the young girl upon her back. Over her was suspended a tackle from the ceiling. It had been there a long time, but unused. It was put there in the hope that by its steady motion she might be lifted to a sitting posture, at intervals, for rest. But it proved a failure. Any attempt to raise her brought nausea and exhaustion, and had to be relinquished. Newton made some passes about her head with his hands, then he put an arm behind her shoulders and said "Now we will sit up, my child."[56]

The nausea and exhaustion Twain writes about would be a part of Livy's life for as long as she would live. And its onset at so common a task, for most people at least, as sitting up would baffle doctors on three continents. Understanding that it was part of Livy's daily existence, no doubt, contributed to her parents' reaction when Newton told her to sit up. Twain says,

> The family was alarmed, and tried to stop him, but he was not disturbed, and raised her up. She sat several minutes, without nausea or discomfort. Then Newton said that that would do for the present, he would come again next morning; which he did. He made some passes with his hands and said, "Now we will walk a few steps, my child." He took her out of bed and supported her while she walked several steps; then he said "I have reached the limit of my art. She is not cured. It is not likely that she will *ever* be cured. She will never be able to walk far, but after a little daily practice she will be able to walk one or two hundred yards, and she can depend on being able to do *that* for the rest of her life."[57]

Twain made it clear that he believed Newton cured Livy: "His charge was fifteen hundred dollars, and it was easily worth a hundred thousand. For from the day that she was eighteen, until she was fifty-six, she was always able to walk a couple of hundred yards without stopping to rest; and more than once I saw her walk a quarter of a mile without serious fatigue."[58] (Resa Willis also puts Newton's fee at $1,500 in her dual biography, *Mark and Livy*, but in her article on Livy in *The Mark Twain Encyclopedia* she says it was "over $2,000."[59])

He also made it clear he believed Newton deserved whatever fame he had while he was alive:

> Newton was mobbed in Dublin, in London, and in other places. He was rather frequently mobbed in Europe, and in America, but never by the grateful Langdons and Clemenses. I met Newton once, in after years, and asked him what his secret was. He said he didn't know, but thought perhaps some subtle form of electricity proceeded from his body and wrought the cures.[60]

Twain's recollections, based on both secondhand information and emotionally involved sources and recorded four decades later, should not be seen as reliable, although there are no known contemporaneous sources to justify dismissing them as entirely inaccurate. Still, those who have written about Livy's ailments tend towards such dismissal.

Dixon Wecter, for example, editor of the love letters that Livy and Mark Twain sent to each other, wrote, "The cosseting of her family — an adoring father and brother and adopted sister Susan, and a mother whose preoccupation with her own ill-health verged upon the neurotic — had probably slowed Livy's recovery with unwise solicitude, as did the whole philosophy about the genteel girl of the period."[61]

His comment about "the genteel girl" is, of course, not exactly the same as Willis's implied diagnosis of neurasthenia, but certainly it is consistent. Much later in Livy's life, not long before she died, according to Willis, "The doctors began to say Livy's illness was due to heart disease and nervous prostration, the catch-all term for the era's ailments."[62] At least those ailments contracted by young women from upper-income families.

Wecter and Willis have similar, if not identical, views of Livy's health problems as a teenager, and both are not in accord with Mark Twain's version. His descriptions of the facts are also inconsistent with the conclusions of the editors of the University of California version of his autobiography. They write:

> The nature of Olivia's ailment has been much debated. She became ill earlier, and recovered later than Clemens allowed for in [his] dictation. Already 'in very delicate health' at the age of fourteen (1860), she was treated by doctors and spent time at the Elmira Water Cure. Showing little improvement, she was sent to a sanatorium in Washington, D.C., and then to the Institute of Swedish Movement in New York City, which prescribed kinesipathy (curative muscle movements). She spent more than two years there before returning home to Elmira.[63]

A more recent commentator on Livy's ailments thinks she suffered a real and, at the time, undiagnosed disease. Laura E. Skandera-Trombley believes Livy had Pott's disease, also known as tuberculosis of the spine. Skandera in 1991 (the Trombley would be added to her name later) told Barbara Wiggans Taylor, a graduate student at Elmira College, about her Pott's disease theory. She later expanded on the theory in her 1994 book, *Mark Twain in the Company of Women*. Taylor, summarizing what Skandera told her, writes, "Because of the lack of diagnostic means, many people thought at the time that Pott's disease was caused by falls. Pott's disease can result in episodes similar to the one described by Julia Beecher to Isabella Hooker."[64]

That last comment is a reference to the fact that at least once the Langdons seemed certain that Livy would die. The circumstances are contained in a letter from Julia Beecher, wife of the Rev. Thomas Beecher, to her sister-in-law Isabella Beecher Hooker. The letter is dated June 6, 1862, when Livy was 16. Julia Beecher writes:

> Mr. Langdon with his wife, Mary Lewis & Susy Crane are in New York attending upon Livy who was brought to Staten Island & then to the city — for a change — direct from Washington — New symptoms became at once acute. She retained nothing upon her stomach — vomited for days — blood at last accounts. She was continually delirious and they are almost certain now that they cannot keep her many more days. Susy went day before yesterday. Mr. Langdon had watched & all had till very weary — This is all I can tell you about the Langdons.[65]

Livy did survive, but surviving is not the same as being cured. Two years later she was still ill, and that's when Newton entered her life.

Some details about the visit of Dr. Newton could not have been known by Twain, but they help to clarify key points. Newton's first visit was on November 30, 1864, and his personal secretary made notes about it. The secretary writes:

> One of these [visits] was at Elmira, N.Y., where Dr. N. went to treat Miss Libbie Langdon, whom he cured, and she has since married the author known as "Mark Twain." Dr. N. found her suffering with spinal disease, could not be raised to a sitting posture in her bed for over four years. She was almost like death itself. With one characteristic treatment he made her to cross the room with assistance, and in a few days the cure was complete.[66]

The mention of spinal disease, which was not noted by Twain and is generally not stressed by those, like Willis, who focus on nervous disorders, leaves open the possibility that Livy suffered from a real and serious medical problem, especially since it's likely that Newton's secretary was repeating a phase given to Newton by the Langdons. Quacks like Newton, then and now, tended to use diagnosis and medical phraseology common to the legitimate medical profession as a beginning point in order to provide the veneer of authenticity to their practice. That is, Newton's use of the phrase *spinal disease* may contain legitimacy only if we accept it as probably originating from something told to him by the Langdons, presumably repeating something doctors had told them.

The most important point that Twain gets wrong, at least by implication, is to assume that Livy was cured by Newton. Less important, but related, is Twain's statement that Newton's second visit was the following morning. Research by later scholars and summarized by the editors of the California version of Twain's autobiography provide different details. The editors write, "Langdon family letters and papers ... show that despite Newton's visits Olivia's health was still seriously impaired. She had a second visit from Newton on 3 June 1865 and was still unable to walk almost a year after that."[67] That is, the second visit was six months after the first, not the following morning as Twain had said. And she was bedridden for four years, not two. These facts cast doubt on Twain's belief that Newton cured her, since she was bedridden nearly a year and a half after his first visit and, more important, a full year following his second. They also tend to not support Willis's thesis that Livy's main ailment was nervous disorder, since a cure by a quack like Newton would be most likely if the patient did not suffer from a condition with an actual physical cause. These facts actually suggest that Newton's secretary was right when he referred to Livy as "suffering with spinal disease."[68] The California editors continue by writing, "A second stay at the [Swedish] Movement Institute [in New York City] in 1866 recovered her considerably; she regained her mobility."[69]

Significantly for Livy's future, she continued to read between Newton's two visits. Her frailty seems never to have lessened her desire to read and to continue her education. Livy read Washington Irving's *The Life of George Washington* in January of 1865.[70] It had been published in five volumes from 1855 to 1859. By being the first American writer to be widely admired by European writers, including Sir Walter Scott, Lord Byron, and Charles Dickens, Irving contributed notably to the creation of an American literary culture at least partly independent of its European roots. His subject matter was American, but his style and structures were derivative of what European, particularly British, writers had used. It's very possible that Livy admired Irving's contributions towards creating an independent American literature. It's something that would reach fruition in her future husband's writings.

Livy also read, in April of 1865, a biography of Charlotte Brontë.[71] *The Life of Charlotte Brontë* by Elizabeth Gaskell was published in 1857 and was the first biography of a prominent female novelist written by another prominent female novelist. While groundbreaking in that sense, the biography is now seen as an attempt to sanctify Brontë. Gaskell knew about but did not report Brontë's love for a married man and generally avoided discussing anything that would have presented her in a negative light. She presented Bronte as a dutiful wife who viewed her main job as running the household. Brontë died in 1855 at age 38, perhaps from tuberculosis or from dehydration caused by excessive vomiting brought on by a difficult pregnancy. Livy may have seen some of herself in Gaskell's loving but incomplete portrait of Brontë, a sickly woman with a love of literature.

Twain knew about Livy's frailty, although his knowledge was faulty. And he would learn about her love of reading. There was a connection between the two.

The passage of time, faulty initial information, the storyteller's impulse to dramatize, not having a chance to fully edit his own dictations, all these factors no doubt contributed to Twain's inaccurate account of Newton's role in treating Livy, but one other factor should be mentioned, and it is, perhaps, most clearly revealed in a letter he wrote to her in Elmira, from New Haven, Connecticut, on December 27, 1869. In that letter, as he often did, he gave his then-fiancée advice on what and what not to read: "I have read several books, lately, but none worth marking, & so I have not marked any. I started to mark the Story of a Bad Boy,[72] but for the life of me I could not admire the volume much. I am now reading Gil Blas,[73] but am not marking it. If you have not read it you need not. It would sadly offend your delicacy, & I prefer not to have that dulled in you. It is a woman's chief ornament."[74]

The phrase *a woman's chief ornament* is revealing. It suggests that Twain found Livy's delicacy, her frailty, attractive.

CHAPTER TWO

Death, Death, Death

Charles Langdon was 17 when his parents sent him on the *Quaker City* excursion, and he became friendly with the then slightly famous Mark Twain near the end of the trip, when in the Bay of Smyrna, which shared its name with the city once called Smyrna, now called Izmir, in western Turkey. On September 5 or 6, 1867, Charlie showed Twain a small photo of Livy. Twain was smitten, and four decades later Twain would dictate (on February 13, 1906) that he first actually met Livy on December 27, 1867, and said that they met again five days later. As so often is the case with Twain dictating his autobiography, some of his facts are demonstrably wrong. In this case the facts involve another famous writer whose locations can be traced. On December 31, 1867, Twain went with the Langdons to hear Charles Dickens read at Steinway Hall in New York City. The invitation to join the Langdons was extended by Charlie, at the suggestion of his father, Jervis.[1]

There was, as might be expected with the passage of time and multiple sources, other confusions on the first and second meetings of Livy and Mark. Susy, their oldest daughter, wrote an incomplete biography of her father when she was 13. In it she said, "Grandpa Langdon, Uncle Charlie's father, told Uncle Charlie to invite Mr. Clemens to dine with them at the St. Nicholas Hotel, in New York. Papa accepted the invitation and went to dine at the St. Nicholas with Grandpa and there he met mamma, Olivia Louise Langdon, first. But they did not meet again until next August, because papa went away to California and there wrote 'The Innocents Abroad.'"[2]

Twain noted that "Susy is not quite correct as to that next meeting. That first meeting was on the 27th of December 1867, and the next one was at the house of Mrs. Berry, five days later. Miss Langdon had gone there to help Mrs. Berry receive New Year guests. I went there at ten in the morning to pay a New Year call. I had thirty-four calls on my list, and this was the first one."[3] The actual sequence is this: They dined together (Samuel, Olivia, the Langdon

35

family) on December 27, 1867, at the St. Nicholas Hotel in New York City. All of them attended the Dickens reading on December 31. Samuel and Olivia met for the third time on January 1, 1868, when he made a courtesy New Year's Day call.

What amounted to their first date was, of course, memorable for Twain for romantic reasons. But it was an occasion that also gave him ideas for future income. Prior to the meeting he had been in the process of building a successful career as both a writer and lecturer, his lectures coming close to being a form of what would later become known as stand-up comedy, although his presentations tended to be much longer, an hour or more rather than 5, 10 or 15 minutes. The central idea he garnered from that event was the literary reading. He later wrote:

> What is called a "reading," as a public platform entertainment, was first essayed by Charles Dickens, I think. He brought the idea with him from England in 1867. He had made it very popular at home and he made it so acceptable and so popular in America that his houses were crowded everywhere, and in a single season he earned two hundred thousand dollars. I heard him once during that season; it was in Steinway Hall [in New York City], in December, and it made the fortune of my life — not in dollars, I am not thinking dollars; it made the real fortune of my life in that it made the happiness of my life; on that day I called at the St. Nicholas Hotel to see my Quaker City excursion shipmate, Charley Langdon, and was introduced to a sweet and timid and lovely young girl, his sister. The family went to the Dickens reading and I accompanied them.[4]

He added, curiously:

> The public reading was discarded after a time and was not resumed until something more than twenty years after Dickens had introduced it; then it rose and struggled along for a while in the curious and artless industry called Authors' Readings. When Providence had had enough of that kind of crime the Authors' Readings ceased from troubling and left the world at peace.[5]

Twain, of course, would give innumerable public readings of his own writings, sometimes pairing himself with such writers as Bret Harte and George Washington Cable. Perhaps Twain felt the fact that his readings were frequently interrupted by jokes and asides and commentaries distinguished them sufficiently from the Dickens variety that he did not think of them as being derivative. In any case, he was clearly wrong to think that authors' readings had died, since they continued to exist while he lived and are alive and well today. Livy later would frequently give him advice on his readings, telling him to pause longer at this point, shorter at that one, change his tone for a certain line, add this, omit that. He willingly allowed her to serve as a dialogue coach and editor of his performances, although he did not always follow her advice.

Twain was clearly impressed by the Dickens reading. He writes:

> Mr. Dickens read scenes from his printed books. From my distance he was a
> small and slender figure, rather fancifully dressed, and striking and picturesque in
> appearance. He wore a black velvet coat with a large and glaring red flower in the
> buttonhole. He stood under a red upholstered shed behind whose slant was a
> row of strong lights—just such an arrangement as artists use to concentrate a
> strong light upon a great picture. Dickens's audience sat in a pleasant twilight,
> while he performed in the powerful light cast upon him from the concealed
> lamps. He read with great force and animation, in the lively passages, and with
> stirring effect. It will be understood that he did not merely read but also acted.
> His reading of the storm scene in which [James] Steerforth [a character in *David
> Copperfield*] lost his life was so vivid and so full of energetic action that his house
> was carried off its feet, so to speak.[6]

The idea of acting rather than simply reading was something Twain would
do, very much with Livy's encouragement.

When Samuel Clemens first met Olivia Langdon, he was five feet, nine
inches tall and weighed 140 pounds. His height and weight are known from a
passport application.[7] Based on the hundreds of known photographs of him
throughout his life, he lost little or any of his height over the remaining four
decades he lived. His weight seems to have gone up slightly, but he never
appears overweight, although later in life there is a visible expansion around
his waistline. Olivia's height and weight need to be estimated, and since in
most of the dozens of known photographs of her she is sitting, and in some
lying down, such estimates turn into guesstimates. In the few photos of her
standing, it is difficult to tell what type of shoes she is wearing and what those
shoes might add to her height. But she seems to have been at least five feet,
two inches tall and perhaps as much as five-five. Her weight when she is
younger must have been around 105 to 115 pounds, and as she grew older she
noticeably put on pounds, perhaps reaching as much as 140 or 150. Samuel
had the advantage of being an inveterate walker, often walking miles at a time.
(He was a walker, not a hiker, and his walks were almost always on streets and
sidewalks, not through woods or fields.) Olivia because of her health problems
did little walking. By Samuel's recollection, only once did she walk as much
as a quarter of a mile at a time, and, more typically, a hundred yards was her
maximum.[8]

Undoubtedly, during their first meeting she spent most of her time sitting.
This can be assumed because, again based on photographs, but also on recollections of her by others, she is most often depicted sitting, sometimes lying
down, seldom standing.[9] Also, in mid–19th-century America, for a woman to
sit while a man stood was a perfectly sociable way to act, while the reverse—
the man sitting and the woman standing—was considered bad manners for

the man. And, of course, their activities that evening, traveling by carriage between the hotel and the Steinway Hall where Dickens spoke and attending the event, would have required sitting by everyone in the group.

The first actual meeting of Samuel and Olivia was in the restaurant of the St. Nicholas Hotel. Jervis had told Charlie to invite his friend from the *Quaker City* trip to join them for dinner, and it was at the dinner, when everyone was seated, that the rest of the Langdon family became acquainted with the character of Mark Twain, that is, the deliberately created character Samuel Clemens had turned himself into.

It's thus unlikely that Clemens on that day would have seen Miss Langdon as being a frail woman. He would have seen a clear complexion, dark brunette hair on a pleasant-looking, quiet-but-not-shy young woman. Probably she would have smiled easily, although none of the photographs of her show a smile. That of course was not unusual in 19th-century photographs. The exposure time needed for the photographic plates in use at the time was typically at least several seconds, and any movement would develop as a blur. Subjects were advised, or knew, to remain as still as possible, and a closed, expressionless mouth was likely to come out less blurry than a bright smile.

But she would have smiled for him and laughed at some of the things he must have said. Samuel Clemens was never without a witty remark, a clever insight, an ability to make himself and what he said the center of attention. And he was a writer, although not yet very famous. She, Olivia Langdon, appreciated wit and loved literature. He, growing up poor, was always attracted to wealth, even if in a general sense he condemned its influence on mankind. And she, while a member of a very wealthy family, would never allow social origin or status to interfere with her evaluation of others. Like everyone in her family, a family that acted against slavery, promoted women's rights, treated everyone with politeness, Olivia could and would accept a person for who he was, not who his lineage said he was. Olivia Langdon and Samuel Clemens were pleased with each other at first sight.

After his *Quaker City* cruise, Samuel had gone to Washington, D.C., to briefly serve as private secretary to William M. Stewart, the senator from Nevada. Stewart made a fortune as a lawyer for the silver-mining industry but developed a reputation for bribing judges and juries. Much later President Ulysses S. Grant would offer the loyal but corrupt Republican a seat on the U.S. Supreme Court, but Stewart would turn him down. Not much opportunity to make money there. Stewart was the principal author of the 15th Amendment to the U.S. Constitution, the one that says, "The right of citizens of the United States to vote shall not be denied or abridged by the United States or by any State on account of race, color, or previous condition of servitude." Clemens and Stewart had personalities that clashed and they argued bitterly.[10] Clemens, who was more interested anyway in building a career as a writer, left and decided to travel to New York to visit Dan Slote, with whom he had roomed on the *Quaker City*.

The Langdon family, coincidentally, also decided to visit New York for the holidays. On such coincidences, lives are shaped.

The third meeting, the one on New Year's Day, 1868, allowed them to get better acquainted. Livy and her friend Alice Hooker, from Hartford and niece of the Langdons' pastor, were receiving New Year's callers at the Manhattan home of a friend, Mrs. Berry. In his autobiography Twain recalled that he arrived at 10:00 A.M. and stayed until 11:00 P.M. Since that was the first of 34 calls he was supposed to make that day, he clearly stayed longer than he intended to when he drew up his call list. With Alice Hooker and, probably, Mrs. Berry, he and Livy would not have had much time alone, if any. (To add to the confusion mentioned earlier, Dixon Wecter, editor of the love letters Livy and Mark sent to each other, believed that the appearances of Charles Dickens at Steinway Hall in New York were on January 2 and 3, 1868, which would mean the Dickens reading was the third time they got together.[11])

After the holidays, the Langdons returned to Elmira and Twain went to Hartford, Connecticut, then a city with one of the highest per capita incomes in America. It was also a literary center, with a dozen book-publishing companies located there. He had an agreement with the American Publishing Company to write a book about his Holy Land travels. Living in Hartford allowed him to work closely with Elisha P. Bliss, Jr., the firm's editor.

(Bliss was Twain's publisher from 1868 to 1880 and published *The Innocents Abroad, Roughing It, The Gilded Age, Sketches New and Old, The Adventures of Tom Sawyer*, and *A Tramp Abroad*. Twain, however, became convinced that Bliss was cheating him out of royalties. At different times Twain gave different estimates of how much he believed Bliss had cheated him, the estimates ranging from $30,000 to $60,000. He broke with Bliss and took his next three books, *The Prince and the Pauper, The Stolen White Elephant*, and *Life on the Mississippi*, to James R. Osgood, whose firm, Osgood and Company, seemed unable to sell many copies of America's most popular writer. Twain then formed his own publishing firm, Charles L. Webster and Company, a decision that contributed significantly to his later bankruptcy. Twain came to detest Bliss but never lost affection for Osgood.)[12]

Because Twain was making good progress on his book, he felt he could accept an invitation to visit the Langdons. Charlie was a friend; the parents seemed amiable; Twain had never been to Elmira and liked to visit new places. And he could not forget Livy.

Mark Twain arrived in Elmira on August 24, 1868. It was the first time he and Livy had seen each other since the holidays in New York. The Langdon mansion took up a full city block and the grounds included elm trees and gardens. There was a glass hothouse for growing flowers. "The interior of the house was somber — with narrow windows, heavy curtains, a sweeping mahogany staircase, and deep upholstery."[13]

Hattie Lewis, first cousin of Livy, was staying with the Langdons at the time (she stayed for a year) and wrote about the Mark Twain–Livy Langdon courtship:

> My cousin Olivia and myself felt a little nervous about entertaining an unmarried man, who had written a book! At this time he had written The Jumping Frog.[14] We wondered how he would look: how he would act: would he be funny all the time? And must we try to be? Etc. as young ladies will. I really felt that I had one advantage over my cousin, but only one. She was rich, beautiful and intellectual, but she could not see through a joke or see anything to laugh at in the wittiest saying unless explained in detail — I could.... He said, "How do you do" ... with that lazy drawl.... We rode, walked, talked & sang together, for Mr. C. had a very sweet tenor voice. But alas — I soon discovered that my quickness at seeing the point of a joke and the witty sayings that I had considered almost irresistible were simply nothing in comparison to my cousin's gifts. Mr. C. evidently greatly preferred her sense to my nonsense. I told him later that I should never understand why he did.... [A]nything I could do to help them along should be done. I had been intending to go on to N.Y. for a visit, but had postponed it on account of Mr. C. coming. I now decided to go, thinking the courtship might progress better if I were out of the way. Olivia was very unsuspicious, therefore, before leaving I gave her a hint of what I thought Mr. C. had in his mind & heart and said that on my return I should ask a question, in regard to a question I was quite sure would be asked her, and I wanted a favorable answer to both.[15]

Twain, according to a story often told in the Langdon family, arrived in Elmira dressed in a yellow duster and wearing a very dirty and old straw hat. Charlie met him at the train station and convinced him to change into something more appropriate before meeting the rest of the family. Probably Twain was simply traveling in comfortable clothing and already intended to change into something else when he arrived. If not, he certainly did not have the personality to allow himself to be talked out of how he wanted to dress.

Twain dressed neither fashionably nor outlandishly. The famous year-round white suit wasn't added until he was in his seventies, but he did wear the white suit during summer months decades earlier. Rather than fashionable or outlandish, his attire was almost always noticeable. He was determined to be the center of attention wherever he went and was usually successful even before his fame made attention inevitable and unavoidable. He often wore a white waistcoat in the summer and a sealskin coat in the winter, and any time of year he might wear socks of bright lavender, pink, or green.[16] His clothing was noticed by the Langdons, but not disapprovingly. It seemed only to add to his charm.

Twain stayed in Elmira two weeks, leaving on September 8. But before he left he asked Livy to marry him. She said no, but she agreed to be like his sister and said he could write to her. On September 7, while still at the Langdon home, he wrote her a letter in which he said, "I ask that you will write to me sometimes, as to a friend whom you feel will do all that a man may to be worthy of your friendship — or as to a brother whom you know will hold his sister's honor as dearly as his own, her wishes as his law, her pure judgments above his blinded worldly wisdom." From Elmira, he started west, on a lecture tour, and in a letter dated September 21, 1868, from St. Louis he wrote, "I *will* 'pray with you,' as you ask." In the same letter he says he accepts her invitation to visit her again in Elmira. The invitation evidently came in a letter to him that has not survived.[17]

Livy was 22 and had never before had a man, or boy, show such interest in her. Her fragility kept her indoors during much of her teen years when she otherwise might have met boys. And she attended an all-girls school and an all-girls college. In addition, being from a wealthy family no doubt kept most of the young men in Elmira at a distance, since they would assume she was out of reach. Being bookish didn't help. And her parents discouraged her from pursuing a romantic relationship with any boy or young man. Mark Twain wrote in a letter dated Dec. 1, 1868, to his older sister, Pamela (pronounced "Pa-mee-la") that "her parents have refused to permit the attentions of any body, before, but I was mean enough to steal a march on them."[18] After Livy did agree to marry Sam Clemens, she confided in him her concerns about leaving home. "To think of having them grow used to my being absent," she wrote in a letter to her fiancé in December of 1868, "so that at last they would come to miss me, made me feel as if I wanted father to put his arms about me and keep me near him always.... He said last night that if he could live as long as I did, he would never let any man take me away from him; and he said that when I left home he was going to sell out — he is good at making threats."[19]

Jervis's protestations of fatherly love may have been gentle and exaggerated teasing, but there is no evidence that the same assertions and mock threats were given to Susan, his older daughter, or Charlie, his son. Rather, Jervis's expressed desire to keep his second-oldest daughter with him always reflects paternal concern for a child, even if she was now a grown woman, who because of her frail health always required special attention. It was the same emotion that drew Sam Clemens to her.

Thus, not having had much experience with boys and men when Sam

Clemens, ten years her senior, proposed in September of 1868, she must have been confused. Did romance move this quickly? She was composed enough, levelheaded enough, to realize she just didn't know him well enough to marry him, as much as she liked him, as interesting as she found him. Livy, as practical as she was romantic, said no.

He proposed twice more and twice more she said no.

But he was not discouraged. Her rejections didn't seem firm, and he believed he only needed more time. More time to spend with her and more time for her resistance to metamorphose into acceptance. He got Charlie to invite him to visit for a week. When it was time to leave for New York, a democrat wagon (a topless, very light wagon with several rows of seats, typically pulled by two horses) waited outside for him with Barney the coachman in the front seat with reins in his hand. It was 8:00 or 9:00 P.M. and dark. Twain said farewell to the Langdon family, which had gathered on the front porch. Twain and Charlie climbed into the backseat, which was a temporary arrangement just for Twain and not fastened into place. Charlie was smoking a cigar. Barney touched the lone horse with a whip and the animal sprang forward, and both Charlie and Twain tumbled out the back of the wagon. Charlie's cigar made a red arc in the darkness. Twain landed on his head, stayed that way, upright, for a moment, and fell to the ground unconscious. He had landed in a cobblestone gutter that was being repaired. His head hit a "dish" formed by four cobblestones touching one another. The depression was filled with sand, which cushioned the fall. He was not hurt, had no bruise, and felt no jolting. Charlie, however, was battered, but the young man paid so much attention to his guest that he ignored his own wounds. The family gathered around Twain. Theodore Crane, husband of Livy's older sister, Susan, poured brandy from a flask into Twain's mouth, but it did not awaken him. Or, more accurately, showed no evidence of awakening him. He was faking the unconsciousness, and he enjoyed hearing the Langdons make pitying remarks about him. He worried that his lack of injuries would soon be discovered. Barney, Charlie, Jervis, and Theodore lifted him up and carried him into the house. They sat him in an armchair in the parlor and sent for the family doctor. Susan brought some type of medicine that was supposed to reduce concussions. She poured it on top of his head and rubbed it in with her hand. Some of it dribbled down Twain's back and made it feel like it was on fire. Twain decided he should soon come out of his unconsciousness, but after a while Theodore suggested that Susan rest and let Livy do the rubbing. Twain gave up his plan to recover from his unconsciousness to allow, and enjoy, Livy massaging his head.

The family doctor arrived, examined Twain, and said there were no concussions or lumps and that the patient only needed rest and would be all right in the morning. Twain, however, said he didn't need a doctor but agreed he needed rest. Which he got, he said, at the Langdon home, for three more days, with Livy nursing him.[20] Actually, he stayed only one extra day. Livy, whose major literary output consisted of personal letters to friends and relatives, wrote to her mother on September 8 and to Joseph Twichell, one of Sam Clemens's closest friends, on November 28, that he stayed only one extra day.[21] Still, Twain's watering the romance with such shenanigans helped it to sprout.

During the courtship he visited Elmira as often as his schedule and his ability to win invitations from Charlie or another Langdon meshed. Twain was lecturing around the East and Midwest and editing his book in progress, *Innocents Abroad*. Bliss wanted him in Hartford as much as possible so he could supervise Twain's editing. When away from Elmira, Twain wrote almost daily to Livy. He was aware that despite what was clearly a growing attachment he and Livy felt for each other, there were aspects of his personality that troubled her. Accordingly, in a letter from Hartford dated October 18 he acknowledged that she was correct (in a letter that has not survived) to "rebuke" him for his "hotblooded needlessness." He was ever apologetic when he thought he might have offended her. It was a trait that would never be absent from their relationship. And he was ever trying to be witty, which he sensed was one of his traits that most appealed to Livy. In early November he traveled to Elmira to deliver a lecture and he showed up at the Langdon home and said, "The calf has returned; may the prodigal have some breakfast?" On a Monday night she attended his lecture. She was polite to him for several days but otherwise avoided him. He wrote to his Hartford friend Joe Twichell that "Wednesday night she said over & over again that she loved me but was sorry she did & hoped it would yet pass away."[22] But he added:

> Thursday I was telling her what splendid, magnificent fellows you and your wife were, and when my enthusiasm got the best of me and the tears sprang to my eyes she just jumped up and said she was glad and proud she loved me!—and Friday night I left (to save her sacred name from the tongues of the gossips)—and the last thing she said was: "Write immediately and just as often as you can!" Huyrra! (Hurricanes of applause.)... I am so happy I want to scalp somebody.[23]

Despite Livy having turned down Twain's marriage proposals at least three times,[24] the Langdons understood the relationship between their daughter and the writer was serious and might, in fact probably would, lead to a wedding. Her father, Jervis, wanted to know more about Twain, but since his daughter's suitor was from out of town, he didn't know who to ask. He liked Twain but felt as a responsible father he needed to know more about him. So Jervis talked to Twain. He told the not-so-young man (Twain was 31) that no one knew him around Elmira except Charlie and that Charlie was too young to be reliable. He asked Twain for references from the West, which Twain willingly provided. He gave his potential father-in-law the names of several prominent men of the West, whose success he hoped would impress Mr. Langdon. He gave him the names of two San Francisco clergymen, and Mr. Langdon also wrote to a bank cashier who used to be a Sunday-school superintendent in Elmira. Twain chose poorly in selecting the names to give to Mr. Langdon, and the name Mr. Langdon chose, by coincidence, was just as bad. All three replies were negative. One clergyman, Horatio Stebbins, pastor of the First Unitarian Church in San Francisco, wrote back to Mr. Langdon that "Clemens is a humbug—shallow & superficial—a man who has talent, no doubt, but will make trivial & possibly a worse use of it—a man whose life promised little & has accomplished less—a humbug, Sir, a humbug." The man Langdon wrote to on his own was Charles Wade Hutchinson, who had once worked for Langdon and later moved to San Francisco, where he became a bank cashier. Langdon asked Hutchinson to find out what he could about this Sam Clemens fellow who wanted to marry his daughter. Hutchinson spoke to James R. Roberts, pastor of the Howard Presbyterian Church, and then wrote back to Langdon that Roberts said, "I would rather bury a daughter of mine than have her marry such a fellow." Twain says he gave Langdon four other references, but the specifics of their replies are unknown. What is known, because Twain himself says this, is that all the replies that were received were negative.[25]

Jervis Langdon was aghast. He asked, "What kind of people are these? Haven't you a friend in the world?"

"Apparently not," a chastened Twain said. Twain realized that he put too much weight on the fact that some of the respondents were clergymen, thinking that would impress the religious Mr. Langdon.

Langdon understood that and was forgiving. He said, "I'll be your friend myself. Take the girl. I know you better than they do."

Sometime later, Jervis heard Twain talk approvingly of Joe Goodman, the editor he had worked for a decade earlier in Virginia City, Nevada, and asked where he lived. The Pacific coast, he was told.

"Why, he seems to be a friend of yours. Is he?"

"Indeed he is. The best one I ever had."

"Why then, what could you have been thinking of? Why didn't you refer me to him?"

"Because he would have lied just as straightforwardly on the other side. The others gave me all the vices. Goodman would have given me all the virtues. You wanted unprejudiced testimony, of course. I knew you wouldn't get it from Goodman. I did believe you would get it from those others, and possibly you did. But it was certainly less complimentary than I was expecting."[26] Jervis was satisfied.

More important, Twain knew Jervis was satisfied and knew what that meant. Twain proposed a fourth time, on November 26, 1868, and this time Livy said yes. The engagement became formal ten weeks later, on February 4, 1869. He gave her a plain, heavy gold ring. The engagement date was engraved inside the ring. A year later, he added the date of the wedding, February 2, 1870, to the inside of the ring. It never again left Livy's finger. When Livy died, someone wanted to take the ring off and give it to the surviving daughters, but Twain would not permit that. It was on her finger when she was buried.[27]

One of the first letters he wrote to her after she agreed to marry him contained two sentences that addressed a point that would constantly be with them. He wrote from New York on November 26, "Tell me the name of that book you were going to lend me, Livy, so that I can get it. I shall send those books by Ed, if I can find him."[28] Talk of books would always be part of their conversations.

Early in their engagement, the proofs of his book *The Innocents Abroad* arrived and Livy helped him edit them. She edited his work from then until three or four months before she died.[29]

The letters they wrote to each other during the ensuing weeks reveal much about the nature of their relationship, and their attraction to each other. The letters contain much that is typical of new love: fawning, exaggerated compliments and teasing. They also contain numerous comments on books and writers. And letters Twain wrote to others provide details of his pursuit of Livy. Far more of the letters that he wrote to her survive than letters she wrote to him, but many of his letters contain replies to specific points she had made, so some idea of what she wrote is detectable.

In a letter to his future father-in-law written on December 2, 1868, Twain noted that he understood Livy's health problems interfered with her everyday activities. "I know from what Miss Langdon said the night I left, that she would have answered my letter if she had been well." He was always aware of her frailty, including throughout their courtship, during his proposals, when she finally accepted the fourth proposal, through their engagement. Her frailty was part of who she was, part of who Twain understood her to be, part of his attraction to her. She was someone to care for and to take care of. In the same letter, he hinted openly for another invitation to Elmira, one directly from Mr. and Mrs. Langdon. He wrote, "If you please, I wish you would say to Mrs. Langdon that I wish to go back to Elmira — for a little while —*only* a little while — only just long enough to say to Miss Langdon a few things which I hadn't quite finished telling her — it will only take a couple of weeks, or a couple of months, of such a matter? Will she let me?— But really, I supposed I *could* get along with just one evening — or just one *hour* — if I couldn't do any better." He was at this point so confident in his relationship with not just his fiancée but with her entire family that he didn't hesitate to tease Jervis. "Now be *good*," Twain wrote, "you are the splendidest man in the *world*!—be generous, now—be merciful—*do* ask her, please? I'll call you all the nice names I can think of if you will enter into this little conspir——Time's up—goodbye—love to all."[30]

A letter he wrote to her on December 4 reveals, teasingly, some of his deepest sentiments towards Livy. In it he lists what he calls her four faults. He wrote:

> They are—1. The using of slang (but you didn't know it was slang, my little angel by brevet, else you wouldn't have used it); 2. The leaving off of blue ribbons at times (which is unconstitutional & unsustained by law); 3. The appearing five minutes late at breakfast, every morning when I have been watching the door for ages & ages to see you enter, radiant and beautiful, & fill all the dull air with sunshine; 4. But your most heinous fault is in loving me—& I pray that it may grow, & grow, & grow, till it shall usurp all your being & leave you nothing but one stately, magnificent, concentrated, sublimated, overwhelming Fault, for all Time![31]

While most of her letters to him do not survive, his references to them reveal they were neither as playful nor as openly romantic as those he wrote to her. For example, he wrote to Joe Twichell on December 12:

> I am honor bound to regard her grave, philosophical dissertations as *love letters*, because they probe the very marrow of that passion, but there isn't a bit of romance in them, no poetical repining, no endearments, no adjectives, no flowers of speech, no nonsense, no bosh. Nothing but solid chunks of wisdom, my boy—love letters gotten up on the square, flat-footed, cast-iron, inexorable plan of the most approved commercial correspondence, & signed with stately & exasperating decorum, "Lovingly, *Livy L. Langdon*"—*in full*, by the Ghost of Caesar!

To make certain Twichell didn't read disappointment into Twain's evaluation of Livy's letters, he added:

> They are more precious to me than whole reams of affectionate superlatives would be, coming from any other woman, but they *are* the darlingest funniest *love* letters that ever were written, I do suppose. She gets her stateliness of [English] epistolary composition from her native dignity, & she gets that from her mother, who was born a countess.[32]

Livy's mother, Olivia, of course was not born a countess, and it's unlikely that she was directly the source of Livy's reserve in her letter writing. More likely, Livy's lack of experience with men and her extensive reading of canonical rather than popular literature are being reflected in the letters she wrote to the man she loved. If she had read more of, say, James Fenimore Cooper and

Sir Walter Scott her letters might have been more flowery. Her future husband would, of course, later famously excoriate both of these adjective-happy, exaggeration-prone authors. Ironically, it's Twain's letters to Livy, not hers to him, that exhibit the traits he would later find so unacceptable in two of the most popular writers of his youth.[33] Books, in fact, were among the most common topics to appear in their letters to each other. For example, in late 1868 and early 1869 Twain wrote to Livy that he liked *The Angel in the House* by Coventry Patmore, that he also liked *Aurora Leigh* by Elizabeth Barrett Browning but found some of it obscure, and that he liked parts of *Tristram Shandy* by Laurence Sterne. He asked Livy if she would explain some of Browning's novel to him but warned her about reading Sterne's. "The book," he wrote, "is coarse, & I would not have you soil your pure mind with it."[34]

His comment about Browning might seem curious. *Aurora Leigh* is not a particularly difficult book to read, and Twain was a careful and insightful reader and would not have needed help in understanding the novel. Rather, he was subtly suggesting to Livy that she read the book in the hope that it would remind her of Browning's most famous work, *Sonnets from the Portuguese*, which she had of course written for her future husband, Robert Browning. Elizabeth and Livy had much in common, something that did not escape Twain. Both were from wealthy families, both suffered from frail health, and both loved to read.[35] (And both of course married famous men of literature.) Twain hoped that Livy by reading Mrs. Browning would adopt her practice of writing openly romantic letters to the man in her life. But Livy, overly protected by loving but fearful parents and unaccustomed to romantic attachments to men, was unprepared and incapable of offering that response.

Twain, meanwhile, provided the same cloak of protection that her parents had provided for two decades. Sensing that her attraction to him was based at least in part on his knowledge and judgments of literature, he especially sought to protect her from certain books. Even if one of them was his. In a letter written on December 31 he gave her what now seems like surprising advice about his first book. He wrote, "Don't read a word in that Jumping Frog book, Livy — don't. I hate to hear that infamous volume mentioned. I would be glad to know that every copy of it was burned, & gone forever. I'll never write another like it."[36] He worried that Livy, raised in the refinement of the East, might not appreciate the rugged silliness of a clearly western yarn. But a year later, on December 14, 1869, more confident in his knowledge of Livy's likes and dislikes and aware that she fully accepted his high judgment of his own literary worth and having discussed with her different ways of telling a story, he wrote to her about a different opinion of the same story. He said "a man might tell that Jumping Frog story fifty times without knowing *how* to tell it — but between you & I, privately Livy dear, it is the best humorous sketch America has produced, yet."[37] He sounds very much like Tom Sawyer trying to impress Becky Thatcher. Just as Laura Hawkins, a childhood friend of Sam Clemens in Hannibal, Missouri, was the model for Becky, a not particularly well-developed character but rather an idealization of youthful beauty and purity, Livy would become the adult Sam Clemens's lifelong model of the same qualities, a woman he would always see as pure and beautiful.

Livy accepted Mark's judgment of both "Jumping Frog" and her character. And so did her parents, who now saw in Sam Clemens a man who viewed her the same way they did and who was on his way to accumulating the financial resources that would allow their daughter, once she left their home, to continue to live in a style similar to the one she had grown accustomed to. Jervis provided the financial resources that enabled Twain to purchase a one-third interest in the *Buffalo Express*, a daily newspaper in one of America's fastest-growing cities, at the western terminus of the Erie Canal. Jervis loaned Twain $12,500, hinting strongly that the loan need not be repaid in any hurry, although Twain insisted he would repay it. Livy, who had been excited by her visits to New York, looked forward to living in a more populous, and presumably more sophisticated, metropolitan area than Elmira. Their engagement was publicly announced on February 4, 1869.

Twain continued touring and lecturing. In May and June he visited Elmira. Charlie, his parents still concerned that he needed a better education, began preparations for a round-the-world tour. And while Twain was away, he wrote to Livy nearly every day. And she wrote back. Always on the day she received a letter from him. Most of her earliest letters to him have been lost,[38] undoubtedly because Twain, constantly traveling, was careless in protecting them. But the letters did reach him. On New Year's Day, 1869, he wrote from Cleveland to his friend Joe Twichell, "I can always depend on an 8-page letter, every day." And the tone of the letters, he told Twichell, was consistent: "Never any whining in it, or any nonsense, but wisdom till you can't rest. Never any foolishness — but whenever she does miss fire & drop *herself* into her epistle accidentally, it is perfectly gorgeous. She thinks about me all the time, & informs me of it with Miltonic ponderosity of diction. She loves me, & conveys the fact with the awful dignity of an Ambassador construing an article of international law." It is sad that Livy's early letters to her fiancé do not survive, but if his judgment of them is correct, she lacked the ability to write truly romantic letters because she misconstrued what good writing is. Big words rather than small, pomposity rather than simplicity, a desire to impress rather than inform seem to have been her guiding principles in writing those letters. Still he treasured them. "Ours is a funny correspondence, & a mighty satisfactory one, altogether," he wrote Twichell. "My letters are an ocean of love in a storm — hers an ocean of love in the majestic repose of a great calm," he wrote. "But the waters are the same — just the same, my boy."[39]

She seemed never to be able to evaluate him without a literary reference. A reunion of travelers on the *Quaker City* had been planned for February 18, 1869, in Elmira with the Langdons as hosts, but Twain, traveling on his lecture circuit, could not attend, so it was canceled, and Livy later said that a reunion without Sam Clemens would be like *Hamlet* without the prince.[40]

They tried to influence each other. In a letter written from Rockford, Illinois, on January 6, 1869, he gently scolded Livy for "daring to sit up & write after midnight." Ironically, in his dateline he noted that he was writing the letter at midnight. In the same letter he wrote, "I bless you for your religious counsel, Livy." She would attempt to influence his religious views for years, always with only superficial success. He would indicate some modicum of agreement, but slowly and inevitably her religious devoutness would move towards his disillusioned skepticism. That letter also contained a note of concern: "'People' made you cross? I wonder what they did. Come to the deserted confessional, Livy — what was it?"[41] Neither his letters to her nor any of her surviving letters indicate what incident or remark she referred to or what trend in society. It is an unusual comment because almost all comments about young Livy depict her as a calm, not easily perturbed person.

Oddly, Twain felt a need to keep his relationship with Livy partly secret. Elmira was a small city with little more than 12,000 residents, and post office employees did not always honor an expectation of privacy. So Twain addressed his letters to Livy to her brother. An outer envelope was addressed to Charlie, an inner one to Livy; the inner one sometimes had notes on it like "Cart it home, Charley, please" and "Courtesy of His Holiness Bishop Langdon."[42]

Even if Livy had difficulty being romantic in her letters, she was still able to let Twain know she loved him. In a letter written on January 13, 1869, from Ottawa, Illinois, he noted that in a recent letter she wrote about marriage and said he was pleased with that.[43]

Perhaps the most frequent distinction in what they said and wrote to each other is revealed in teasing. There is very little in what she wrote or is known to have said to him that can accurately be classified as teasing, but there are hundreds of examples in his letters to her and his known conversations with her that clearly are teasings. And there's no indication that she ever reacted with annoyance or hurt. Quite the opposite, she took his teasing as proof that he loved her, for while humor was ever present in his novels and essays and travel literature, much of it self-deprecatory, teasing was reserved for her. And later for their children. For Mark Twain, teasing was an act of love.

And there's nothing he teased her about more frequently that her spelling. In a letter written January 16, 1869, from Chicago, he wrote:

"Sicisiors" don't spell scissors, you funny little orthographist. But I don't care how you spell, Livy darling—your words are always dear to me, no matter how they are spelt. And if I fancied you were taking pains, or putting yourself to trouble to spell them right, I shouldn't like it at all. If your spelling is never criticised till *I* critise it, it will never be criticised at all.[44]

And of course his teasing was not criticism, but rather a statement of affection.

The letter in which she misspelled *scissors* does not survive, but Twain remembered it into his seventies, and provided more details when dictating his autobiography. He said that while traveling on his lecture tour he was receiving letters regularly from both Livy and her sister, Susan. Between them they spelled *scissors* seven different ways, and they wanted him to tell them which was correct; he added that four decades later he didn't remember the circumstances. One of the spellings was *sicisiors*, but he didn't remember the others. He did remember that they were all wrong. The sisters never consulted dictionaries. Later in life, he noted, Susan Crane kept near her a little 30-page book with a list of words that she used regularly in her letters. But she still didn't use a dictionary.[45]

His teasing of Livy's spelling was something he handed down to their daughters. Once while Livy was away from home a few days, Clara, their second-oldest daughter, wrote her a short letter each day. When Livy returned, she praised Clara's letters but said, "But in one of them, Clara, you spelled a word wrong."

Clara said, "Why mamma, how did *you* know?"[46]

Neither the teasing nor the negative recommendations he received from supposed but unkind friends in California deterred either Livy or her parents in their love for Clemens. On February 4, 1869, Jervis and Olivia Langdon gave their formal approval for Samuel Clemens and their daughter Livy to be engaged. A public announcement was made on February 5.[47] Livy was 23½ years old at the time. He was 10 years older. Neither the ages of either nor the age gap was particularly uncommon in mid– and late–19th-century America.

About two weeks before the engagement, already a de facto reality, was formalized, Livy told Twain that her parents called him a "wanderer."[48] Although they were merely stating a fact that was hard to not notice and were not criticizing him, he felt obligated to defend his wandering ways. He wrote:

I have been a wanderer from necessity, three-fourths of my time—a wanderer from choice only one-fourth. During these later years my profession (of correspondent) made wandering a necessity—& *all* men know that few things that are done from necessity have much fascination about them. Wandering is not a *habit* with me — for that word implies an enslaved fondness for the thing. And I could most freely take an oath that all fondness for roaming is dead within me. I could take that oath with an undisturbed conscience before any magistrate in the land.[49]

Twain was clearly a bad prophet. For the rest of his life he would wander. He would go on long lecture tours leaving Livy at home. He would live years in country after country in Europe, in England and France and Germany and Austria and Italy and elsewhere, Livy and their daughters with him. For a decade. He would travel around the world, at least that part of it where English was widely spoken — Australia, New Zealand, India, Ceylon, South Africa, Great Britain, Canada, the United States — for more than a year, Livy and their second-oldest daughter, Clara, with him. He would in fact spend almost as much time during the remainder of his life span wandering as he did settled in an American home. And even his American homes would change frequently. Despite his willingness to take an oath to the contrary, he remained a wanderer for decades, and Livy often wandered with him.

Twain continued to build a close relationship with Livy's parents. Jervis had already said he would be Twain's friend, and in a letter written from Ravena, Ohio, on February 13, 1869, he worked on solidifying his friendship with the mother, Olivia, whom he called Mrs. Langdon. Referring to himself and Livy, he claimed in the letter, "Neither of us are much afflicted with a mania for money-getting, I fancy. She thinks we *might* live on two thousand a year (& you know she is an able & experienced housekeeper & has a sound judgment in such matters,) but if I thought I couldn't earn more than that, I would not be depraved enough to ask her to marry me yet awile."[50] The sentence is clearly intended to convince Mrs. Langdon that he is capable of providing for her daughter in a manner similar to how she had been living, with servants, in a large house, without having to worry about financial matters, and to praise in advance the contributions the daughter would make to that lifestyle by properly managing the family finances. It's the life Livy was educated for at Miss Thurston's and at Elmira Female College. The life her parents assumed she would live. And agreeing to the engagement meant that Mrs. Langdon believed Twain could provide her daughter with the life wealth offered. Mrs. Langdon no doubt sensed that Twain's claim that he was not afflicted with a mania for money getting was not true. He would not only make a great deal of money; he would also seek to make even more through some remarkably bad investments. Jervis Langdon had invested well, especially in an anthracite mine in Shamokin, Pennsylvania, and his influence would both inspire Twain and lead him astray, making him believe that any investment

was likely to produce wealth. Jervis Langdon never made a major bad investment. Twain learned only part of the lesson: invest. He didn't learn the part
about the investment needing to be sound.

Writing from Lockport, in northwestern New York, on February 27,
1869, Twain told Livy that he likes the fact that she likes him to mark up the
books he reads and then sends to her. He wrote that he marked more books
than he sent to her but threw some away, not realizing she enjoyed his mark-
ings. She told him she was thinking of their future home together, and he said
he looked forward to them reading and studying together. She had noted in
an earlier letter that she was not getting enough sleep, and he responded by
saying she was too selfless and not thinking enough of herself. And he particularly liked a joke she made in a letter to him: Livy called the ring Twain gave
her "the largest piece of furniture in the house." He liked it so much he called
it "a burst of humor worthy of your affianced husband, you dear little Gravity."[51] This long letter (more than 2,000 words) to Livy was a much better pre-
dictor of their future than his February 13 letter to her mother. In this one
there is evidence of the sharing of literature that will become a permanent
part of their lives, of his constant concern with her health, and of one of the
earliest uses of what became his favorite nickname for her: Gravity.

Two days later, writing from Rochester, where he was continuing his lecture tour, he praised *Gulliver's Travels, Don Quixote*, and Shakespeare but
added that *Don Quixote* and Shakespeare were not proper for virgins to read.
Remembering that little more than two months earlier he had told Livy he
preferred that she not read his *Jumping Frog* collection of stories, he now
wrote:

> I had rather you read fifty "Jumping Frogs" than one Don Quixote. Don Quixote
> is one of the most exquisite books that was ever written, & to lose it from the
> world's literature would be as the wresting of a constellation from the symmetry
> & perfection of the firmament—but neither it nor Shakespeare are proper books
> for virgins to read until some hand has culled them of their grossness. No gross
> speech is ever harmless.[52]

Livy always appreciated her fiancé's literary judgments and seldom disagreed
with them. Her admiration of him as a litterateur never wavered, but she
believed she, too, understood great literature and would not be swayed from
reading it.

Livy's letters to Twain reveal a young woman confident enough in her
relationship with her fiancé to not worry that her attempts to remold him
would drive him away. In an effort to make him value religion as much as she
did, she regularly sent him copies of *Plymouth Pulpit*, leaflets containing sermons delivered by Henry Ward Beecher in his Brooklyn church and in which

she underlined parts for his edification; and Twain sometimes prayed on his knees with clergymen and read Bibles in hotels, more in an effort to impress Livy with an alleged religiosity than from true belief.[53] Henry Ward Beecher was the brother of Thomas K. Beecher, the Langdons' pastor at the Park Church in Elmira. The Beecher brothers were fine from Twain's perspective, but their sister Isabella was not. She had married John Hooker, a descendant of the founder of Connecticut who waited a lifetime to be appointed to that state's supreme court. His dream was never realized. Twain could not abide Isabella. With his current lecture circuit completed, he returned to Hartford to complete work on *Innocents Abroad*, and as long as he was there, Livy said in a letter, he should visit John and Isabella. Livy was a friend of Alice Hooker, and she wanted her fiancé to also be friends with the family. Twain had gone to Elmira and stayed until mid–June, when he and the Langdons traveled to Hartford for the wedding of Alice Hooker and John Day. Livy was a bridesmaid. Twain, trying to please his bride-to-be, visited some members of the Hooker family in Connecticut's capital, but he was unable to ever bring himself to like Isabella, whom he found, and many people agreed with him, insufferable. She believed she had been selected by "my adorable brother Jesus" to become a sort of matriarch in a new millennium following an apocalypse.[54] Livy failed in her attempt to make her fiancé a friend of Isabella.

That and other failures created enough anxiety for Livy that at times she felt compelled to say something. A letter from her to him in Hartford was enclosed with a letter from his sister, Pamela, that had been sent to Elmira, and he jokingly scolded Livy for that, saying he thought he received a much longer letter than he had. In the same letter he repeated his teasing about her spelling: "I notice how you always spell John with a G."[55] The teasing she could accept. But in a March 1869 letter she said he had, to use Wecter's phrase, "come perilously close to wearing out his welcome."[56] The revelation was startling enough to him that it led to a thorough apology. "I *apologize* Livy," he wrote. "I will make it my business to forget that [visit] ever caused you uneasiness, & remember only that it gave me my darling, my matchless, my beautiful Livy my best friend, my wise helpmate, my teacher of the Better Way — my wife."[57] It was not any particular incident that led to Livy's scolding but rather Twain's general demeanor.

Clearly there was some loving manipulation in Livy's comment, and clearly she succeeded. And it had a larger purpose than seeking an apology for an incident that did no lasting damaging to their love. Twain, always seeking the witty remark, often said things that offended others or that at least could potentially offend others. In April of that year, for example, he penned a letter to Pamela saying he had time to write because Livy was taking a nap. He wrote that he had been "outraging" Livy's feelings and that she was trying to cure him of what she called his "dreadful" speeches. When he had visited Elmira in the middle of the winter, he told his sister, many people in town had recently died and relatives and friends came to the Langdon hothouse (greenhouse) to get free flowers. Mrs. Langdon raised flowers in the hothouse and freely gave them to people who needed them for weddings or funerals. This time most of the flowers had already been taken because of the higher than normal number of recent deaths, and Twain made some joke about that. Livy, Twain wrote, didn't like him to joke about people dying. On the April trip he told Pamela, "I have been in the conservatory, and there is a perfect world of flowers in bloom, and we haven't a confounded corpse."[58] It is a typical Twain witticism, the type that would never desert his repertoire. The fact that their marriage lasted is proof that her machinations, her attempts to reform him, were no match for those aspects of his personality that attracted her.

His teasing attracted her. In a letter to her from Hartford on May 12, 1869, he teased her again about her spelling, this time noting that she spelled *terrible* correctly and pretending he didn't like that because it made her "un-Livy-ish." And his constant concern about her health attracted her, even if she found talking about that unpleasant. In a letter in early May to Mary Mason Fairbanks, a woman he met on the *Quaker City*, he wrote that when he tries to talk to Livy about her bad health "she turns crimson" and doesn't want to talk. He told Mrs. Fairbanks that Livy "is as sensitive about it as I am about my drawling speech & stammerers of their infirmity."[59] She was attracted by her occasional ability to control him. He had planned when his current lecture tour was completed to make a trip to California, where he had achieved his first substantial success as a journalist, short story writer, and lecturer, but she asked him not to go and he didn't. He never saw California again.[60] She was attracted by the fact that he displayed trust in her literary judgments. On May 17 he sent her, from Hartford, duplicates of his proofs of *Innocents Abroad* and asked her to help edit them.[61] Gentle teasing, constant concern for her health, a willingness to sometime acquiesce to her wishes, and a trust in her literary opinions would all remain part of their relationship for as long as they lived together.

The Langdons wanted Twain to settle down, preferably not far from Elmira. Twain considered buying an interest in a newspaper in Cleveland, New York City, or, his first choice, Hartford, a city he came to admire as clean, safe, and sophisticated. Jervis suggested his future son-in-law purchase an available interest in the *Buffalo Express*, and Twain, who was amendable to any suggestion from Jervis Langdon, agreed. Especially when Jervis offered to lend him $12,500 to close the deal.[62] The purchase was made and Twain became part owner of the newspaper on August 14, 1869. He was close enough to Elmira, about 150 miles away, to make frequent trips to see his fiancée.

Less than a week after taking partial control of the paper, he wrote to Livy (on August 19), "I simply want to educate them to modify the adjectives, curtail their philosophical reflections & leave out the slang." He said she should thank Charlie for him for inviting him to Elmira.[63] Twain, now a de facto business partner of Jervis and fiancé of Livy, no long needed an invitation to visit Elmira whenever he wanted, but Charlie didn't seem to realize that. Twain, however, did feel a need, or at least wanted Livy to believe he did, to seek her opinion about literary matters, like writing style in the newspaper.

Another trait that would become common to Twain, perhaps his least admirable one, worked its way into a September 3 letter he wrote to Livy. He had refused to print an advertisement that condemned a coal cartel in Buffalo. Other Buffalo papers ran the ad for free. The advertisement sought to promote coal "for the people," hoping to reduce the price per ton so more people could afford it. Twain said of those who wanted to place the advertisement, "The effrontery of these people transcends everything I ever heard of."[64] What he did not have to say in the letter, and what Livy very well knew, was that the cartel under criticism in the advertisements had two members, the Delaware, Lackawanna & Western railway and J. Langdon & Company. The cartel that kept coal prices artificially high in Buffalo and elsewhere made and helped keep Livy's father a very wealthy man. And much later in life Twain would defend the ruthless Standard Oil Company because one of its top executives, Henry H. Rogers, would befriend him.[65] Concern for the poor and condemning slavery did not deter Jervis Langdon from ruthlessness in business, nor his future son-in-law from defending him, nor his daughter from acquiescing in the practice and accepting its rewards.

In early September, Twain sought to make amends for the joke he told about flowers four months earlier. He told Livy he liked wearing the button-hole bouquets she made for him, and also that he liked the abundance of flowers around the Langdon home, adding that he liked to imagine they were put on display for him. But a newer crisis needed to be addressed in the same letter (written from Buffalo on September 3). Livy had suggested that their wedding, scheduled for late winter, be delayed until spring. Twain would have none of it. There was a possibility that he might be giving some lectures in February, and Livy had said in her letter that to allow for that the wedding could be moved back several weeks, or longer. Twain was determined that he would marry Livy and did not trust that a delay would be temporary. He insisted they keep to their original plans, an early February wedding.[66]

Livy became upset when Twain mentioned the around-the-world trip

Charlie was being sent on by his parents, who worried that he needed to be better educated, something that clearly was not happening in a classroom. Twain, as often happened, apologized to Livy in a September 8 letter for having mentioned it. "Livy darling, I ought not to have told you about Charlie's trip, & yet after all, I ought, for we must begin to do something for that boy." He added, in a reference to Charlie's fiancée, a comment that revealed much about how he viewed his own relationship with Livy, "I suspect that the most promising course will be to set Ida [Clark] to reforming him. Judging by my experience, you energetic & persistent little task-mistress, if any body can change his style of conduct it is the darling that has her nest in his heart." He then repeated his apology: "I am sorry I made my darling sad about it."[67]

The oldest letter written by Livy to Mark that survives is dated November 13, 1869, but most of it was written the next day. Much of it concerns the land the Clemens family owned in Tennessee, a bad investment that contributed to the financial ruin of Twain's father. A few months before Livy wrote the letter, there was a report of coal being found on the land. Mark turned his share of the land over to his mother, Jane, and his older brother, Orion, but the Clemens family in Missouri was hoping for more. They wanted Mark to convince his future father-in-law to invest in the land, or at least in the coal deposits that might be there.[68]

Livy wrote:

> I read Father what you wrote about the Tennessee land, he said, it was too bad for your brother to be such a drag to you, he did not make any remark about his working the land, and I did not like to press the matter because I know that he has a good deal on his hands.... God gives diversities of gifts, he has not given to your brother money making wisdom, but from what you say, he has given him a beautiful spirit never the less....
>
> ... I cannot but have a great desire to do all I can to lift the burdens from those who are carrying a heavy load — I feel that I have no burden, that I am so richly cared for, that I cannot but have a tender yearning for those whose backs seem almost broken with the heavy load under which it is bent.... I believe dancing and singing is a true way to give praise to God....
>
> Don't let your sister stay away from our wedding because she fancies her clothes are not fine enough — We want her, and her daughter here we don't mind about their clothing.[69]

Twain, always adhering to Livy's lead in matters concerning the Langdon family, also refrained from in any way pressuring Jervis on the Tennessee land matter.

Because Livy and Mark were both uneasy about discussing the possibility of having Jervis invest in the Tennessee land, they quickly turned to writing about other matters less likely to put stress on their relationship. In late

November he wrote saying Twichell had given him a copy of Charles Kingsley's 1853 novel, *Hypatia*, about the first famous female mathematician, who was murdered in 415 in Alexandria, but added that he couldn't read it because it was so bad. Twichell also gave him Charles Reade's *Hearth and Cloister*, a novel based on the life of Erasmus, the 15th-century Dutch Catholic scholar, and he liked that one so much that although he kept a pencil handy while reading it he could find nothing to mark up.[70] And on January 10, 1870, he wrote saying he loved the silk quilt Livy's mother gave them that was made from an old dress Livy wore as a little girl and said they must never sleep under it.[71]

Twain met Livy and her parents at the St. Nicholas Hotel in New York City in mid–December and stayed with them three days. They were there to purchase Livy's trousseau or, as Jervis jokingly called it, her *trowsers*. Jervis was extremely attentive, staying up on one occasion until 11:00 P.M. for the arrival of packages containing items purchased earlier in the day. He did not retire for the night until he had opened and inspected each item to ascertain it was in acceptable condition. Livy was so touched by her father's solicitude that tears welled in her eyes when she told her fiancé what had happened.[72]

With the wedding only five weeks away, Twain's writing career, already showing signs of future success, spiked upward. *Innocents Abroad* sold 12,000 copies in December, making it the best-selling American book in its first month of publication since *Uncle Tom's Cabin*.[73] He was on his way to becoming a national celebrity. Livy could imagine no better wedding present, even if her response was limited to expressing pride and pleasure in her husband-to-be's success.

In a December 27 letter he continued his tutoring on literature, telling Livy he had read but did not like *Story of a Bad Boy* by Thomas Bailey Aldrich, a semi-autobiographical novel about a teenage boy in Rivermouth, New Hampshire. Twain also read and advised Livy not to read *Gil Blass* by Alain-René Lesage, an 18th-century novel, saying it "would sadly offend your delicacy.... It is a woman's chief ornament."[74]

His career on the rise, her family happy in her choice of a husband, Samuel Langhorne Clemens and Olivia Louise Langdon were married on February 2, 1870, in Elmira.

CHAPTER THREE

Disease

Two ministers performed the wedding service, Twain's friend Joseph Twichell and the Langdons' minister, Thomas K. Beecher. Both were Congregationalists, Twichell at Asylum Hill Church in Hartford and Beecher at Elmira's Park Church. But the wedding was held in neither church. Instead it was held in the large parlor of the Langdon home in Elmira, large enough to hold nearly a hundred people, including Mark's sister, Pamela, and her daughter, Annie, but not his mother, Jane, who declined to attend because of her sense of fairness to her other children. She had not been able afford to attend the weddings of either Orion to Mollie Stotts or Pamela to William Anderson Moffett, and although Twain offered to pay all of her expenses to attend his, she declined. She insisted all of her children would be treated equally. Twain did pay for Pamela and Annie to attend, including making certain they had new clothes to wear.[1]

When Pamela (sometimes called Mela) pointed out to Jane that the $100 Sam sent for them to travel to Elmira would pay the train fare for everyone, Jane told her, "Since I didn't see you married, Mela, nor Orion, I'd not feel right to see Sam married." Jane Clemens's biographer, Rachel M. Varble, suggests that Jane also felt she would be socially out of place among the wealthy Langdons. For reasons that remain unexplained, Orion and Mollie never received an invitation to attend the wedding. Annie, 17 years old, arrived in Elmira early enough to help Livy address wedding invitations. Annie would later tell Jane how Livy so easily gave orders to servants, like the cook and coachman. The coachman was white, something fairly unusual in Missouri, and he wore the funny livery outfits coachmen in the East used as uniforms. And Annie told about the parlor walls covered in blue satin. And when Annie told Jane about the "reception room," Jane wanted to know if Sam sat in that room. Annie said, "Yes, he does, and even brings in mud on his shoes. But Aunt Livy won't let him smoke in those places. She's firm about that. And she has him asking the blessing at meals. Another thing—Uncle Sam has stopped swearing. And if he drinks now, I never saw a sign of it. Aunt Livy has simply made him over, and he appears to like it. They kiss and laugh a lot."[2] Annie was clearly not a good observer of her uncle. Uncle Sam curtailed his drinking, smoking, and swearing only in the presence and home of Jervis and Olivia. Livy understood from before the wedding that as much as she might want her beloved to become a non-drinking, non-smoking, non-swearing man, if she were to succeed in her attempts at reformation he would cease to be the man she loved.

One example of Livy's limited willingness to actually reform Sam was her repeated request that he stop smoking. Three weeks prior to the wedding, writing from Cambridge, Massachusetts, he told her that he had smoked since he was eight years old, that it did not make him nervous, and that the only thing that could make him stop smoking now was for him to believe that that was what she truly wanted. But the overall tone of the letter is that he thinks she is willing to accept him with his faults, including his heavy smoking. "If you had ever harried me," he wrote, "or persecuted me about this thing, I could not speak as I do—for persecution only hardens one in evil courses." And, "Ah, Livy, if the whole matter had been left solely in your hands, I would have been quit of the habit of smoking, long ago, & without a pang or a struggle ... there could be little prospect that other means would succeed if your gentle ministrations failed."[3]

"She made him over," Jane said. "A real feat." If Annie's report sounded incredulous to Jane, Pamela's was just as startling. "The Langdons are richer than I supposed," she said. "Coal." The Clemenses had heard about but never known anyone so rich. When Pamela told Jane that the son, Charlie, was going around the world on a cruise, with a tutor no less, Jane said, "You can't mean it." Pamela went on to praise the Langdons but noted a tidbit that surprised Jane. "They're very kind to people," Pamela said. "Livy's older sister, Mrs. Crane, has provided a milk route for the poor. I believe you'd call Mr. and Mrs. Langdon freethinkers. They attend a Congregational church without a creed, and sometimes they entertain Frederick Douglass, the Negro abolitionist, at dinner."[4] Jane had always had doubts about the morality of slavery and she particularly thought the practice of breaking up slave families to be evil, but she still did not feel comfortable thinking of a black as a social equal. "You don't mean it," she said incredulously.

And there was one more piece of incredulous news. Pamela told her that Sam wanted them to move to Fredonia, New York, a small town on Lake Erie, about 40 miles south of Buffalo. Jane was shocked. How dare her son think he could move her about without even consulting her. "I shall not leave St.

Louis," she said. "My friends are here. The river's here. Orion's here." Sam had inherited his love of the big river from his mother. Pamela had other news. Sam had arranged for Orion to become editor of a new magazine that Bliss was starting in Hartford. "Where is Hartford?" Jane wanted to know. Pamela told her and told her also that Sam would soon double the amount of money he sent her regularly. Orion going to another city? Jane was more prescient on the meaning of that fact than her daughter. "Do you think for a minute, Mela, that Sam will stay in Buffalo? Do you give him more than a year or two there?" But Pamela had already rented a house in Fredonia, and Jane realized she was defeated. Sam was the only one in the family with money, and that meant that in many things what he said would happen was what would happen. Sam had lectured in Fredonia and found it a pleasant town, and it was both close enough to Buffalo for him to look in now and then on his mother and far enough away for her to not be a constant presence. Jane reluctantly agreed to the move.[5]

Twain had arrived in Elmira twelve days prior to the wedding, allowing him plenty of time to take care of myriad details associated with a major life change. Some of the details were already in progress. He purchased a $10,000 life insurance policy with his mother as the intended beneficiary, although Livy's name was on the document. He assured his mother Livy intended that she, Jane Clemens, would receive the money in the event of Sam's death. Livy's family was all too well off for a mere $10,000 to be significant. For Jane, 67 years old at the time of her son's marriage, such an inheritance would be enough to last the remainder of her life. And he sent his mother a bank draft for $500, part of which Jane deposited in a bank and another part of which was used to go shopping in St. Louis with Mollie. Some of the money was spent on having a tailor make a suit and a topcoat for Orion.

Livy and Mark wanted a small wedding, with only family and friends in attendance, but Jervis and Olivia were too prominent in Elmira and the rest of the city's social elite could not be excluded without hurting feelings and relationships, both personal and business, and if some people were invited from out of town, like the Twichells from Hartford, other people from other towns needed to be invited, like Mr. and Mrs. Fairbanks from Cleveland. Livy wanted to be married on February 4, the anniversary of their engagement, which would save money, because Clemens would not have to buy a second ring and could simply change the date already engraved on the inside of the engagement ring. Twain removed the ring from Livy's finger, not to change the date already there but rather to add a second date, the date of the wedding, February 2, 1870. Livy herself never removed the ring from her finger, and it was buried with her.[6] Olivia, Livy's mother, thought that February 4 would create problems with the housekeeping staff, being too close to the weekend, when some were entitled to time off, so the wedding was moved up from Friday to Wednesday. It was also moved up from 8:00 P.M. to 7:00 P.M. to accommodate the Reverend Beecher, who had an 8:00 P.M. meeting at the Park Church, which was just across the street from the Langdon mansion (close enough to allow escaped slaves in pre–Civil War days passage from one to the other via an underground tunnel).

Livy, certainly a virgin at her wedding, wore a white dress with long white gloves extending up to her biceps. Twain was probably also a virgin, although he may have visited prostitutes in Nevada or California more than a decade earlier.[7]

The wedding ceremony was immediately followed by a formal dinner of boneless turkey. And toasts were made without alcohol, the Langdon family being temperance-minded. Then Mark and Livy danced. Followed by Livy and Jervis dancing. Then others joined in on the dance floor.

An unexpected wedding present arrived in the mail the morning of the wedding. The Blisses in Hartford had sent Twain a royalty check for $4,000 for sales of *Innocents Abroad*. His and Livy's marriage was starting off extremely well, and the next day, thanks to the loving machinations of Jervis and Olivia Langdon, the start got even better.

The anxiety realized by a young couple so inexperienced in sex called for time alone. But this was Victorian America and interfering with sexual union was not a matter for discussion. It was simply expected. The morning following the evening wedding, more than a dozen people who had attended boarded a private car on the Pennsylvania Northern Central railroad and traveled to Buffalo. Not just the bride and groom, but the bride's family, the ministers, and friends. Use of the private car was a wedding present from the president of the railroad, a business friend of the bride's father. Livy had never been to Buffalo and Twain had little knowledge of or fondness for the city. It paled, he believed, compared to Hartford, a city he found attractive and appealing. He had written to J.D.F. Slee, the manager of the Langdon coal business in Buffalo, and asked him to make arrangements for a pleasant but inexpensive boardinghouse in the city. If necessary, Mark and Livy could look for something else after they resided in Buffalo for a while. Already, however, he was hoping to persuade Livy that Hartford would be a better choice for a home. He did, meanwhile, have to figure out how to make such a move without offending his father-in-law, whose generosity made the move to Buffalo possible and who preferred to have his daughter less than three hours away. Hartford was twice as far away. And more of that generosity was still to come.[8] And just as the generosity had stifled Livy's social life while she was growing to womanhood,

it would threaten to stifle her independence from her parents that she needed
to help build a successful marriage. But since the overprotectiveness stemmed
from love, it was difficult to identify as damaging or to counter. Jervis's wealth
made protecting his frail daughter with stifling generosity all the more possible.

The train arrived in Buffalo about 9:00 P.M., and Slee met them with the
three or four snow sleighs needed to carry everyone in the party from the station to the new home. Livy and Mark were both anxious to see where they
would be living. But the sleighs turned one corner and then another, and still
another, and Twain developed a feeling that there was a deliberate effort to
delay their arrival. And then one of the sleighs in the entourage seemed to get
lost, but no one seemed concerned. Livy knew what was happening. She had
happily plotted with her parents. Twain made a few jokingly derogatory comments about Slee, but he dare not be too harsh, since Slee was both an employee
and friend of Jervis.

Finally the sleighs turned onto Delaware Street (now Avenue), a fashionable neighborhood of large houses, near mansions, just north of downtown.
Twain knew enough about Buffalo to realize they were now in a neighborhood
beyond his financial resources. Livy was delighted with the homes she saw.
Smaller of course than her home in Elmira but still nice, large houses with
plenty of trees, on wide streets, with a sense of stateliness.

Finally the sleigh with the newlyweds pulled up in front of a large home
at 472 Delaware Street. The sleigh that left on its own earlier was already
there. The house was three stories high, with three large arched windows on
each floor in the front. The main entrance was to the left of center, with six
steps leading up to a small porch. The front yard was about 10 feet deep and
contained two towering trees, each reaching well above the 30- to 35-foot
height of the house. The trees were barren in the winter but even in that season
looked majestic. Light from the inside lit every room. Twain stepped out of
the sleigh and helped Livy out, always careful of her delicacy. He made some
more remarks about Slee but this time had difficulty hiding his annoyance.
This was more than he could afford, if indeed this was the place Slee had rented
for them. It didn't seem to be a boardinghouse at all but an entire house for
one family, something they could ill afford. Everyone went inside, where the
people from the missing sleigh had already assembled. A male servant and a
female servant stood near the front door. Twain wanted to take Slee aside and
say something harsh to him. But that would have to wait. This was, after all,
the day after Twain's wedding, and his loving bride smiled so broadly and no
one other than Twain showed the least sign of being upset. In fact, they seemed
to all smile at him, as if he were the only one left out of a joke. Then Jervis

from someplace produced a small and prettily carved wooden box, stepped towards the newly married couple and opened the box. He took from it a piece of paper and handed it to Twain. It was a deed. A deed to the house they now stood in. Jervis had purchased the house for $20,000 as a surprise wedding present to his son-in-law. Livy knew about the surprise, and the indignation and annoyance on her husband's face until the moment he read the deed were worth a fortune in quiet amusement.

Twain was placated, and appreciative, but he could not help but wonder how much privacy he and his new wife would have with such a father-in-law. Would Jervis never give up his suffocating intrusion into his daughter's life? Everyone sat down to dinner. The house was fully furnished, even including servants, paid for by Jervis Langdon. Even a horse for the carriage. The house had a blue satin drawing room and a "sanctum" with scarlet upholstery. A cook and maids were introduced. The errant sleigh had arrived first at the new home to assure the staff, who came with the house — another element of Jervis's generosity and control — would have a meal ready and ensure that all the lamps would be lit, that the heat would be turned up, that everything would be ready. The way Jervis thought everything should be ready. Midnight had passed before everyone from Elmira and elsewhere finally departed, leaving the newlyweds, at long last, alone. Except of course for the servants.

In the morning the cook, Ellen, said she was going shopping for food and asked Livy and Mark what she should buy. Making up a grocery list was something neither Livy nor Mark had ever done. Livy's mother had supervised the servants, and Mark was entirely unaccustomed to living with servants. "Neither of us knew," Twain said, "whether beefsteak was sold by the barrel or by the yard. We exposed our ignorance, and Ellen was full of Irish delight over it."[9] And then a tall, slender black-haired man in his early twenties approached them. He was energetic and Irish. He said his name was Patrick McAleer and he would be their coachman. (For 25 years. When McAleer died 35 years later, Twain traveled from New York to Hartford to attend the funeral.)

Finally with time to themselves, Livy and Mark settled into their new lives. Livy supervised the household, giving instructions to servants, arranging social events, writing letters. Twain had his job as an editor and part owner of the *Buffalo Express*. He wrote an unsigned article praising a speech given in Buffalo by humorist Petroleum Vesuvius Nasby backhandedly in defense of women's rights.[10] Another was an obituary filled with praise for Anson Burlingame, who had served as a member of the U.S. House of Representatives and as Lincoln's minister to China.[11]

The playfulness of newlyweds became part of the Clemenses' letter writing. On February 20, 1870, a little more than two weeks after their wedding,

Twain wrote a letter to Livy's parents with Livy watching over his shoulder, and he provided the earliest known example of a joke he would play on Livy for the rest of their lives together. He wrote things he knew she would find outrageous. He praised her housekeeping and said "this morning she had a mackerel fricasseed with pork & oysters," and Livy wrote "False" on the letter. Twain then wrote, "I never saw anybody look so unearthly wise as Livy does when she is ordering dinner; & I never saw anybody look so relieved as she does when she has completed her order, poor child." Livy wrote at this point, "This is false too, mother dear, prettie nearly."[12] In fact, the family had a cook, Ellen, and a housemaid, Harriet, and a coachman, Patrick, and Livy's role therefore was mostly supervisory. She had not been raised to prepare meals or to clean but rather to supervise those who did that work.

Letter writing and teasing were always part of the way Twain courted Livy. Even before they were married he sometimes inked out something he had written to her and at other times cut out words with a scissors, all to make her wonder what had been eliminated.[13]

In the first letter she wrote after her wedding, to her parents, she remarked that "I wish that I could remember some of the funny things that Mr. Clemens says and does." Often in her letters during the following decades, she would refer to "Mr. Clemens." In speaking to others she sometimes referred to him as Samuel. But she never liked that name. And she would later object at least occasionally to the name Mark Twain, because she thought it had become associated in the public mind with a humorist and she believed her husband deserved to be ranked with the great writers. Mr. Clemens (too formal), Samuel (doesn't like the sound of it), Mark Twain (wrong connotation). She needed another name for him. Before they were married she started to develop a habit of calling him Youth. He was 10 years older and it seemed a way of glazing over the difference in age. The name seemed to emphasize what she liked most about him, his liveliness and humor, contrasted to her somberness and seriousness. He was 10 years older but so much younger in his attitude towards life. In Elmira she had tested Youth on him, and in Buffalo she adopted it as her lifelong name for him. (Jervis occasionally also called Twain Youth, but no one else in the family did with any regularity.)

In a February 9, 1870, letter written by Mark with annotations by Livy, we learn that Livy went shopping and to visit the Slees. Twain says that together they visited the Slees once, the Slees visited them once, he visited them once alone, and now Livy was visiting them alone. He also says the Twichells visited for 24 hours and that he and Livy showed them the house and made Joe Twichell wipe his feet and blow his nose before entering each room. To tease Livy Mark wrote that "Mrs. T. [i.e., Julia Twichell] says Alice

Day's house [in Hartford] is vulgarly showy & out of taste. I am awful glad of it. (So is Livy, but she don't say so — at least she don't want it mentioned outside.)" Livy wrote, "It's no such thing and Mrs. T. did not say so — ahem! Naughty youth."[14] Here *youth* is lowercase, as if it's a generic reference. In the future it will usually be capitalized, as a nickname.

The same letter continues the teasing, even including an oblique sexual reference. Twain wrote:

> Livy has a dreadful time making her cash account balance; & she has a dreadful time economizing a turkey in such a way as to make him last a week; & she has a dreadful time making the servants comprehend that they must buy nothing whatever on credit & that whatever they buy they must make the butcher or the grocer set down in the pass-book to be critically scanned by her eagle eye. These are all the dreadful times she has on the surface. She naturally has her little sad moments within, & she confesses it — but you may take an honest man's word for it that I think she secretly reproaches herself for not being sad oftener.

He adds,

> She is become so boisterous, so noisy, & so lawless in her cheery happiness that I, even I, am forced to put on an irksome gravity & decorum in order to uphold the dignity of the house. She pulls & hauls me around, & claws my hair, & bites my fingers, & laughs so that you might hear her across the street.... We sit alone in the loveliest of libraries, in the evening, & I read poetry — & every now & then I come to a passage that brings the tears to my eyes, & I look up to her for loving sympathy, & she inquires whether they sell sirloin steaks by the pound or by the yard. Ah, the child's heart is in her housekeeping; not in the romance of life.... We get up at 6 o'clock every morning.... We have three meals a day — breakfast at 10 o'clock, lunch at 1 P.M. & dinner at 5.... [W]e have heard that early rising is beneficial. We then go back to bed, & get up finally at half past 9.[15]

In a separate note to her parents, Livy focuses on the purely domestic and includes nothing playful. She writes that she has purchased a clothes bar, a bread box, a flat iron stand, a blower stand, and other unnamed items. "We are as happy as two mortals can well be."[16]

The playfulness and happiness was not without interruption. The first piece of mail Twain received in his new Buffalo home was a letter about his income tax. Someone in the Internal Revenue Department had read an article in the New York *Tribune* saying Mark Twain would make $100,000 from *Innocents Abroad*, so an assessor was sent to drop off a form. At the time, income above $1,000 was subject to a 5 percent tax.[17] In a March 26 letter to the Langdons, Twain noted that he was making $1,400 a month from the book.[18] He turned the incident into a humorous piece of journalism for the *Buffalo Express*, "The Mysterious Visit," which was published on March 19, 1870. In the article he claims that he had an income of $214,000 that year (clearly exaggerated) and should have paid $10,650 in taxes, but that he went to a very wealthy friend who advised him on a long list of deductions (all of dubious legality), so he had to pay taxes on only $250.[19]

Livy's bond to her father remained strong. A wedding present, a marble statuette of "Peace," broke during her and Mark's first month of marriage and Livy was nearly in tears, but the Langdons shipped a replacement. Twain wrote to the Langdons on March 2, 1870, that the new "Peace" statue had arrived but Livy didn't yet know about it because she had company in the drawing room, but later in the same letter he added, "She went into convulsions of delight when she entered" and saw it.

Earlier Twain, on February 26, wrote to Jervis Langdon that he told Livy "it is not showing proper respect to a father who pulls his house to pieces all the time— Move the wash tubs into the wood house, Madam, pile the wood in the stable & put the horse in the laundry—I tell you something must be altered quick, or your father won't like it." Jervis replied, "You may put the carriage in the cellar, the horse in the drawing room, & Ellen in the stable. Please your own tastes, my boy.... I am for liberty." Clearly Samuel and Jervis possessed meshing senses of humor.

Twain wrote in the March 3 letter that Livy's cash accounts had balanced only once (Livy wrote "false" at that point) and that she increases an item, say, butter, from 78 cents to 97 cents or reduces another, say, gas, from $6.45 to $2.35, so everything balances. Livy, both jokingly and seriously concerned with her father's opinions of her abilities, inserted: "Father it is not true— Samuel slanders me."

And when Livy could not find something she wanted to buy in Buffalo, she sent to Elmira, a much smaller city, to have her parents send polishing irons. Her husband wanted his shirts done up with them, she said.[20]

And in March Livy became pregnant. The baby was due to be born in December. For Livy and Mark, a daughter of wealth and privilege and a man well on his way to great success and fame, life seemed wonderful.

But as Livy already knew, life can be filled with unkindness. Just days after the wedding, she wrote to her parents, "I cannot but expect that the clouds will come some time, but I pray that when they do I may be woman enough to meet them."[21] Her father, 61, had been robust and energetic throughout Livy's childhood and into her earliest adulthood, but now he moved slowly, sometimes ate less than a full meal, and complained occasionally of not feeling well. The complaints were general and not specific. Except for his stomach. It now always seemed to bother him. Even before Livy's wedding, his health problems had become obvious to everyone who knew him well. He worried too much about his businesses, many thought. Doctors prescribed what in the late 19th century they often prescribed to the wealthy, that Jervis go south to rest in a warmer climate. In March he went to Richmond, Virginia, and wrote cheerful, joking letters. To his daughter and son-in-law in Buffalo, he wrote, "Samuel, I love your wife and she loves me. I think it is only fair that you should know it, but you need not flare up. I loved her before you did, and she loved me before she did you, and has not ceased since. I see no way but for you to make the most of it."[22]

Six weeks in Virginia did not cure him or even make him feel better. He returned to Elmira, and now his doctors had a more certain diagnosis. He had stomach cancer, and everyone knew that meant death was imminent. Livy and Mark went to Elmira, which that summer was very hot, the temperatures often in the eighties and nineties, and Livy and Sue took turns sitting at their father's bedside, up to eight hours each at a time, often moving a large fan made from a palm leaf to cool him. Twain sat at his bedside sometimes at noon, sometimes at midnight, usually for four hours at a time. Looking now and then at the large grandfather clock in the room made time move more slowly. Sometimes, when his time to sit at the bedside arrived, neither Livy nor Susan would come to get him. He had to remember the time on his own. But when he was sitting next to the bed, Livy or Susan always showed up on time. Doctors suggested the family hire professional nurses to sit with Jervis, but neither Livy nor Susan would agree. As his stomach worsened, Jervis could eat nothing. Even drinking water was difficult. He was administered the foam of champagne. In his condition, this man of temperance may not have known what he was taking. Twain would later recall that each morning, about an hour before the sun rose, a bird somewhere outside sang a mournful song. Twain canceled plans to vacation in the Adirondacks. He remarked to Susan that he thought Livy would never smile again. Jervis would sometimes recite lines from a poem by John Greenleaf Whittier, "God Is Love." He had sent Livy a newspaper clipping containing a copy of the poem on August 29. He particularly liked the lines

> I long for household voices gone,
>   For ravished smiles I long,
> But God hath led my dear ones on,
>   And He can do no wrong.[23]

One day Jervis seemed a little better, and the Reverend Thomas K. Beecher visited on August 6 and Jervis told his pastor and friend, "Beecher, I'm going home ... and I'm almost there."[24]

Then he died.

In the same parlor where six months earlier Jervis had watched his daughter's wedding he now lay in a coffin as family sat by and friends from the community paused in silence to say farewell. Jervis had been well liked in Elmira. His success, many believed, brought prosperity to the small city. He was interred in Woodlawn Cemetery, where 3,000 Confederate prisoners of war already rested and where, one day, his wife and three children and famous son-in-law would also rest. And because so many people wanted to pay formal respects to Mr. Langdon and could not be accommodated in the Langdon mansion, as large as it was, on August 21, two weeks after he died, the Reverend Beecher delivered a formal oration in his memory at the Elmira Opera House.[25]

Livy, in a tribute to her father, pasted the newspaper clipping with the Whittier poem ("God Is Love" or "The Eternal Goodness") into her common-place book. Then she copied it in longhand into the same book. Above the clipping she wrote, "Father died August 6th 1870."[26] A few months later she wrote to her friend Alice Hooker Day, "He was my back bone ... what energy I had came from him."[27]

Jervis's estate was worth about $1,000,000 at the time of his death. For the decade following the Civil War, it was an enormous amount of money, equal to several tens of times that amount today. Sue, the older daughter, received Quarry Farm, a 250-acre piece of land, with a house, on East Hill about two and a half miles from downtown Elmira that the family often used as a weekend retreat. Olivia, the wife, received the Elmira mansion. And they along with Livy and Charlie shared in the Langdon businesses. Livy's inheritance was worth about a quarter of a million dollars. She was a very wealthy woman.

Many years later, in 1885, Susan would write to her sister, comparing their father to Ulysses S. Grant. Grant was at the time near death and newspapers reported his condition daily. A record of Livy's response to the letter does not survive, but she did save Susan's letter and give a copy that same year to her 14-year-old daughter, Susy, to include in the biography the child was writing of her father, a clear indication that Livy agreed with the sentiments expressed in the letter. Susan wrote,

> Are you not reminded by todays report of Gen. Grant of father? You remember how Judge Smith and others whom father had chosen as executors were going out of the room, he said "Gentlemen I shall live to bury you all," smiled and was cheerful. At that time he had far less strength than Gen. Grant seems to have, but that same wonderful courage to battle with the foe. All along, there has been much to remind me of father, of his quiet patience — in Gen. Grant. There certainly is a marked likeness in the souls of the two men. Watching day by day the reports from the nations sick room brings to mind so vividly the days of the summer of 1870. And yet they seem so far away, I seemed as a child compared with now, both in years and experience. The best and the hardest of life have been since then, to me, and I know this is so in your life. All before seems dreamy — I

sepose this because our lives had to be all readjusted to go on without that great power in them. Father was quietly such a power in so many lives besides ours Livy dear,—not in kind or degree the same to any one, but oh a power! The evening of the last company, I was so struck with the fact, when Mr. Atwater stood quietly before fathers portrait a long time, and turning to me said, "we shall never see his like again"—with a tremble and a choking in his voice,—this after 15 yrs. And from a business friend. And some stranger a week ago spoke of his habit of giving as so remarkable, he having heard of father's generosity × X × X × X × X.[28]

There may be some grown children who chose a spouse because that person is a reminder of a parent, an I-want-a-girl-just-like-the-girl-that-married-dear-old-Dad syndrome.[29] And some may be drawn to a potential spouse because he or she seems exactly the opposite of a disliked parent. But neither of these is the case in Livy's attraction to Samuel Clemens. She loved her father, but the two men had little in common, at least on the surface. Jervis Langdon did not smoke; Samuel smoked cigars nearly every adult moment he was awake. (In 1882, in reply to an editor in England, Samuel wrote that he quit smoking for a year and a half to please Livy but that once he started writing *Roughing It* he had to return to his habit of 300 cigars a month.)[30] Jervis did not drink; Samuel loved alcohol, particularly hard liquor, so much so that some of his earliest acquaintances considered him an alcoholic (although that was seldom said about him later in life). Jervis was a religious man and active in his church. Samuel pretended early in his relationship with Livy that he was willing to be converted, but he never successfully convinced anyone that he would really change. Although Joseph Twichell, a Congregationalist minister, would for decades be one of his closest friends, the older Twain grew the less he attended church and the less kind his comments and writings would be about organized religion. In fact, Livy would eventually be more embraced by his skepticism than he would be by her early religiosity. Jervis never swore. Samuel considered swearing an honorable use of the English language. Jervis had a knack for making successful business investments, Samuel a knack for making disastrous ones.

Yet there was much they did indeed have in common. Both came to believe that slavery was a great moral evil, although Jervis grew up with that belief and Samuel did not develop it until he was an adult.[31] Both had Victorian ideas about women, reflecting a mixture of beliefs that saw women as deserving of rights equal to those of men but assuming they were in many ways in need of the protection and guidance of men. Both were amiable men who found making and keeping friends easy to do. Both were very generous with their wealth, often helping near strangers financially. Both loved reading and joking and working long hours. Each took great pride in his success. And both loved

Livy. Because he knew Livy loved Jervis, Samuel could not help but love his father-in-law, and because Jervis knew Livy loved Samuel, he could not help but love his son-in-law. Beyond that, the two men did have a fondness for each other.

For Livy, Buffalo was a lonely place. Mark's mother and sister had moved to Fredonia, as Mark wished, and visited Livy and Mark in late May. And Mr. and Mrs. Slee, the Langdon agent in Buffalo and his wife, had also stopped over. And so had Mr. and Mrs. David Gray, the editor of the *Buffalo Courier* and his wife.[32] Livy liked Jane and Pamela, but none of her in-laws ever became part of her family the way the Langdons became part of Mark's. And the Slees were business friends, nice people but folks she shared so little with. The Grays were her only real friends in Buffalo, and she just didn't know them well enough to turn to them for emotional support when her father died. So she invited an old friend from her days at Elmira Female College, Emma Nye, now a schoolteacher. Nye was on her way from visiting her parents in Aiken, South Carolina, to Detroit to begin a new teaching position when she stopped in Buffalo to visit her college friend. Emma arrived in late August and within a day or two showed signs of a serious illness. Doctors diagnosed her with typhoid fever, which in the second half of the 19th century was often, but not always, fatal.[33]

Emma's temperature rose to more than 100 degrees, spiking to 104. Sometimes her nose bled. She had a constant headache and no energy, and sometimes she complained of abdominal pain. Mark hired private nurses to care for both the visiting Emma and the pregnant Livy, who, despite her frailty and now her exhaustion from the emotional drain caused by the death of her father and her friend's illness, insisted on caring for her friend. But the nurses spent much of their time on the job sleeping, and Livy often had to get up in the middle of the night to make certain the nurses had Emma take the medications the doctors had prescribed. Livy also arranged for Clara Spaulding, also a college classmate, to come to Buffalo and help with the nursing.[34]

Emma at times seemed delirious, unable to recognize anyone around her, and her pulse was inconsistent. Red spots appeared on her abdomen. Livy, her frailty and exhaustion apparent, still insisted on nursing her friend. Mark urged Livy to rest, to let the hired nurses do the caring, but it was an effort doomed to failure. Livy for her entire life would feel obligated to personally aid anyone ill in her household. Emma's abdomen swelled, and episodes of diarrhea occurred six or more times every day. Her stools were a dark green. Wherever she was touched around her midsection she was tender.

Then, the doctors said, everything became worse. She was, they were convinced, bleeding internally. Emma began picking at her clothing and bedding for no apparent reason. It was an action without thought, as if she had no sense of what she was doing or what was happening to her. Her fever no longer went up and down. It stayed up, at 104 degrees for a week. Then it started to drop. And the doctors told Livy and Mark there was nothing more they could do, that now it was only a matter of time. But didn't the lowering of the fever mean there was hope? No, not now. She will die. There's nothing that can be done. On September 26, Livy decided to stay as close to her friend as possible, even though Emma did not have enough awareness of her surroundings to know Livy was there. For three days Livy did not go to bed, did not change clothes, ate little, stayed at her friend's bedside or sat outside her room.

On September 29, eight weeks after the death of Jervis Langdon, Emma Nye died in a guest bedroom in the Clemenses' home in Buffalo.

On October 12 Livy's younger brother, Charlie, married Ida B. Clark, who had been a college classmate of Livy's. The death first of her father and then of Emma Nye made what should have been a happy celebration a somber occasion.

A few weeks later, near the end of October, Mary Mason Fairbanks, who had befriended both Twain and young Charlie on the *Quaker City* excursion, visited Livy and Mark in Buffalo. When it was time for Mrs. Fairbanks to leave, she asked Livy to accompany her to the train station. Twain, concerned for his wife's general frailty, her delicate condition in the seventh month of her pregnancy, and the strain that the deaths of her father and friend had burdened her with, objected. But Mrs. Fairbanks insisted, and Livy acquiesced. Because Mrs. Fairbanks then delayed her departure, Patrick had to rush the carriage ride to get her, and Livy, to the station on time. Over cobblestone streets. Twain compared the ride to a "Channel passage in a storm." It was too much for the delicate and always frail Livy and, as a direct result, according to Twain, their son was born a week later, November 7, more than a month prematurely. He weighed only four and a half pounds.[35] They named him Langdon in honor of Livy's father.

Langdon had eyes such an unusual shade of blue that 14 years later Livy was unable to describe them to Susy. Livy had never seen that shade of blue except in her baby son's eyes. Langdon often carried a pencil in his hand as a plaything. When Aunt Susan picked up Langdon, he would hold out his hands for Livy to take him, but he held out the backs of his hands, not the palms.[36] Clearly something was wrong. Premature babies frequently develop more slowly than full-term babies, and Langdon's slow development worried his parents.

Twain had been in Albany to lecture a year earlier and wrote a letter to Livy comparing her interest in his writing with that of the wife of his friend Joe Goodman in his:

I am glad and proud that you take such an interest in my scribblings. I plainly see now, why Joe Goodman gradually lost all interest in his poetry (he was a born poet) and finally lost all ambition in that direction and ceased to write. The one whose applause would have been dearer to him and more potent than that of all the world beside, could not help him, or encourage him, or spurt him, because she was far below his intellectual level and could not appreciate the work of his brain or feel an interest in it. When I told him you took care of my sketches for me and listened with a lively interest to any manuscript of mine before it was printed, he dropped an unconscious remark that was so full of pathos — so fraught with "It might have been" — that my heart ached for him. He could have been so honored of men and so loved by all for whom poetry has a charm, but for the dead weight and clog upon his winged genius of a wife whose soul could have no companionship save with the things of the dull earth. But I am blessed above my kind, with another self — a life companion who is part of me — part of my heart and flesh and spirit — and not a fellow pilgrim who lags far behind or flies ahead, or soars above me. Side by side, my darling, we walk the ways of life.

His praise of her contributions to his writing was part of a lifelong pattern.[37]

The death of her father, the death of her friend Emma, the premature birth and slow development of her son, all this would have taken a toll on anyone, but the difficulties in Livy's life continued to accumulate. In February 1871, she was diagnosed with typhoid fever. The same disease that had killed Emma Nye less than five months earlier. Livy wanted a doctor she would trust, and she sent for Dr. Rachel Brooks Gleason, who had treated her as a teenager. Gleason was co-founder with her husband of the Elmira Water Cure Spa, a health resort that the Langdon family frequently visited. It was near the bottom of East Hill, upon which stood Susan Crane's new home, Quarry Farm. After a week, Dr. Gleason said Livy had to return to Elmira. Twain asked her to stay three more days, but she said she couldn't. So Twain hired a private policeman to stay at the front door of the house with instructions that no one was allowed to leave without his permission. Dr. Gleason stayed three more days.[38] Just as important for Livy's recovery, her sister, Susan Crane, arrived from Elmira.

Livy had red spots on her lower abdomen, and headaches, and was listless, and Twain said he thought she was going to die. But the disease did not progress as far with Livy as it had with Emma, and at times she could sit up in bed for a few minutes. And by April she could walk a few steps if aided by Mark or if holding a chair. The always frail Livy managed to summon a physical strength many thought she did not possess in order to overcome her attack of typhoid fever.

Langdon was just as frail. His parents loved him and wanted to share that love with others. On November 11, 1870, Mark wrote a letter to Olivia, Livy's mother, and playfully signed Langdon's name. It said, "My mother has mashed potatoes, & gruel, & tea, & toast, & all sorts of sumptuous fare, but she never gives me a bite."[39]

But nothing could make Mary and Livy want to stay in Buffalo. Since they moved there life had become unbearable. Jervis's death. Emma's death. Langdon's health problems. All that coupled with Twain's dislike of newspaper work. This was not the writing he wanted to do, not the writing that allowed him the depth and freedom he yearned for. On March 2, 1871, the Buffalo house and Twain's interest in the *Buffalo Express* were put up for sale. And on March 18 they moved to Quarry Farm outside Elmira to stay with Livy's sister, Susan, and her husband, Theodore.

In June, while at Quarry Farm and fully recovered from her typhoid fever, Livy again became pregnant. And in August 1871 Twain went to Hartford to look for a new place to live. In early autumn he rented a house from John Hooker in a section of Hartford known as Nook Farm and the family moved to Hartford.[40]

Orion had also moved to Hartford because, through Mark's influence, he became editor of a trade newspaper, *The Publisher*, put out by the Blisses. And Jane Clemens, their mother, also moved to Hartford and lived in a boardinghouse.[41] And emphasizing how certain they were that they would actually make the move, Livy sent a box of clothes to her husband in Hartford.[42]

The Buffalo house was sold for $25,000, $5,000 more than Jervis had paid for it, but Twain sold his interest in the *Buffalo Express* at a $10,000 loss.[43] Buffalo, a city that had promised him and Livy so much happiness and provided them with so much pain, was no longer part of their lives.

On October 1, 1871, they moved to Hartford to live in a rented house in Nook Farm. Twain, however, without an income from the *Buffalo Express*, was now compelled to return to lecturing, which kept him away many days at a time from his new home.

On October 31 he wrote to Livy from Milford, Massachusetts, saying he read *Eugene Aram* by Bulwer Lytton, an 1832 novel based on a real-life 18th-century Englishman who murdered his business partner and who also was the subject of a poem by Thomas Hood. Twain, who always shared his literary opinions with Livy, said he found the book "tedious" and that he skipped four out of every five pages.[44] On November 16, writing from Haverhill, Massachusetts, he thanked Livy for sending him a newspaper clipping, "[n]ot a stage trick," and noted that she mentioned a "Brooklyn note" but that she didn't include it. Also, Livy had told him she was having trouble finding a cook, so he said she should increase the offered salary to $5 a week.[45] Their letters were often so numerous that they could engage in the same type of chatter they would have if they were sitting in the same room.

But, of course, it was not the same. On November 20 Livy wrote to Mark:

> I do hope that this will be the last season that it will be necessary for you to lecture,...
>
> ... It was a pleasure to be writing letters for you,...
>
> ... I am going over to "the club" [a discussion club in Hartford that Twain belonged to called the Monday Evening Club] now in a few minutes....
>
> ... I do trust that we shall be a thoroughly united loving family — it certainly is the heaven here below —
>
> Youth in certain things you must teach me a "don't care" spirit, as regards cooks and the like,... I believe there is nothing that sooner ruins the happiness of a family than a worrying woman —
>
> ... I have slept and visited with the baby most of the day —
>
> Mother sits near me at work on her silk quilt.[46]

The day after Livy wrote that letter, Ida, wife of her brother, Charlie, gave birth to a baby girl, Julia Olivia Langdon.

On November 27, referring to Livy's earlier reference to writing many of his business letters, Twain wrote from Bennington, Vermont, saying, "I particularly hate to have to inflict on you the bore of answering my business letters. That's a hardship indeed."[47] But, of course, Livy willingly accepted the task. She had, after all, been raised to be a helpmate to a husband. Twain closed that letter with a reference to the many Olivias in the Langdon family. Twain sent his love to his wife, Olivia, his mother-in-law, Olivia (whom he called Mother), his niece Olivia, and his future daughter Olivia. Twain and Livy had already decided on the name of their daughter and that's the name that would appear on her birth certificate, but she would be called, from the date of her birth, Susy. Just too many Olivias to not cause confusion. And Julia Olivia was always called Julia. (Susy was originally Susie, but the child, at about age 13, changed the spelling on her own and everyone went along with her wishes.) Among Langdon males there would be almost as many named Jervis.

Mark and Livy usually wrote to each other every day when he was away from home, but sometimes the letters arrived a day or more late. On November 28 Livy wrote, "I hope that I shall get a letter from you tomorrow morning. I do like to hear from you little man, because you know — well you know all about it."[48]

The death of her father, the death of her friend, the premature birth and health problems of her son, her bout with typhoid fever all combined to create in Livy doubts about some basic beliefs she had lived with as a child. The doubts were particularly strong when she was alone at night.

On December 2 she wrote to Mark:

> It is just after dinner, I guess I will not write more until bed time, ... As you go further west it will take longer and longer for letters to reach me.... Mother and I

went to church this morning ... we were the first people in the church, so went over to Mr. Twichells and staid there until they were ready for church — It is so long since I have been to church.... Mr. Twichell's prayer touched me and made me cry, he prayed particularly for those who had fallen away and were longing to come back to God — Youth I am ashamed to go back, because I have fallen away so many times and gone back feeling that if I ever should grow cold again, it would be useless trying, because I never could have more earnest and prayerfull and even at times heart broken determination to keep by the truth and the right and strive for God's spirit.... [I]f I felt toward God as I did toward my husband I should never be in the least troubled ... how almost perfectly cold I am toward God —[49]

She had labored to make Mark more religious and he had put no effort into making her as much a religious skeptic as he was, and she was the one who was converted, not him. William Dean Howells would later recall that Livy once said to her husband, "Well, if you are to be lost, I want to be lost with you."[50]

The subject depressed her and she switched her letter to more mundane matters, writing:

I think I have about decided what we shall do about building, I have decided so you will not have to decide you see, Dear Heart — ... Charlie says I can perfectly well have from three to five hundred dollars a month.... If after a time we find, that the estate is not worth a living to us we will change entirely our mode of living — ... we will not be in debt for our house — ... We will either board or live in a small cottage and keep one servant, will live near the horse cars so that I can get along without a horse and carriage — I can not and I will not think about your being away from me this way every year ... — if in order to sustain our present mode of living you are obliged to do that, then we will change our mode of living —... I have not commenced French yet. Clara [Spaulding] wants to study German when she comes, and I know with Baby, house and all, both would be more than it would be best for me to undertake —.[51]

On January 7 Twain wrote from Wooster, Ohio, to say he had made about $10,000 on the lecture tour but adding, "I do hate lecturing.... Lecturing is hateful, but it *must* come to an end yet, & *then* I'll see my darling, whom I love, love, *love*." And continuing his decades-long discussions of his literary judgments with Livy, he said he was reading a novel called *The Member from Paris*, but he does not say who wrote it. He calls it "a very bright, sharp, able French political novel, very happily translated." He also said he had sent home the *Golden Legend* [by Jacobus de Voragine, a medieval book about saints], *The New England Tragedies* [by Longfellow], *Edwin of Deira* [by Alexander Smith, published in 1861, a book about the sixth-century King of Northumbria, in what is now northern England, who became a Christian saint], *Erling the Bold* by R.M. Ballantine (1869), and an unnamed book by Dinah Mulock Craik, an author best known for *John Halifax*.[52]

The family moved to the Cranes' home at Quarry Farm, outside of Elmira, in time for their daughter to be born there on March 19. On April 22 Twain wrote to his Hartford neighbor Charles Dudley Warner and said, "The new baby ... keeps one cow 'humping herself' to supply the bread of life for her—and Livy's relieved from duty." At this point he crossed out the words "Livy is very inefficient in some respects." He went on, "Livy drives out a little, sews a little, walks a little—is getting along pretty satisfactorily."[53] They were relieved that Susy was healthy. The family told the Cranes and Langdons they would stay in Elmira until the end of summer, but there was nevertheless some traveling to do. Twain had called his latest lecture tour "the most detestable lecture campaign that ever was,"[54] but he didn't object when Livy traveled with him. In early May they went, along with Jane Clemens, to visit Fair Banks, the Fairbanks family estate in Cleveland. While there he wrote to the infant Susy, who, along with Langdon, remained in Elmira with Grandmother Langdon and the Cranes. The letter was no doubt intended as a gift to be appreciated in the distant future. He wrote, "Many's the night I've lain awake till 2 oclock in the morning reading Dumas & drinking beer, listening for the slightest sound you might make, my daughter."[55]

Discussion of books, concerns about the home, expressions of love—their lives, after the tragedies, were settling into a mundane pleasantness.

Then, they returned to Elmira to pick up Susy and Langdon. The boy still had what seemed to be an almost constant cough, and he had not yet, at a year and a half, learned to walk. He could hardly sit up alone without the aid of supporting pillows. Livy had developed a habit of taking him for an early morning carriage ride. The fresh air, she believed, would help both her and her son. One day, however, Mark was the one to take Langdon for the carriage ride. Mark sat next to his son as the driver rode them around the hills to the east of Elmira. Twain wrote decades later:

> It was a raw, cold morning, but he was wrapped about with furs and, in the hands of a careful person, no harm would have come to him. But I soon dropped into a reverie and forgot all about my charge. The furs fell away and exposed his bare legs. By and by the coachman noticed this, and I arranged the wraps again, but it was too late. The child was almost frozen. I hurried home with him. I was aghast at what I had done, and I feared the consequences. I have always felt shame for the treacherous morning's work and have not allowed myself to think of it when I could help it. I doubt if I had the courage to make confession at that time. I think it most likely that I have never confessed until now.[56]

The dictation of this event was made in 1906, 36 years after it occurred. He never told Livy what he had done.

In late May, Livy, Mark, Langdon, and Susy went to Hartford. They intended to return to Elmira later in the year. Langdon's always present ill health seemed to worsen, and when Mark and Livy arrived in Hartford they contacted a doctor, who diagnosed the problem as diphtheria. Langdon was white-faced, coughed constantly, his neck was swollen, and from the way the doctor spoke Livy and Mark knew their son was close to death. Jervis. Emma Nye. Now little Langdon. The pattern produced inevitability. The boy, 19 months old, died on June 2, 1872.

Twain's late-in-life confession that he caused his son's death is, without doubt, mistaken, more a result of grieving memory than factual accuracy. Diphtheria is a contagious disease that spreads by contact with someone already infected. If an infected person coughs or sneezes in the proximity of an uninfected person, it can spread. Or if infected saliva ends up on food or drink that is consumed by someone else. A cold carriage ride would not cause it.[57]

Livy's grief resulted in failing health, and Mark feared she, too, might die.[58] Livy wanted Langdon buried in the family plot in Woodlawn Cemetery. But when he was interred next to his grandfather, for whom he had been named, neither Livy nor Mark could be present. Livy was too ill to make the trip, and Mark would not make it without her. Instead they went, with little Susy, to Saybrook, 43 miles south of Hartford, on the north shore of Long Island Sound. Orion and his wife, Mollie, stayed in the Hartford house.[59] Susan and Theodore Crane and members of the Langdon family attended the funeral services.

Livy had learned a terrible truth. It was not Buffalo or any particular locale that brought tragedy. It was life.

CHAPTER FOUR

The Picturesque Life

The rest of the summer was spent at Saybrook, and Livy's health then seemed strong enough for the family to return to Hartford. Twain sailed alone to England to give some lectures, to make notes for a travel book on the British Isles, and to arrange to protect the copyright on his new book, *Roughing It*, about his travels in the West with his brother Orion. Twain was particularly worried that a British publisher named John Camden Hotten would steal his work.[1] Hotten had made a fortune publishing Victorian pornography and, almost as a sideline, stole copyrighted works from writers living in other countries. Hotten never published *Roughing It* and Twain never wrote his planned travel book on England, but the trip was a precursor to something that would be become a major part of his and Livy's lives: living in Europe. On September 11 he wrote to Livy from London, "I would rather live in England than America—which is treason.... Real pleasant people here."[2] And he wanted to send her something English, so on October 3 he wrote that he had purchased a cloak for her.[3]

He returned to the United States and on January 16, 1873, signed a deed purchasing a piece of land in the Nook Farm section of Hartford and on March 22 purchased an additional strip of land to add to the property. They would build a home in Hartford.

One night early in the year, Livy and Mark were having dinner with their neighbors and friends, Charles Dudley Warner and Susan Warner. The two writers, Twain and Warner, both complained about the stupidity of modern novels, so Livy, with the support of Mrs. Warner, challenged them to write a better one. It took only seconds for the two men to agree to collaborate, and very quickly they began to write *The Gilded Age*.[4] Most of the novel was, in fact, written by Twain. An April 16, 1873, letter to Livy, who took Susy on a trip to Elmira while Twain remained in Hartford to work on the novel, noted that the first 11 chapters were his.[5] Started in February, the novel was completed by the end of April. The sections written by Twain do not mesh well with those written by Warner, and most reviewers noted that. It was Twain's only literary collaboration. The title is better known than anything else in the book. "The Gilded Age" now commonly refers to the corruption and graft common in big business and politics in the United States following the Civil War. Most Twain fans consider it a minor work, but it's Warner's best-known book.[6]

The book done and arrangements for the start of construction of their new house under way, on May 17 Livy, Mark, and little Susy set sail for England and Scotland.

Innocents Abroad made Twain a literary celebrity in the British Isles, and he had no trouble arranging meetings with the most celebrated European writers who happened to be in London in June and July, when he was there, including Thomas Hardy, Robert Browning, Ivan Turgenev, Herbert Spencer, and Anthony Trollope. Even their neighbor in London Joaquin Miller was an author. Miller had just published *Life Among the Modocs*, about a Northern California Indian tribe that continued fighting the U.S. Army late into the 19th century, the last group of Indians to wage war against the United States. Twain started calling baby Susy The Modoc, partly because her haircut resembled the hair worn by members of that Northern California tribe and partly because of his friendship with Miller.[7] There were so many social occasions in London that the Twains had no time for the sightseeing they wanted to do. They had taken along a nursemaid for Susy named Nellie, a secretary for Twain named Samuel C. Thomson, and a friend to keep Livy company, Clara Spaulding. But they were unprepared for the demands placed on their time by invitations to visit famous writers. So they went to Scotland, where, oddly, they were delighted to meet a famous writer. In Edinburgh they stayed at the Veitch, a hotel on George Street that catered to families.[8]

When Livy became ill and needed a doctor, Mark went looking for one and, knowing that Dr. John Brown, a famous author of children's books, lived in the neighborhood, looked for his office, found it, and was happy to learn that Brown still actively practiced medicine. Brown treated Livy,[9] and a lifelong friendship between the Brown family and the Clemens family developed. Brown's most famous book, *Rab and His Friends*, about an English mastiff, a huge dog that can weigh over 200 pounds, was a favorite of Twain's. (It was actually a short story that was published as a book.) Twain liked Brown's *Pet Marjorie* (also a short story published as a book) even better. *Pet Marjorie* was based on a fictional relationship that a real girl, Marjorie Fleming, supposedly had with Sir Walter Scott. Livy was very pleased when Brown gave her a copy of the book. The Twains and the Browns saw each other every day for the next six weeks.[10]

While they were in the British Isles in August, construction began on their new home in Hartford.

Livy became pregnant again, in early September (1873), when she and her husband were visiting either Scotland or Ireland. They then returned to Hartford so Livy could rest, and about November 8, Twain returned to England alone so he could lecture with C.W. Stoddard, a poet and travel writer who had been friends with Twain from their days together in San Francisco. But Twain missed Livy and reminded her of that frequently in his letters. On December 29, he wrote from London that reading her letters to him made him want to take her in his arms.[11] In January, Twain returned to his family in Connecticut. He and Livy jointly supervised the construction of their new home, and it contained much that Mark wanted, but in conception, design, and execution it was far more Livy's creation than his.

When they first moved to Hartford in 1871, Livy and Mark rented a three-story L-shaped cottage on Forest Street, in the Nook Farm neighborhood, from their friends John and Isabella Beecher Hooker. Hartford at the time had the highest per capita income of any city in the country, and the Nook Farm section was home to many writers and artists. After Livy and Mark purchased land on Farmington Avenue in the same neighborhood, they hired New York City architect Edward Tuckerman Potter to design the house. Livy drew sketches to show to Potter. To guide him. For Potter it was an ideal assignment, a client willing to spend a great deal of money and who was willing, also, to do unusual things. From one angle, the house looks like a steamboat, evoking Livy's husband's days as a riverboat pilot. The kitchen and servants' quarters are in an extension of the house, architecturally connected but visibly separated from the family quarters, a design typical then and today of many mansions of the very rich. A large library on the first floor, a schoolroom for children to be educated at home on the second floor, and a billiards room on the third show Livy's influence. Construction commenced in August 1873, and the family moved into the still-unfinished house on September 19, 1874. Mark was very pleased with the house, and Livy was very proud of her creation.[12]

They might have moved in earlier but, as became their standard procedure for 20 years, they spent the summer at Quarry Farm, the home of Livy's sister, Susan, outside of Elmira. And it was at Quarry Farm that Clara, their second daughter, was born on June 8.[13] When the newborn Clara was shown to her older sister, Susy, then two years and three months old, she said, "Lat bay got boofu' hair." *Lat bay* was as close as Susy could come to saying the "baby" had beautiful hair. Livy and Mark accepted the pronunciation and called their newest child Bay, a nickname that stayed around until Clara became an adult.[14]

Quarry Farm, as much as the new Hartford house, would help shape the Clemens family.

Livy loved Quarry Farm. The way it blended into nature. It was so heavenly. Youth loved it and her sister, Susan, was so kind and the children adored its open spaces. And views of the river and the distant hills and the city below—if ever there was a perfect home for summers, away from the heat of Hartford, it was Quarry Farm.[15]

It was picturesque not by accident, by design. Livy had read and talked to Susan about Charles Locke Eastlake's *Hints on Household Taste in Furniture, Upholstery and Other Details*. Eastlake's book was first published in England in 1868, and in America four years later. Eastlake's ideas were shaped by *Essay on the Picturesque* by Uvedale Price, a work that influenced many wealthy people in both the United States and Europe. The essential philosophy of the picturesque found beauty in the irregularity of nature, and to whatever extent was practical architects, gardeners, furniture makers, and others sought to incorporate that philosophy into their designs.

Quarry Farm was about two miles north of downtown Elmira and about 800 feet higher, atop a hill—East Hill—that afforded a view of the city, of the Chemung River, even of hills in northern Pennsylvania. There were no neighbors within hearing distance.

A man named Cornelius Roberts is the first known owner of the land, 287 acres that he acquired in 1788. He sold 37½ acres sometime after 1800 to Robert Covell. That sale also included 30 "perches," for another one-fifth of an acre. Covell, a land speculator, in turn sold the land to John Henry Fausnaught in the 1850s. Fausnaught was a farmer and sometime stonemason, who dug out a quarry on the farm. Jervis Langdon and members of his family would sometimes ride up East Hill in a carriage for relaxation and often passed the small house on the farm. On May 14, 1869, he bought the land from Fausnaught for $3,553.12, probably more than it was worth, but Langdon wanted the land as a weekend getaway, a place that would be cooler and quieter than his mansion near downtown. He was the richest man in the city and he could afford the small extravagance. Fifteen months later, he was dead.

Jervis had purchased the house in Buffalo for Livy and her husband, and his son, Charles, would eventually inherit the house that his widow, Olivia, lived in. So the land on East Hill and the small cottage on it were left to Susan and her husband, Theodore Crane.

The Cranes, like Livy, were adherents of the picturesque, and the changes they made in the house and land reflect that. The house Susan's father purchased was a cottage, but he quickly added on to it, and by the time Susan and Theodore moved into it, it contained a bedroom on the ground floor and another on the second, which might have been intended for a servant. A veranda, a wide porch with a roof and partly enclosed by latticework, was added, and Livy spent long hours sitting there, talking with her sister and brother-in-law, with her husband and daughters, with visitors. She found the distant view of the Chemung and the Pennsylvania hills relaxing and pleasing. She lacked the physical energy that allowed Youth to spend hours and hours walking, in the woods, around the grounds, down the hill into the city where he played pool and drank beer and scotch with town residents. Sitting on the veranda was a substitute way for her to be part of nature.

The colors of the cottage — which would over the years expand into a near mansion — allowed the building to blend into its surroundings: grays and browns. White was almost always unacceptable to anyone designing a picturesque home, as it stood out; it separated the home from its land.

The interior colors were also subdued, but the furnishings were clearly expensive: Oriental rugs, statues, sturdy and attractive couches and lounging chairs. The large windows in the parlor slid into slots in the wall, creating a large doorway leading to the veranda.

The Cranes added, during the first few years they owned the property, rooms in the rear to serve as servants' quarters, a room to store wood for the fireplaces, and bedrooms for Livy's three daughters. The Cranes had no children of their own, and Susan loved Susy and Clara and Jean as if they were her own. Susy and Clara shared a room, and Jean shared another with her nurse; their parents had the large bedroom on the first floor for many years and later a large room on the second floor.

Many homes of wealthy Americans, especially second homes, summer-retreat or weekend homes, espoused the picturesque principles. And like those homes, Quarry Farm exhibited sunburst designs in much of the woodwork, including on the bookcases, on the wooden blinds, on brackets that held curtain rods.

While Jervis was alive, Quarry Farm was an occasional retreat and it was taken care of by a tenant farmer. When Jervis died and Susan and Theodore made it a year-round home, it ceased to be "ornamental" (a favorite word in the late 19th century to describe such farms by those rich enough to own one) and was expanded and converted into a near mansion.

In the following years, the Clemens family would spend most of each year in the Hartford home and most of each summer at Quarry Farm. Parts of *Roughing It*, *The Adventures of Tom Sawyer*, *The Adventures of Huckleberry Finn*, *Life on the Mississippi*, *A Connecticut Yankee in King Arthur's Court*, *The Prince and the Pauper*, *A Tramp Abroad*, and other books would be written at both homes, but more of the writing was done at Quarry Farm, mostly because

Hartford was filled with socializing. The Clemenses invited others to their home for dinner and parties and attended dinners and parties at the homes of friends. Even at Quarry Farm there could be distractions, so Susan and Theodore Crane surprised their brother-in-law in 1874 with an enclosed study about a hundred yards from the main house where he could do his writing in relative peace. He would walk up a small hill to get to the octagonal study most mornings, after breakfast, and stay there through lunch, which he seldom ate. Livy seldom went to the study because walking up the small hill was a chore that taxed her physically, and Susan and Theodore tended to let him write in peace. As his daughters grew, however, they would sometimes want to visit him, and although he had supposedly strict rules about not being disturbed while he worked, he frequently entertained them inside and outside the study. The study, which took just four or five steps to cross from one side to the other, had one door, windows in seven of the sides, and a fireplace. There was a writing table and several chairs. From inside the study, and from the front porch of the main house, he could see downtown Elmira, the Chemung River, which flowed through the city, and in the distance the hills of northern Pennsylvania.[16]

In the evening, Twain often read what he had written to the assembled family, whether in the parlor in the Hartford home or on the front porch of Quarry Farm. And Livy offered advice. This was the time and place Livy was born and raised for, a Victorian daughter of wealth and privilege married to a man who would benefit from her care and love.

She was sometimes frustrated by her husband's behavior, but disapproval was always gentle. Novelist and editor William Dean Howells, a Cambridge, Massachusetts, resident and a frequent visitor to the Twain home in Hartford, said that Mark once entered the drawing room there wearing white cow skin slippers, his hair sticking out sideways, and imitated an elderly black man, and everyone there was entertained, except Livy, who in a "low, despairing cry" said, "Oh, Youth."[17]

Another time, when Howells, as editor of *The Atlantic*, sent Twain a proof of something Twain had written, Howells observed that Twain had left out the profanity. Twain wrote back, "Mrs. Clemens opened that proof, and lit into the room with danger in her eye. What profanity? You see, when I read the manuscript to her I skipped that."[18]

When *The Adventures of Tom Sawyer* was published in 1876, Livy did not want readers to think that the title character was too autobiographical. She wanted her husband to be known not just for his humor but also for the beauty, kindness, and natural piety she saw in him, and she considered Tom Sawyer lacking in those qualities, too rough, too unrefined.[19]

Her love for her husband now included admiration, and admiration included acceptance. She never drank alcohol and knew little about it, but by 1874 she was no longer trying to get Mark to stop drinking. She accepted his consumption of beer and whiskey, understood that he was not a drunkard and that what he called "temperate temperance" was a reasonable policy.[20]

On November 12, 1874, Mark and Joe Twichell started to walk from Hartford to Boston, estimating they could make the 102-mile trip in 24 hours, but after little more than a dozen miles they took a carriage to a train station and finished the trip by railroad. Mark said that was enough to prove the trip could be made by foot. Along the way he received a letter from Livy that does not survive, but in his reply he praises what she had written: "You had a sentence in your letter that all the culture & all the genius & all the practice in the world could not improve." His frequent praise of his wife's writing, however, always sounded like a loving parent's reaction to a child's drawing, an appreciation based more on deep affection than artistic merit.[21]

As much affection as Livy and Mark displayed for each other, one never became the clone of the other. They had their individualized ways of responding to the world and those ways were not the same. In 1877 Twain and Bret Harte wrote a play together, *Ah, Sin*. It was performed in Washington and on Broadway and required that the two spend a good deal of time together. Twain came to consider Harte a sponger, a plagiarist, and tricky, but his biggest complaint was that Harte, while visiting the Clemenses, made an insulting remark about Livy. The remark has not been recorded, but it forever soured Twain against a man he once considered a friend.[22] Livy, ever aware of what she considered her Christian obligations, was more forgiving.

When Harte visited in Hartford and made many sarcastic remarks, Mark endured them because of Livy, but on Harte's last day there he said something that Mark interpreted as being rude about Livy and he told him that, but Harte denied that Livy was the target. Twain told him:

> Harte, your wife is all that is fine and lovable and lovely and I exhaust praise when I say she is Mrs. Clemens' peer — but in all ways you are a shabby husband to her and you often speak sarcastically, not to say sneeringly, of her, just as you are constantly doing in the case of other women; but your privilege ends there, you must spare Mrs. Clemens. It does not become you to sneer at all; you are not charged anything here for the bed you sleep in, you have been very smartly and wittily sarcastic about it, whereas you ought to have been more reserved in that matter, remembering that you have not owned a bed of your own for ten years; you have made sarcastic remarks about the furniture of the bedroom and about the tableware and about the servants and about the carriage and the sleigh and the coachman's livery — in fact about every detail of the house and half of its occupants; you have spoken of all these matters contemptuously, in your

unwholesome desire to be witty, but this does not become you; you are barred from these criticisms by your situation and circumstances; you have a talent and a reputation which would enable you to support your family most respectably and independently if you were not a born bummer and tramp; you are a loafer and an idler and you go clothed in rags, with not a whole shred on you except your inflamed red tie, and *it* isn't paid for; nine-tenths of your income is borrowed money — money which, in fact, is stolen, since you never intended to repay any of it; you sponge upon your hardworking widowed sister for bread and shelter in the mechanics' boardinghouse which she keeps; latterly you have not ventured to show your face in her neighborhood because of the creditors who are on watch for you. Where have you lived? Nobody knows. Your own people do not know. But I know. You have lived in the Jersey woods and marshes and have supported yourself as do the other tramps; you have confessed it without a blush; you sneer at everything in this house but you ought to be more tender, remembering that everything in it was honestly come by and has been paid for.[23]

Harte at the time owed Twain $1,500. The amount would go up to $3,000 and Harte eventually offered Twain his note, but Twain refused it, saying, "I was not keeping a museum and didn't take it."[24]

Livy's generosity, or at least her willingness to offer forgiveness, is revealed in a letter she sent to Mark from Elmira while he was on the road with his play. On July 29, 1877, she wrote, "I am so thankful that all the arrangements about the play [*Ah, Sin*] suit you so well, how I do wish that I was going to be with you on the opening night.... [D]on't say harsh things about Mr. Harte, don't talk against Mr. Harte to people, it is so much better that you be reticent about him.... [H]e is so miserable, we can easily afford to be magnanimous toward him."[25] In the same letter she reported to her husband the tidbits of their child's developments that loving parents so love to share with one another:

Today I had the baby all undressed but her little under shirt — she said, "oh if Susie see me she will say I am all legged.... I asked her if she would like to sleep on a high pole," she said, "No, for the world, I wouldn't" — once afterward during our conversation she used that expression "for the world" — I spoke about our riding on the clouds the[y] were so beautiful as we sat looking at them, she said in quite a fretful voice, "there isn't any chair up there on the clouds" — I love you a bit.[26]

Sometimes Livy and Mark traveled together, but more often he traveled without her and she endeavored to keep him informed about the family. In 1877, on July 15, she wrote to him from Elmira (he was at the St. James Hotel in New York) that "I made wreaths & crowns of Golden rod for the children this morning — This afternoon Susie and I had a rather sad time because she told me a lie — she felt very unhappy about it — This evening after her prayer

I prayed that she might be forgiven for it, then I said, 'Susie don't you want to pray about it and ask for your self to be forgiven?' She said 'Oh one is enough.'"[27]

Most of the traveling they did together was outside of the United States, especially to Europe. On April 11, 1878, they sailed as a family to England; from April 25 to early August they lived in Germany; from August 12 to September 16 they were in the Swiss and French Alps; from September 16 to November 14, they visited Italy, and from November 15, 1878, until February 1879, they lived in Munich, Germany.

As on their earlier visit to England together, Livy and Mark taught their daughters "little scenes of drama," learned languages with them, led them in singing. And almost always the parents and children ate dinner together. Livy sometimes had dinner in England with ladies who snubbed each other, and sometimes while in England as a guest at someone's house she was often left on her own, while in America hosts and hostesses felt obligated to entertain guests. At first Mark liked the English more than Livy did, but later she liked the English more than he did, according to their friend William Dean Howells.[28]

But they were always in agreement that they liked Dr. Brown, the Scottish doctor and author of children books. On June 22, 1876, Livy wrote to Brown from Quarry Farm, saying, "I wish you could come over to us for a season; it seems as if it would do you good, you, and yours would be so very welcome. We are now where we were two years ago when Clara (our baby) was born, on the farm on the top of a high hill where my sister spends her summers. The children are grown fat and hearty, feeding chickens and ducks twice a day, and are keenly alive to all the farm interests."

In an earlier letter from Livy, undated but written in 1875, she said:

> Susy is very motherly to the little ones.... I speak from experience that one must get good every time they meet and chat with you. I receive good every time I even *think* of you.... You ask if Clara is "queer and wistful and commanding," like your Susy. We think she is more queer, (more quaint) perhaps more command-ing, but not nearly so wistful in her ways as "your Susy." The nurse that we had with us in Edinburgh had to leave me to take care of a sister ill with consump-tion. We have had ever since a quiet lady-like German girl.... Affectionately, Livy L. Clemens.

Mark added a note to the letter, also inviting the Browns, and then wrote, "P.S. Livy, you haven't *signed* your letter. Don't forget *that*. S.L.C.," and Livy added, "P.P.S. I hope you will excuse Mr. Clemens's P.S. to me; it is characteristic for him to put it right on the letter. *Livy* L.C."

After Dr. Brown died on May 11, 1882, Twain wrote a letter to his son,

Jock Brown, dated June 1, saying Livy regretted not going to see Dr. Brown one more time before leaving Edinburgh, but that they didn't make the trip because he, Twain, wanted to get to Liverpool to sail to the United States.

The deaths of friends sometimes led the two Clemenses to think of their own mortality. Mark often told Livy if she died first the rest of his life would be spent reproaching himself for making her cry so often, and she would reply that if he died first she would not have to reproach herself because she never loved him less when he made her cry. They had the conversation many times, including just before she died.[29]

Livy's delight in the joys of her children was ever present throughout their growing years. When Susy was six and the family was visiting the Scholls Gardens in Heidelberg, Germany, Susy and Livy saw dozens of snails creeping around. A few days after that Susy saw a dish of snails on the lunch or dinner table, and she asked, "Wild one, mamma?"[30] That same year, 1878, Livy told Susy the biblical story of Joseph, of how his brothers sold him and how his coat was stained with the blood of a slaughtered kid. Susy said, "Poor little kid."[31] While in Munich that year, Susy had a dream with a bear in it and said she was "never the one that ate, but always the one that was eaten" and when Livy tried to console her daughter with the observation that it was only a dream Susy replied, "But mamma, the trouble is that I am never the bear but always the person."[32]

Little in these pleasant years could upset Livy, and even when something did occur that worried her it always seemed to eventually turn out all right. In December 1877, Twain was one of numerous literary luminaries invited to speak at the 70th birthday party of John Greenleaf Whittier. Twain told a story, entirely fiction, about a western miner who was unimpressed with meeting "Mark Twain" because he recently had met three other famous writers, Henry Wadsworth Longfellow, Ralph Waldo Emerson, and Oliver Wendell Holmes, Sr., all of whom, not by coincidence, were attending the party. The fictional acquaintances of the miner were drunks who cheated at cards, stole the miner's boots, and threatened to beat him up. Most of those in attendance recognized that Twain was joking about literary fame, but some people thought the joke was in poor taste and Livy had worried about that. She did not want her husband to be seen as a social lout. She and Mark had both heard that Emerson in particular was upset with the story. So when in Venice in October 1878 they met a man named Augustus P. Chamberlaine and his wife, both of whom were friends of Emerson, Livy and Mark raised the point and were assured that Emerson was not offended. The Chamberlaines must have written to Emerson about Livy and Mark's concern, because on December 31, 1878, Emerson's daughter Ellen wrote to Livy on behalf of her father saying that while the family was "disappointed" in the speech, "no shadow of indignation has ever been in any of our minds. The night of the dinner, my Father says, he did not hear Mr Clemens's speech he was so far off, and my Mother says that when she read it to him the next day it amused him."[33]

These were times of travel and entrée into a world of fame. From the end of February to early July of 1879 they stayed in Paris, where they met and talked at length to Henry James, James Whistler, and Charles Darwin. A week in the middle of July was spent visiting Belgium and the Netherlands. From there they went to England and stayed until near the end of August. And on August 23 they sailed from Liverpool, arriving in New York on September 3. They stayed in their Hartford home for most of the rest of the year. The exception was an October visit to see Livy's family in Elmira.

There was more travel, and there were more opportunities for Livy to continue to try to mold Mark. Livy would hold small dinner parties about twice a week when they lived in Paris. Mark often did things at the parties that she didn't approve of. She often said to him after one of the parties, "I have told you over and over again, yet you do these same things every time, just as if I never had warned you." Their daughters often hid at the top of the stairs to hear the scolding. They called it "dusting off Papa." Mark said:

> Why, Livy, you know that dusting me off *after* these dinners is not the wise way. You could dust me off after every dinner for a year and I should always be just as competent to do the forbidden thing at each succeeding dinner as if you had not said a word, because in the meantime I have forgotten all these instructions. I think the correct way is for you to dust me off immediately before the guests arrive, and then I can keep some of it in my head and things will go better.

Livy agreed, and the two of them worked out some signs Livy could give to Mark during a dinner so he would know what his offense was. Their daughters positioned a screen to hide behind during dinner. If Livy missed some offense of Mark's, one of the daughters would whisper, "Blue card, Mama" or "Red card, Mama" or "Green card, Mama." Livy would say to Mark something like, "What did you do with the blue card that was on the dressing table?" Mark knew the blue card meant, "Let the lady on your right have a reprieve, destroy the one on your left." A reference to a red card meant, "Oh, are you going to sit there all the evening and never say anything? Do wake up and talk." The card system worked, Twain said, and kept him from committing many "crimes."[34]

This anecdote, related three decades after the fact as Twain dictated his autobiography, tends to paint a portrait of Livy with a loving sense of the dictatorial. Howells noted the tendency to talk about Livy in that manner, as did others. There is not a single indication in the memoirs written by the people who knew the couple, whether written by daughters, friends, or a servant, that Livy and Mark ever had any emotion to extend to each other except for love. The anecdote about the blue and red cards, while no doubt based on something factually accurate, is merely an extension of the teasing that Twain often offered to Livy and Livy's understanding that the teasing was an act of love. That it was dictated in 1906 proves only that the teasing extended beyond Livy's death.

Livy and Mark both loved all their daughters, but they took special delight in the oldest, Susy. In 1879 when they were in Hartford, Susy, then seven, on several occasions cried over things that went wrong in her life, once over a broken toy, once because a picnic was canceled because of thunder and lighting, another time because a mouse that was becoming friendly in the nursery was killed by a cat. Livy told her, "There, there, Susy, you mustn't cry over little things." Susy said, "Mamma, what is 'little things?'" Livy tried to answer but seemed to Susy to be confused in defining little things, so Susy tried to help. Livy was planning to go downtown to buy a toy watch for Susy, so Susy said, "If you forgot the watch, mamma, would that be a little thing?" The answer has not been recorded, but the parents decided that by asking the question Susy was now old enough to decide for herself what was a little thing.[35]

Twain believed his wife had a special knack for hiring and supervising servants, no doubt a result, he believed, of having been raised with servants. And many of their servants did develop a special fondness for her. Katy Leary was one of them. When Katy was 17 and living in Elmira, she was making baby clothes for Mrs. J. Sloat Fassett when a Mrs. Stanchfield, a friend of Livy's, came in. Katy mentioned she would like to leave Elmira, and Mrs. Stanchfield said, "I know somebody would love to have you. She lives in Hartford, and Hartford is a beautiful place; she has three children and her name is Mrs. Clemens." Livy sent a note to Katy saying they should meet at her mother's, Mrs. Langdon's. Livy was staying at Quarry Farm then. Katy went and waited in the library of the Langdon home when Livy came in. Livy was wearing a white silk dress, and her hair was combed "down plain and done in a coil."

"Why, is this Katy Leary?" Livy asked.

"Yes.

"Would you like to come and live with me?"

"Oh, yes. Yes, I would."

"Well, when could you come?"

"Well, I need about a week or ten days to get ready."

"Why, you could come about the nineteenth." That is, October 19, 1880.

"Yes, I'll be ready. I'll come to Hartford then."

"Mr. Langdon will give you all the details of the traveling."

Livy called to another room, "Youth, Youth, dear, will you come in here!" When Mark came in, Livy said, "Now this is Katy Leary that is coming to live with us in Hartford."

Mark looked at her carefully, then said, "Have you got any money?" He gave her a $5 bill. "If that isn't enough, you can charge it to us when you come to Hartford, but I think maybe that will buy your ticket anyway."

When she arrived in Hartford, George the butler showed her in and Livy entered the room and took her upstairs to the nursery and introduced her to the children; Jean was still a baby in the nurse's arms.

Later Katy overheard a conversation between Mark and Livy.

"So you hired that girl after me giving you the money?" Mark asked.

"Yes," Livy said.

"Well, did you notice them wide, thick black eyebrows of hers?"

"No," Livy said. "No, I didn't."

"Well, you know," Mark said, "she's got a terrible fierce temper, I believe, nothing halfway about her. Yes, I think you'll find she has a temper. She's Irish!"

Livy laughed. "Yes, maybe — we'll see."[36]

Around that time, Twain's interest in politics heightened. On October 16, 1880, he gave a speech welcoming former president Ulysses Grant to Hartford, and ten days later Twain gave another speech in support of James Garfield's successful campaign for president. Both Grant and Garfield were Republicans, and Twain's admiration for Grant as a military leader and for Grant's efforts during his presidency to improve the status of freed slaves led to Twain's support, although he later had no difficulty supporting Democrat Grover Cleveland. Livy's interest in politics was largely confined to support of women's suffrage, something that her fiancé and later husband was at first opposed to, believing that women should not soil themselves by becoming involved in something that was often so dirty. Livy was instrumental in getting her husband to become an ardent supporter of both women's suffrage and women's equality in general.[37]

There is an indirect but revealing connection between Livy's hiring of Katy Leary as her maid and her support of women's equality. Both reflect the sense of social equality for everyone that was part of the values her parents instilled in her as a child. When Katy told her mother she had been hired by the Clemens family, her mother wanted to meet Livy before agreeing to allow her daughter to move to Hartford. Livy went to Mrs. Leary's home, although normally Mrs. Leary would have been expected to visit Livy's home, since both the Clemens and Langdon families were far wealthier. Mrs. Leary told Livy she thought Katy was too young to leave home, and Livy said, "Oh, now, Mrs. Leary, don't worry about Katy. I'll take good care of her. I'll take just as good care of her as I would of my own children. I'll always look after her. Nothing will happen to her, and if she's sick, I'll take care of her, and when she's well, I'll take care of her just the same."[38] That sense that social standing was unimportant led inevitably to a belief that women must be seen as the equals of men.

Katy was both the family maid and Livy's personal maid. She combed and brushed Livy's hair every day. The hair was long and dark brown, although Livy seldom let it just hang down. It was always up in one style or another, so its length was not visible to most people. Katy liked to comb Livy's hair. She combed and braided it every night just before Livy went to bed. Much of the rest of Katy's day was spent sewing.

The servants ate breakfast about 7:30 A.M. Livy and Mark didn't have breakfast until 11:00 A.M. Katy would go into the bedroom before that and brush Livy's hair and help her dress. Mark never ate lunch. After breakfast, Mark, when in the Hartford home, went to his billiards room to write. No one was to disturb him. "Oh, for nothing!" Katy said. Dinner was usually at 6:00 P.M. Livy always dressed up for dinner and there was always music during dinner from a music box in the hall, and George the butler wound it up to play every day just before the family sat at the table. The music box was from Vienna and it was not a Victrola. It was, Katy implied, better than that. After dinner, in wintertime, the family gathered in front of the large fireplace in the library. Livy and Mark sat in big chairs. The daughters, Susy and Clara, and later Jean, sometimes sat on the floor. Mark would often read Browning or Dickens aloud. Before Clara knew how to read, she would take a big book and make up a story as if she were reading from it. After a while, Mark would say it was his turn to read, and he would read until 9:00 P.M. The children always went to bed without a fuss. Then Mark would drink scotch and Livy would drink a cup of tea. Then Livy and Mark would talk, often laughing, and go to bed at 10:00 P.M.

When the daughters started to get older, Livy would teach them herself. She would have breakfast at 8:30 A.M. and would teach the children in the schoolroom on the second floor from 9:00 to noon. The schoolroom was next to the nursery. She taught them like that for "a couple" of winters, then hired a governess. Katy gives the governess's name only as F——. F—— later became a Christian Scientist and a Spiritualist, Katy said, and "that spoiled her."[39]

Katy, according to Mary Lawton, who transcribed her memoirs, spoke in a "soft, deep, rather quiet voice." (Lawton says Katy was illiterate, but Katy in the memoirs talks of having read many books.)[40]

Patterns changed when the family spent the summer at Quarry Farm. Livy spent more time watching the children at Quarry Farm than she did in Hartford. If they were sick, she took them out of the nursery and into her own bed and Mark would have to sleep in another room. The fire in the fireplace was kept lit all night. Livy had a very large bed, a Dutch bed with four posters, each with a fat cherub that unscrewed, and the daughters liked to unscrew the cherubs and play with them. Clara, more so than Susy or Jean, when they were little, had the croup a lot, with its horsey cough that often interfered with her sleep.[41]

Once at Quarry Farm Susy hit Clara with a stick during an argument, so, according to Livy's family rules, Susy went to her mother to report her offense and she also, the rules said, was required to suggest a punishment. Livy and Susy both suggested various punishments, but when Livy mentioned depriving Susy of the opportunity to go on a hayride that had been promised Susy's expression clearly indicated that was the one punishment she must feared.

Livy said, "Which one do you think it ought to be, Susy?"

Susy asked, "Which do you think, mamma?"

Livy said, "Well, Susy, I would rather leave it to you. You make the choice, yourself."

Susy paused, not wanting to make the choice, but finally said, "Well, mamma, I'll make it the haywagon, because you know the other things might not make me remember not to do it again, but if I don't get to ride on the haywagon I can remember it easily."

Once when Susy was seven, a woman visited who was dressed nicely to attend a ball. Susy complimented her on how nice she looked, and the woman was very pleased until Susy added, "I wish I could have crooked teeth and spectacles."

When Susy was six and a half years old, she did something that Livy disapproved of, and Susy later told her mother, "Well, mamma, you know I didn't see myself, and so I couldn't know how it looked."

On a hot day in Hartford, Livy borrowed Susy's child's fan, a Japanese one that cost a nickel, cooled herself with it for a few seconds, and then gave it back to Susy with thanks. Livy, of course, had more expensive fans upstairs, but Susy took a nickel from her money box and gave it to Patrick, the carriage driver, and asked him to go downtown (about a mile and a half) and buy a Japanese fan for her mother, which he did.

When Susy was nine or ten, she went to her mother's room to report that Jean, still a baby, was crying and asked if she should call for the nurse. Livy said, "Is she crying hard?"

Susy said, "Well, no, mamma. It is a weary, lonesome cry."

When Susy was 11, Livy let her see the Christmas presents she had purchased for Patrick's children. One of the presents was a sled for Jimmy, Patrick's son, with gilt lettering saying, in capitals, "DEER." Susy had liked all the presents until she saw the sled, which made Susy "sober and silent." Livy said, "Why Susy, doesn't it please you? Isn't it fine?"

Susy said, "Well, mamma, it is fine, and of course it did cost a good deal, but, but, why should that be mentioned." She pointed to the word *DEER*. (Thinking it was a statement that the sled was expensive; as Twain comments in his autobiography, "It was her orthography that was at fault, not her heart. She had inherited both from her mother.")[42]

Mark seldom praised any new clothes Livy purchased, but when she had been wearing them six months he did praise them. Livy liked that, because it meant he would not tire of those clothes.[43]

When Livy and Mark went to New York, they always brought back presents for their daughters. George, the butler, would serve supper to the parents on a small table in front of the library fireplace. Susy and Clara always sat nearby, waiting for their presents. Once Twain gave them each a small silver watch he and Livy had purchased. He said to Clara, using his favorite nickname for her, "Well, Bay, are you disappointed?"

"Oh no! But it is too beautiful!" Clara said.

"It won't be in a few days," Twain said.

But Clara, decades later, wrote that she never broke or bruised it.[44]

When there were dinner parties for adults, Susy and Clara sat on the stairs and listened to the conversations of their parents and guests. Neither Livy nor Mark sent them to bed.[45]

Livy usually made a big fuss for Christmas. Every Christmas Eve, the three daughters hung stockings in the second-floor schoolroom and Livy recited "'Twas the Night Before Christmas." Their father sometimes, but not always, dressed as Santa Claus.

Prior to Christmas Livy helped her daughters write letters to Santa Claus, and they always received replies. They learned only as adults that the replies were written by their father. One reply to Susy said, "I have received and read all the letters which you and your little sister have written me by the hand of your mother and your nurses." Later in the letter he added, "There was a word or two in your mama's letter which I couldn't be certain of. I took it to be 'trunk full of doll's clothes.' Is that it? ... Your mama will help you to name a nice color and then you must tell me every single thing in detail which you want the trunk to contain."

Livy and Mark always slept late on Christmas Day because they were up late the night before, and their daughters had already opened their presents by the time their parents woke up.[46]

Santa Claus was not the only illustrious visitor to the Hartford home. Just as when they visited Europe, Livy and Mark attracted the attention of celebrities. Sir Henry Irving arrived one day and bowed deeply at the front door when greeted by Livy. Irving was the first British actor ever to be knighted, and some of his biographers speculate that he was the model for Bram Stoker's character Dracula. Sir Henry Stanley, the explorer, and his wife, the artist Dorothy Tenant, stayed at Clemens's Hartford home several days. William Dean Howells was among the most frequent visitors. He and his wife often stayed several days at a time. Susy, Clara, and Jean did not dine with company if they stayed only for the meal or only one night. But if they stayed several days, the daughters joined them at the dinner table.[47]

And Mark wrote, and Livy read what he wrote and commented on what he wrote. According to Clara, her mother served as her father's critic, providing both "constructive criticism" and "applause." Mark said to Livy's sister, Susan Crane: "Do you know, Sue, whenever I have failed to follow the advice of Livy to change this or that sentence or eliminate a page, I have always come to regret it, because in the end my better taste in thoughts and their expression rises up and says, 'You should have done as she said; she was right.' And never once can I remember wishing I had left something as I had originally written it after it had received the censure of her unfailing vision."

"What would you do without her, Samuel?" Sue asked.

"I don't know, nor do I know what my publishers would do without her."[48]

This is what Livy lived for, what she was born for, what she was educated for, the feeling that she was important to her husband's success.

He had a temper that Livy and his daughters considered harmless, but sometimes it would lead him to do things he regretted, so she helped him with that, too. Livy suggested to Mark when he was angry at some man in a distant town that he write a letter to that man but not mail it, and Mark followed that advice frequently.[49]

The irregularity of the architecture of Quarry Farm, its picturesque quality, both paralleled and contrasted with the life Livy led in Hartford. During summers at Quarry Farm there were patterns that pleased her sometimes sober nature. And she was reminded of her childhood.

Clara described the Langdon home in downtown Elmira as "full of mysterious staircases and unexpected hallways that led to remote rooms, unused except by the people of our imagination." She added, "The long drive down the hill [from Quarry Farm], which always seemed dangerously steep.... Then the iron gates at the entrance ... swung magically, in response to a mechanical arrangement.... The wheel of the carriage passed over an elevated iron bar so arranged in the earth that, when pressed down by the weight of the carriage, it lifted the lock of the gates." Inside, she said, "The hall and spacious living-room were rather dark.... The house gave forth a certain ... perfume ... wide mahogany staircases ... three entrances to the grounds by iron gates which made a ringing noise when they clinked into place after being opened and closed."

Mark got more work done at Quarry Farm than in Hartford because there was less entertaining to host and attend, but there was some. Clara said, "Every summer there was a big celebration" for Mrs. Langdon's [i.e., Livy's mother's] birthday. Charlie sent carriages to bring down some people from Quarry Farm." The children often sang poorly or performed bad theater as part of the celebration. Entertainment included children playing piano and violin. Sometimes Mark sang with the children, usually Negro spirituals. He also played piano and sang with more enthusiasm than talent. Mrs. Langdon displayed remarkable tolerance.

Except for the grandmother's birthday party, the three daughters were not allowed to go to parties during summers at Quarry Farm, and Livy and Mark seldom entertained there. The farm was for relaxation and quiet. And Mark's writing.

In the summer heat of Elmira, Twain wore the white linen suits that would later become part of his public image, but he did not wear them year-round until after Livy died. He seldom ate lunch; once he wrote to Livy that he was eating one meal a day and "[i]t consists of four boiled eggs and coffee. I stir in a lot of salt and then keep on dusting and stirring in black pepper till the eggs look dirty."

The Clemens family spent about three and a half months each summer at Quarry Farm, mid–June to late September. Livy brought her own German and Irish maids, while Sue Crane had black and white American servants.[50]

Life in the Hartford home could be more complicated, partly because it was a more complicated home, at least as Mark viewed it. And that required great patience on Livy's part.

One night in the 1880s, Mark told his wife, "Livy the mahogany room won't go on, I have just opened the window to see." He was talking about the burglar alarm.

Livy said, "Why Youth, if you've opened the window why of course the alarm will ring."

Mark: "That's what I've opened it for. Why I just went down to see if it would ring!"

Livy said that if he wanted to see if the alarm will go off while the window was closed he must not open the window, but Mark didn't understand. Susy said her father became impatient with her mother.[51]

Another time Mark told Livy about wanting F.G. Whitmore, his business agent, to drive the buggy around the starboard side of a small garden that divided the road leading from the gate to the house so he could get out on the house side, but Whitmore said it didn't make any difference, and it didn't, so Mark called Whitmore an ass, and when the buggy pulled up to the house with Mark on the starboard side he insisted it was an accident and insisted Whitmore do it again, and again the buggy pulled up on the starboard side. Mark lost his temper, told Whitmore to apply to an asylum, and said he didn't want to see him for a week. Then Mark went inside and told Livy what happened, expecting her to sympathize with him. Instead, he wrote, "she merely burst into peal and peal of laughter as the tale of my adventure went on, for her head was like Susy's. Riddles and complexities had no terrors for it."[52]

But the greatest patience required of Livy must have come once in the 1880s in the month of March, at 2:00 A.M. The burglar alarm went off in the Hartford home, and Mark went into the bathroom, looked at the "annunciator," determined that the alarm came from the basement door, and turned off the alarm. When he got back to bed, Livy asked, "What was it?"

He said, "It was the cellar door."

"Was it a burglar, do you think?"

"Yes, of course it was. Did you suppose it was a Sunday-school superintendent?"

Livy said, "No. What do you suppose he wants?"

"I suppose he wants jewelry, but he is not acquainted with the house and he thinks it is in the cellar. I don't like to disappoint a burglar whom I am not acquainted with and who has done me no harm, but if he had had common sagacity enough to inquire, I could have told him we kept nothing down there but coal and vegetables. Still, it may be that he is acquainted with this place and that what he really wants is coal and vegetables. On the whole, I think it is vegetables he is after."

"Are you going down to see?"

"No. I could not be of any assistance. Let him select for himself. I don't know where the things are."

Livy said, "But suppose he comes up to the ground floor?"

"That's all right. We shall know it the minute he opens a door on that floor. It will set off the alarm." At that point, the alarm went off, a "terrific buzzing." Mark said, "He has arrived. I told you he would. I know all about burglars and their ways. They are systematic people." Mark went into the bathroom, saw that he was right, and shut off the dining room alarm. And went back to bed.

Livy said, "What do you suppose he is after now?"

"I think he has got all the vegetables he wants and is coming up for napkin rings and odds and ends for the wife and children. They have families — burglars have — and they are always thoughtful of them, always take a few necessaries of life for themselves, and fill out with tokens of remembrance for the family. In taking them they do not forget us: those very things represent tokens of his remembrance of us, and also of our remembrance of him. We never get them again, the memory of the attention remains embalmed in our hearts."

"Are you going down to see what it is he wants now?"

"No. I am no more interested than I was before. They are experienced people — burglars, they know what they want. I should be no help to him. I think he is after ceramics and bric-a-brac and such things. If he knows the house he knows that that is all that he can find on the dining-room floor."

"Suppose he comes up here?"

"It is all right. He will give us notice."

"What shall we do then?"

"Climb out of the window."

"Well," Livy said, "what is the use of a burglar alarm for us?"

"You have seen, dear heart, that it has been useful up to the present moment, and I have explained to you how it will be continuously useful after he gets up here." No more alarms went off, and after a while, Mark said, "He is disappointed, I think. He has gone off with the vegetables and the bric-a-brac and I think he is dissatisfied."

Mark and Livy then went to sleep. At 7:45 A.M., Mark got up and was getting ready to make the 8:29 A.M. train to New York City. On the first floor, he found all the gas lamps were turned on. He also found that his new overcoat, his old umbrella, and his new patent-leather shoes were all gone. A large window opening to the ombra, a small garden shaded by trees, at the back of the house was wide open. Mark climbed out the window and had no difficulty following the trail of the burglar, because the burglar had dropped, along the way, imitation-silver napkin rings, the umbrella, and other things.[53]

But Livy, as much as she was prone to at times gently scold Mark, would never fail to accept him for the man he was. Once he told her that a woman acquaintance of theirs interrupted often, and said, "I am glad Mrs.—— wasn't present when the Deity said, 'Let there be light.'" But there were limits to how much Mark would misbehave in Livy's presence. He said that in the first ten years of his marriage he did not swear around Livy because "I prized my wife's respect and approval above all the rest of the human race's respect and approval." But one morning he went into the bathroom and did not close the door tightly. Shaving often made him swear. This time, in addition, he had trouble with his shirts. Some had buttons missing, and each one that did he threw out the window, swearing as he did. The buttons were in the back, a design Twain came up with himself. After throwing three shirts out the window, swearing with each one, he saw that the door was open. He delayed leaving the bathroom for fear of how Livy would react. When he did leave the bathroom he pretended nothing had happened and avoided eye contact with Livy. Then Livy spoke, the exact same words Mark had used in the bathroom, the same profanities. Twain years later wrote, "The language perfect, but the expression velvety, unpractical, apprentice-like, ignorant, inexperienced, comically inadequate, absurdly weak and unsuited to the great language.... I tried to keep from laughing."

Livy said, "There, now you know how it sounds."

Mark laughed hard and loud and long. He said, "Oh, Livy, if it sounds like that, God forgive me. I will never do it again."

Livy, realizing his meaning, could not keep herself from also laughing.

At breakfast that day, Livy remarked that the children shouldn't use profane language and one of the girls said, "Why, mamma, papa uses it."

Mark said, "How did you know, you little rascals?"

One said, "Oh, we often listen over the balusters when you are in the hall explaining things to George."[54]

There were always cats, and Livy accepted them. Mark and the children loved them, and their names clearly revealed Mark's never-ending desire to be clever: Lazy, Stray Kit, Abner, Motly, Freulein, Buffalo Bill, Soapy Sal, Cleveland, Sour Mash, Famine, Susan, Sin.[55]

The cats sometimes sat and watched as Livy and the children helped edit Mark's books. Livy would sit on the porch at Quarry Farm and read Mark's manuscripts aloud to her daughters, holding a pencil in her hand. The children believed that when Livy came to a "particularly satisfactory passage" she would cross it out. Mark often wrote something he knew Livy would cross out just to hear the children's protest when she did. He always sided with the children, but Livy usually struck out the passage anyway. It was "three against one" (Jean was too young to take part in the family editing). Sometimes, not often, Mark and Susy and Clara won and Livy kept the passage in, and then Mark privately would strike it out.[56]

Livy usually taught the children lessons while Mark was writing, but he sometimes tried to act as the teacher. Once in Hartford Mark gave an arithmetic lesson to Susy and Clara and he started by saying if A buys a horse for $100, and Jean (less than five years old at the time) interrupted by saying, "Two hundred dollars," and Mark said, surprised, "Who is doing this example, Jean?" And he started again, "If A buys a horse for one hundred dollars," and again Jean said, "Two hundred dollars," and Livy "went into convulsions of laughter." So Mark changed the example to $200.[57]

Livy was also usually in charge of disciplining the children, although Mark had his own ideas about the subject. Susy noted their views: Livy believed that if a child was old enough to misbehave she was old enough to be "whipped." Once at Quarry Farm Livy had a conversation with a doctor (whose name Susy did not record) and Livy said:

> Suppose the boy has thrown a handkerchief onto the floor. I tell him to pick it up, he refuses. I tell him again he refuses. Then I say you must either pick up the handkerchief or have a whipping. My theory is never to make a child have a whipping and pick up the handkerchief too. I say, "If you do not pick it up, I must punish you." If he doesn't he gets the whipping, but I pick up the handkerchief, if he does he gets no punishment. I tell him to do a thing if he disobeys me he is punished for so doing, but not forced to obey me afterwards.

If Susy and Clara were naughty, the nurse would call Livy and Livy would appear and look at them ("she had a way of looking at us when she was displeased as if she could see right through us"). Then Livy would say either "Clar" or "Susy, what do you mean by this? Do you want to come to the bathroom with me?" Going to the bathroom evidently meant getting spanked. That meant being whipped by the "paper cutter." Livy would never punish a child when she, Livy, was angry. If she showed anger while punishing a child, she stopped the punishment until she was no longer angry. After the punishment was over, the child could not leave until she, the child, was happy and there was no bitterness. After the punishment, Livy would not show any signs of being displeased.

One summer while at Quarry Farm, Mark wrote an article about punishing children for the *Christian Union* and he let Susan Crane and Susy and Clara read it in manuscript, but he did not tell Livy about it. He didn't want Livy to know about it until it was published. But after he wrote it, he thought maybe it was too personal, even though it praised Livy, so he went to New York to see if he could stop publication, but it was too late.

However, as Susy and Clara were reading it Livy appeared and asked why they were not in bed. They told her it was a secret and tried to hide the article. Livy chased them but couldn't catch them, so she left, and the girls hid the article under Clara's bed.

Mark eventually told Susy and Clara they could give their mother a copy of the article. Livy read it while the rest of the family sat around. At first she was pleased, but when she realized it would be read by strangers she was upset.

Mark received letters about the article, some of them "very disagreeable." Livy read the worst one. When someone told Susy how much she or he enjoyed the article, she laughed because both of her parents came to wish the article had never been published.[58]

Livy considered it her job to protect Mark's writing time. Clara, later in life, recalled that when she and Susy and Jean took up too much of their father's time, perhaps requiring him to tell them a story, Livy sent George, the butler, into the room to tell Mark he had to get ready for dinner. Or at times to tell him that a visitor was waiting downstairs, even if there was no visitor, or even if it was just a deliveryman with some produce, someone George or Livy or Katy could attend to.[59] From Livy's perspective, Mark was a wonderful husband and a wonderful father, but he was also a writer and, more than a writer, a great writer. And she tried hard to assure that he had the quiet and alone time he needed to continue to be a great writer.

This was an idyllic life for Livy, a daughter of the Victorian era. She accepted, even gloried in, her role as wife and mother. She existed to make the lives of her husband and three daughters as pleasant and productive as possible. And she understood that her husband made the important financial decisions in the family.

Sam, Samuel, Mark, Youth. Not Livy. He made the business decisions. He decided where to invest their money. Even the quarter-million-dollar fortune she inherited from her father. That was her role: acceptance.

CHAPTER FIVE

Money

Livy's father made business investments that were both sound and lucky. He purchased timber rights that made enough money for him to invest in an anthracite mine in Pennsylvania, and then the Civil War commenced and anthracite became enormously profitable. And he made tough, close-to-ruthless decisions, like creating a near monopoly in anthracite distribution in the Buffalo area. That, too, made him a great deal of money.

Livy's husband by contrast made business decisions that seemed sound but were often plagued by bad judgment that only superficially seemed like bad luck. Chief among these were investments he made in the Webster Publishing Company and the Paige typesetting machine.

Livy, with both her father and her husband, watched and seemed to learn, but she was never much of an influence with either man when it came to their business interests.

Twain clearly had something close to an addiction when it came to investments. He wrote in late 1890, justifying his first investment, of $2,000, in the Paige Compositor (i.e., typesetting machine) that "I was always taking little chances like that; and almost always losing by it, too—a thing which I did not greatly mind, because I was always careful to risk only such amounts as I could easily afford to lose."[1] Anyone related to or friends with a heavy gambler has heard pretty much the same words in the earliest stages of the addiction. And in early March 1906 Twain wrote that during all his years of losses, losses that would drive the family into bankruptcy, Livy "endured the economies of that long stretch of years without a single murmur."[2] Livy did not consider it her place to advise her husband in business matters, even though much of what he lost was her inheritance, even though she and her children suffered from the losses. Her major reaction to the bankruptcy was after the fact; she insisted that he pay back everybody every single penny. He did. And the world honored him for that with newspaper editorials of praise, letters of congratulations, favorable comment after favorable comment. She helped earned that praise for him.

Setting type in the years after the Civil War for the thousands of newspapers in the United States, and thousands more around the world, was a laborious process, done by hand, time-consuming, prone to errors. Numerous attempts at inventing a machine to do the job had met with limited success. Twain had set type as a teenager while working for his brother Orion on the Hannibal *Journal* and knew how valuable a good typesetting machine would be to newspapers, book publishers, magazines, all types of printing. So when, in the early 1880s, a friend, Dwight Buell, visited him in Hartford and the two went to the billiards room on the third floor and Buell told him about a typesetting machine being built at the Colt Arms factory by a man named James W. Paige, Twain was intrigued. And immediately addicted. He bought $2,000 worth of stock. Over the years Paige would say he needed more and more money and Twain, always with some hesitation, would give it to him. Twain found numerous contradictions in Paige, but his addiction would not allow him to act in the best interests of his family. Paige, Twain wrote, was

a most extraordinary compound of business thrift and commercial insanity; of cold calculations and jejune sentimentality; of veracity and falsehoods; of fidelity and treachery; of nobility and baseness; of pluck and cowardice; of wasteful liberality and pitiful stinginess; of solid sense and weltering moonshine; of towering genius and trivial ambitions; of merciful bowels and a petrified heart; of colossal vanity and— But the opposites stop. His vanity stands alone.... It is the only unpleasant feature in him that is not modified, softened, compensated by some converse characteristic."[3]

Twain added $3,000 to his original investment almost immediately. Over the next five years he gave Paige $40,000. He said the machine still needed a little more work. The sum rose to $80,000. At one point Twain was putting in $4,000 a month. Early in his contact with Paige, Twain came to believe he would have to invest up to $30,000. By the time he was done close to a decade later, the total exceeded $150,000. By some counts, $300,000.[4]

Paige at one point said the only real remaining problem was that the machine could not "justify" a line. That is, it could not set type so the right-hand margin was even. He could fix that, he said, if only he had more money. Twain wanted to market the machine the way it was and perfect it later. But Paige said no. Twain made suggestion after suggestion, and Paige said he needed more time. And more money. Meanwhile, the potential market for a typesetting machine was so obvious that competitors in several different countries were working on their own versions. And Ottmar Mergenthaler in Germany beat Paige. Mergenthaler's Linotype machine quickly became the standard. A majority of newspapers and other printers in North America would be using his machine before the end of the century.

Paige's machine had 19,000 parts. The number alone assured that something would keep breaking or failing or malfunctioning. Only once, in a test run with the *Chicago Herald*, did the Paige Compositor operate without breaking down. The Mergenthaler Linotype machine, by contrast, often worked without failure for years. The Mergenthaler machine, in fact, significantly contributed to the reputation of the superiority of German engineering and manufacturing. The last known Paige Compositor was donated to Cornell University, which donated it for scrap metal during the Second World War. A war against Germany. If Twain had lived he would have no doubt seen the irony in donating the machine that destroyed his finances to join the effort to defeat the country of the inventor who beat it in the first place.

Even if Livy didn't interfere with Mark's addiction, she worried about its effect. She told Katy Leary, her longtime maid, "Oh, dear, I am afraid I'll have to lose my help. I'll have to send them all away."

Katy said, "Oh, Mrs. Clemens, you won't have to send me off, for I won't go. If you just give me something to eat, never mind my pay, I'll stay."

Livy cried when Katy said that. "Oh, Katy, Katy. How lovely. But, I hope it will never come to that, that we'll have to let you go."

"Well, I wouldn't go if you sent me. Nothing could drive me away. I'll never leave you, no matter what happens."[5]

Livy was also concerned with how the family's financial setbacks would affect her husband's reputation as a writer, because one of his reactions was to write more and more articles for the best-paying magazines in the country, magazines that sometimes had less prestige than Livy thought worthy of her Youth. In 1893, she wrote to him from Europe, where the family moved because living expenses for the wealthy, not necessarily for the poor, were cheater there. He was visiting New York and Chicago in search of a patron for the typesetting machine. "You did not tell me anything about sending an article or articles to the Cosmopolitan," she wrote with obvious dismay. "Why did you do that? I should greatly prefer appearing in the Century or Harpers. What made you do it? ... My darling child you must not blame yourself as you do. I love you to death, and I would rather have you for mine than all the other husbands in the world and you take as good care of me as any one could do."[6]

But her darling did blame himself. He wrote years later, in describing how he allowed Paige to talk him into signing contracts he knew that he should not have signed, that "I quite understand that I am confessing myself a fool."[7] If Livy was guilty of any sin in the affair it was only in not talking Youth out of being a fool when it came to investments.

Not that the Clemens family was living in poverty. Twain himself estimates that during the decade or a dozen years when his poor investments were
draining their financial resources his annual income — not counting Livy's
holdings in the part ownership of the companies inherited from her father —
ranged from $12,000 to $20,000 a year.[8] That alone put them into what today
would be called the upper middle class. But, of course, both Livy and Mark
had become accustomed to living better than that.

The problem with the Webster publishing company was more complicated but less financially severe. It involved family. Twain became dissatisfied
with Elisha Bliss and his son Frank at the American Publishing Company[9]
and decided to form his own publishing company to handle his books. So he
formed the firm of Charles L. Webster & Co., named for his nephew by marriage. Charles Webster had attended Fredonia Normal School (now Fredonia
State College) and become an engineer. He met, wooed, and married Annie
Moffett, the daughter of Twain's sister, Pamela, who had moved to Fredonia
with her mother at Twain's insistence when he and Livy moved to nearby Buffalo. Technically, Webster and Twain were partners in the firm, formed in May
1884, with formal legal papers being filed the following year, but in reality
Webster managed the day-to-day operations and Twain made most of the
major decisions, especially regarding which books would be published. The
first book the firm published was *Huckleberry Finn*, which sold very well. It
earned Twain $54,500 in the first three months.[10] That same year (1885) Web-
ster & Co. published *Personal Memoirs* by Ulysses S. Grant, which also sold
very well. Twain arranged for Grant's *Memoirs* to be sold door-to-door by
Union Army veterans, some of whom chose to wear their old uniforms while
making their rounds. Grant died on July 23, 1885, just weeks after completing
the manuscript, and Twain had Webster rush it into print, so it was being sold
while the nation still mourned its greatest war hero. An estimated 350,000
copies were sold within months, and Twain generously calculated Grant's share
at 30 percent of the selling price, which ranged from $3.50 to $12 depending
on the binding. Twain presented Julia Grant, the general's widow, a check for
$450,000, making her a wealthy woman.

Webster and Co. would go on to publish other Twain books, including
Mark Twain's Library of Humor (1888), *A Connecticut Yankee in King Arthur's
Court* (1889), *The American Claimant* (1892), *Merry Tales* (1892), *The
£1,000,000 Bank-note and Other New Stories* (1893), and *Tom Sawyer Abroad*
(1894), all of which made money for the Webster company. The success of the
Grant memoirs led Twain to sign other military men to write books, including
memoirs by George B. McClellan (1886) and Philip Sheridan (1888). Twain
also published *Tenting on the Plains; or, General Custer in Kansas and Texas*

by Elizabeth Custer, a tribute to her husband, who had been killed at the Battle of Little Big Horn in 1876. While not selling as well as the Grant book, these works also made money for the Webster company.

But not all of the books the firm published were moneymakers, and that led to trouble in the family.

In December 1886, Twain decided to publish a biography of Pope Leo XIII,[11] naively assuming that every Catholic family in the United States would buy a copy. When Livy hesitated to buy an expensive sofa she wanted because of the cost, Mark wrote to her, "You can order 100 such sofas now, if you want to — the future bank account will foot the bill & never miss it. The Pope's book is ours, & We'll sell a fleet load of copies."[12] Livy's primary and most frequent contribution to Mark's bad business judgments was to believe him. She wrote to Charley Webster telling him to buy her a bureau with drawers at least 19 inches long. And it must cost less than $40. When her husband explained that Pope Leo XIII was "head of two or three hundred millions of subjects, whose empire girdles the globe, & whose commands find obedience somewhere in all the lands & among all the people of the earth," Livy accepted his misguided logic. He believed, and she accepted his belief, that all Catholics would feel obligated to buy the biography. It was a bit of prejudice that was as wrong as social analysis as it was as a business decision. Twain sent Webster to Rome to give the pope a gift of a leather-bound, gold-lettered copy of Grant's *Memoirs*, and when Webster reported back that he had traveled to the Vatican in a carriage accompanied by footmen in uniforms and that he had been granted a private audience with the pope Livy regretted not making the trip. "Ah, why didn't we go, too!" she complained. The biography was written by Father Bernard O'Reily with the cooperation of the pope. An overly enthusiastic advertisement for the completed book called it "The Greatest Book of the Age!" and said, "Every Catholic in the land should possess this volume as it is issued with the approbation and blessing of the pope as a souvenir of his golden jubilee." It was selling for $3.75 a copy, or $3 for the "plain edition." Twain was convinced it would outsell Grant's *Memoirs*. It didn't come close, although it didn't lose money, either. Twain became convinced the problem was not his poor judgment based on a misunderstanding of how Catholics think and behave but rather that his nephew-in-law Charley Webster must have mishandled the advertising or distribution or something. It was Charley's fault. Twain was convinced of that.

He overlooked the fact that he had a history of bad business decisions. Like the $25,000 he invested in a steam generator that flopped. The $25,000 that went into a steam pulley that was a financial failure. The $25,000 that he put into a marine telegraph and the $50,000 for Kaolotype, an engraving

process. Flop, flop, and flop. He even tried to invent things to make money,
like a vest strap that self-adjusted, and a memory improvement game based on
history questions, and "Mark Twain's Self-Pasting Scrapbook." He patented
all three. Only the scrapbook, sold by Putnam & Davis, "Booksellers & Sta-
tioners" in Worcester, Massachusetts, made a little money, no doubt because
Twain's name and picture were on it.[13] He was a gambler, and the excitement
of gambling intoxicated him. He gambled pennies and dollars at cards and billiards. At business, he gambled tens of thousands of dollars. And like almost
all gamblers, he lost. And like almost all gamblers, he couldn't admit his addiction. Someone else had to be blamed. And when after some early successes the
Webster publishing company began to lose money, poor nephew Charley was
blamed. Even though most of the losses came after Charley left the firm under
pressure from Twain in 1888. It was, in fact, Webster, not Twain, who talked
Grant into writing his memoirs and who convinced him to use a stenographer
after he said he was too "lazy" to write.[14] Webster, a broken man, unsure what
he had done wrong, returned to Fredonia and died three years later, at age 39,
from internal hemorrhaging caused by inflammation of his peritoneum, the
tissue lining the inside of the abdomen.[15] Webster was a nervous man prone
to ailments, and the pressure he felt from his treatment by Twain could not
have helped his health.

Livy didn't criticize Mark for his treatment of Charley, but it did make her
think of his relationship with his own family. He had been close to her father
and remained close with her sister, Susan, and had cordial relations with her
mother and her brother, Charlie. But she sensed that Mark needed to pay
more attention to his own family. His mother, Jane, was increasingly frail, so
when she turned 83 on June 18, 1886, Livy urged Youth to visit her. She had
moved to Keokuk, Iowa, and was living with Orion and his wife, Mollie. Livy
particularly thought Jane should see Jean, who would turn six that summer,
and who was named for her grandmother. Although named Jane, she was from
birth called Jean. Livy, Mark, and their three daughters made the trip by train
to Buffalo, then by boat across the Great Lakes to Chicago, then by train to
St. Paul, where they switched to a steamboat to travel south on the Mississippi
River. Travel always tired Livy. On the steamboat, Clara, now 12, heard the
leadsman call out the standard cry to indicate the water was deep enough for
safe sailing. "Mark Twain," he bellowed. Clara searched and searched for her
father, and when she found him she said, "Papa, I have hunted all over the
boat for you. Don't you know they are calling for you?" That summer in the
Midwest was unusually hot, with temperatures often reaching into the nineties
and little breeze. Livy, as so often happened with her, had difficulty enduring
the heat and spent much of the trip sitting or lying down.[16]

In Keokuk, relations between Livy and Mollie were strained. The two women never cared for each other. Mollie thought that her brother-in-law, Mark, had an annoying sense of importance, and Livy thought her brother-in-law Orion had made a very bad choice in picking a wife. Mollie did try hard to be a good hostess on this trip, for Jane's sake. Orion, who always seemed genial and easygoing, often seemed not to notice the tension between his wife and sister-in-law. Mollie arranged for plenty of ice to be available, for Livy's and the girls' lemonade and for Mark's scotch. Mollie and Orion had a boarder that summer, a young professor named George Edward Marshall, who almost always wore a white suit of linen or cotton. Mark asked him about it. "I do it to be clean and comfortable," Marshall said. "These suits tub nicely. It takes courage to wear them, though. Some people are inclined to stare." Mark took note. He didn't mind people staring at him. He enjoyed being a celebrity. Livy enjoyed being married to one.[17]

Livy's tolerance of Mark's small eccentricities in dress and habit was mirrored by his acceptance of her judgment of people, even the woman who married the older brother he loved. He wrote, decades later, that Orion fell in love with two girls in Iowa, one from Muscatine and one from Keokuk:

> He was always falling in love with girls but by some accident or other he had never gone so far as engagement before. And now he achieved nothing but misfortune by it, because he straightway fell in love with a Keokuk girl [Mollie Stotts]—at least he imagined that he was in love with her, whereas I think she did the imagining for him.... He didn't know whether to marry the Keokuk one or the Quincy [i.e., the one from Muscatine] one, or whether to marry both of them.... But the Keokuk girl soon settled that for him. She was a master spirit and she ordered him to write the Quincy girl and break off that match, which he did. Then he married the Keokuk girl and they began a struggle for life which turned out to be a difficult enterprise and very unpromising.[18]

Howells, Twichell, and other friends sometimes gently prodded Twain to be more careful with his investments, and finally even Livy would join the quiet chorus suggesting that he refrain from putting money into every invention or enterprise that interested him. They had some success, but it was far too late.[19]

On April 25, 1886, Twain made Fred J. Hall a partner in Webster & Co. to replace Charley, and at first he praised Hall's business skills, but in the end he called him incompetent and blamed him for the company's failure. There was always someone else to blame. Only Livy possessed enough influence with Mark to persuade him to not make more investments, but she was far to gentle in her admonitions. The good Victorian housewife did not interfere with a husband's business decisions.

But Livy was not completely without fault in contributing to the family's financial decline. While she hesitated to interfere in Mark's business decisions, she was very aware of monetary setback after monetary setback. Still she did not do much more than express caution for personal spending and seldom exercised fiscal restraint. The mahogany room of the Hartford house, so-called because much of the furniture in the room was made from that wood, was used to store and wrap Christmas presents every year. Livy was adept at wrapping presents, but the task still tired her because of her general and permanent frailty. And there were so many presents, for relatives, friends, neighbors, the needy. Livy wrote lists of names and the presents each was to be given. Then wrapped them, later helped deliver them. Each year the list grew longer. When the family finances reached the point that the extensiveness of the gift giving needed to be greatly curtailed, Mark told Clara, "I am glad, for one reason, that financial losses have struck us! Your mother will have to give up that infernal Christmas-suicide."[20]

Beginning in June 1891, because of losses from the Paige typesetting machine, the Webster publishing company, and Twain's generally bad investments, the family decided to move to Europe, where they could live more cheaply than in their Hartford mansion. They could have moved to a less expensive home in a less expensive city in the United States, but that would mean a downgrading of their lifestyle, something neither Livy nor Mark was willing to endure. Decades later, to help justify his memory, Twain would also say one of the reasons for moving to Europe was to seek treatment for Livy.[21] They stayed in Europe for nine years.

Livy never seemed to fully comprehend the extent of and damage done by her husband's investments. After nearly a decade of serious loses, she wrote to him from Hartford while he was in New York on business, on December 17, 1893:

> Youth my darling ... seems as if perhaps you were beginning to see your way through financially. How is Webster & Co. situated now? Are they working out of debt? ... You should have been here today to see Clara imitate you telling them stories and eating at the same time, it was just as funny as it could be. She bit a piece of bread exactly as you bit it. She said "I don't know what it is but Papa always seems to be having a quarrel with his piece of bread to make it let go" ... sometimes it has been hard to keep cheerful with her [Susy] so down hearted.[22]

The ease with which Livy could move from a discussion of the loss of tens of thousands of dollars to family chatter reveals a disconnect with financial reality. She had not been raised to worry about money.

Mark Twain was too well known for word of his difficulties not to become public knowledge. According to Katy Leary some newspapers suggested collecting a nickel apiece from people all over the world, but when Livy heard about it she opposed the idea.[23]

In March of 1888, Twain went to Washington, D.C., on business and Livy was supposed to join him to have dinner with their neighbor and friend Joseph Roswell Hawley and his wife. Hawley, who had been a general in the Civil War, was now a U.S. senator and owner of the *Hartford Courant*. But on March 11, a four-day snowstorm began, now known as the Great Blizzard of '88.[24] The blizzard dumped up to 50 inches of snow on Connecticut, New York, New Jersey, and Massachusetts. The temperature in Central Park, in New York, was six degrees, the lowest ever recorded for March. Railroads shut down and people were confined to their homes for up to a week. Telegraph poles were knocked down, rendering long-distance communication on the East Coast impossible. More than 100 ships were grounded or sunk, killing more than 100 seamen. On land more than 400 were killed directly by the storm, and another 100 from the lingering effects of the cold. Among the fatalities was former U.S. senator Roscoe Conkling, who was hit by falling ice while walking in New York City.[25]

Two years later another trip was canceled, this one because of Twain's bad investments. Livy and Mark had planned to begin a summer trip to Europe in 1890, hoping to expand their daughters' cultural education, but they abandoned those plans because of losses from the Paige machine. Livy wrote to Mark on May 2, 1890, "Youth don't let the thought of Europe worry you one *bit* because we will give that all up.... I want to see you happy much more than I want any thing else even the childrens lessons. Oh darling it goes to my very heart to see you worried."[26]

Twain was destroying the family finances, and Livy, who never hesitated to offer advice to her husband about his writing, remained silent on his business decisions. She seemed to be the only person capable of dissuading him from continuing his business blunders, but she wouldn't speak up. She would suggest that a sentence not be included in a novel, but not that a thousand dollars not be invested in an unworkable contraption. And there was no one else who could have had that kind of influence with him. Until Henry Huttleston Rogers befriended him.

At first glance, Rogers and Twain should never have become friends. Rogers was a robber baron, one of the class of men Twain and Warner had pilloried in his first novel, *The Gilded Age*. Rogers's ruthless dealings in oil, railroads, and other ventures made him one of the richest men in American history. He first fought the equally ruthless John D. Rockefeller, then joined him at Standard Oil. But Rogers enjoyed reading Twain and read Twain's books to his five children. And he gave away a great deal of money to causes he liked. He funded libraries. And, after he befriended Booker T. Washington, schools for blacks in the South. He paid for Helen Keller to attend Radcliffe College.[27]

He had once attended a lecture Twain gave on Hawaii (then called the Sandwich Islands), which Twain had visited long before he met Livy, and was so struck by his presentation that he eventually read every book Twain published. Long after that lecture, Twain and Rogers happened to be in New York at the same time and a mutual friend, Dr. Clarence Rice, introduced them. Rice, Twain's sometimes doctor, privately told Rogers about Twain's financial woes and asked the robber baron if he could help. Rogers loved Twain's writing, loved spending his ill-gained fortune on worthy causes, and quickly developed a liking for Twain the man. So Rogers asked Twain how he could help. Money was never offered or requested, but advice was proffered and received. Livy was relieved. Rogers was in so many ways like her father, a man who was not born into wealth but who acquired a great deal of it, and clearly his advice must be unassailable.

Rogers offered advice; Twain needed advice; Twain took advice. And unlike Livy, Rogers, who admired Twain immensely, could be blunt. Twain took and benefited from his robber baron friend's guidance. Livy, remembering her admiration for her father, was delighted with the friendship.

He offered three main pieces of advice: declare bankruptcy, pay back every penny you owe, and stop investing. Twain hesitated on the first, agreed wholeheartedly with the second, and simply could not obey the third. Livy and Mark both had doubts about bankruptcy, feeling it was in some way dishonorable, but Rogers convinced them it was simply a way of managing their affairs, that if they did indeed pay back every penny they owed there was no dishonor. And he told them, in case they needed to distinguish what he did for a living from what Twain did, honor was important to a writer, his most valuable commodity. Livy and Mark both reluctantly became convinced that Rogers was right. They would later disagree on some of the details of the bankruptcy, but they came to accept the wisdom of his overall plan. In particular Livy wanted to pay the smallest creditors first, and Mark quickly agreed with her. People with money and large businesses could wait. But Rogers convinced them to let him handle the repayments. He intended to pay back first those most likely to be able to do damage to Twain's reputation. Twain, and later Livy, acquiesced. The investment warning wasn't discussed much, probably because Rogers didn't know Twain well enough to realize how much he had been infected with his business-gambling disease and Livy as always refrained from advising her husband about such matters.

Rogers had Twain transfer the copyrights of all of his writings to Livy, on the legal technicality that Charles L. Webster & Co. owned her $60,000. By this time Twain was, probably, the most famous writer in the world, and maybe the second best-known American in the world second only to the president, his copyrights were undoubtedly worth far more than that and the debt Webster & Co. owed to Livy could have been satisfied with one or two copyrights of the better-known books or maybe even of the lesser-known books, since by now everything with Mark Twain's name on it sold well. But Rogers had a different standard from mere logic. His advice for Twain's benefit was based on the same legal underpinning Rogers based his own business decisions on: if legally you can get away with it, it's all right to do it. And sometimes even the legality part could be safely avoided. Rogers's later advice that they not automatically pay off smaller creditors first, people most in need of money, was based on his belief that a creditor owed more money might challenge in court the legality of transferring all copyrights to Livy, and he knew that Livy and Mark might lose on that point.[28]

The copyrights now safe from creditors, the Charles L. Webster & Co. publishing firm declared bankruptcy in April, 1894. Webster owed 96 creditors an average of $1,000 each. The Panic of 1893, the worst financial crisis the country would face until the Great Depression, stopped Livy's income from her father's inheritance, which was being managed by her brother, Charles, and Twain's income from his books. Henry Robinson, onetime mayor of Hartford and two-time Republican nominee for governor of Connecticut, told Twain, "Hand over everything belonging to Webster and Company to the creditors and ask them to accept that in liquidation of the debts. They'll do it. You'll see that they'll do it. They are aware that you are not individually responsible for those debts, that the responsibility rests upon the firm as a firm." Mark told Livy what Robinson advised, and both she and Mark were very much against it. They wanted to pay off the debts in full. Livy said, "This is my house. The creditors shall have it. Your books are your property — turn them over to the creditors. Reduce the indebtedness in every way you can think of— then get to work and earn the rest of the indebtedness, if your life is spared. And don't be afraid. We shall pay a hundred cents on the dollar yet." That's when Rogers took over. He spoke to the creditors. He told them they could not have Livy's house, that she was a preferred creditor and that they could not have Twain's copyrights, because they belonged to Twain (and later to Livy), not to Webster & Co. Eliminating the $60,000 owed to Twain and the $65,000 owed to Livy, Twain would pay off all the other debts, Rogers said. But he emphasized that this was not a legally binding promise. Rogers's reputation as a ruthless businessman was well known and when the creditors heard him speak they might not have liked what they heard, but they listened with considerable trepidation. Who knew what he might do if they caused trouble for his friend.

At the time Webster & Co. failed, its liabilities exceeded its assets by 66 percent. Twain felt morally but not legally bound to pay the debts. During the panic, businesses all over the country were failing and creditors were settling for a company's assets. Business friends said, "Business is business, sentiment is sentiment — and this is business. Turn the assets over to the creditors and compromise on that; other creditors are not getting thirty-three percent." Rogers disagreed with them. He sided with Livy and said, "Business has its laws and customs and they are justified, but a literary man's reputation is his life. He can afford to be money poor, but he cannot afford to be character poor. You must earn the cent per cent and pay it."

Twain approvingly quoted his nephew, Samuel E. Moffett, son of his sister, Pamela, who once said, "Honor knows no statute of limitations."

Livy estimated Mark would need four years to clear his debts. Rogers estimated a minimum of seven. Twain privately thought seven was more reasonable but didn't tell that to Livy. He once overheard a conversation between Rogers and two "Men of Affairs." One man asked, "How old is Clemens?" and Rogers said "Fifty-eight," and the man said, "Ninety-five percent of the men who fail at fifty-eight never get up again," and the second said, "You can make it ninety-eight percent and be nearer the mark." Livy, upon hearing about that conversation, sat down with a pencil and a piece of paper and calculated the four-year figure.

Of the 96 creditors, only 3 or 4 wouldn't agree with Rogers's plea that they give Twain time to raise the money. Twain said he believed those three or four would undoubtedly end up in hell.

On June 6, 1891, Livy and Mark closed their Hartford home to save money, and eight days later they sailed for Europe, where they would stay, moving from country to country, for nine years. Living in Europe, they said, was less expensive than living in the United States. That was not true for poor people or anyone of modest means. But for the wealthy, the cost of luxury living was indeed less, and Livy and Mark did not intend to live in poverty. They moved from expensive hotel suite to expensive hotel suite, ate well, dined often with the wealthy and with members of royal families, met famous writers. In Europe Mark Twain was the best-known American and the most admired.

Rogers was given nearly full control of all of Twain's business affairs. He told Twain to have Webster stop publishing his *Library of American Literature* because it was losing money, and Twain, who originated the series, complied.[29] If Rogers said do this, Twain did it; if Rogers said don't do that, Twain didn't do it. Livy of course agreed with Mark.

In July 1894, Twain traveled to New York to consult with Rogers and Livy and the daughters stayed in the expensive Hotel Brighton at 218 Rue de Rivoli, in Paris. On July 31 she wrote to Mark:

> You say that Mr. Rogers wanted to ask the creditors 25 cents and that you felt that .20 was enough for Puddin' head Wilson. In that case if I were over there I should probably ask them .10 or .15[.] What we want is to have those creditors get all their money out of Webster & Co. and surely we want to aid them all that is possible. Oh my darling we want those debts paid and we want to treat them all not only honestly, but we want to help them in every possible way.... You say Mr. Rogers has said some caustic and telling things to the creditors. (I do not know what your wording was) I should think it was the creditors place to say caustic things to us.
>
> My darling I cannot have any thing done in my name that I should not approve. I feel that we owe those creditors not only the money but our most sincere apologies that we are not able to pay their bills when they fall due.... I do not want the creditors to feel that we have in any way acted sharply or unjustly or ungenerously with them. I want them to realize & know, that we had their interest at heart, more, much more than we had our own. You know my darling, *now* is the time for you to add to or mar the good name that you have made. Do not for one moment [let] your sense of our need of money get advantage of your sense of justice & generosity. Dear sweet darling heart! You will not throw this aside thinking that I do not understand will you? You will always consider at every proposition whether it is one that I would approve will you not?[30]

Livy would not interfere with Mark's business decisions, but she was insistent that he remember that more than money was involved. Family honor was at stake. She was not arguing with her husband on how to settle their debts, only reminding him of what she knew he already believed and helping to give him the strength to not be tempted by the opportunity to save some money.

Their financial debts were not the only things going on in their lives. They were still a literary family with literary friends. In the same July 31 letter she praised *The Golden House* by Charles Dudley Warner, their Hartford neighbor and friend, published that year. As a postscript she added a poem that appeared, she said, in the *Critic* and which "expresses exactly what I feel for you." The poem is called "Light" and was written by Francis W. Bourdillon and was first published in 1897. It was well known at the time:

> The night has a thousand eyes
> And the day but one
> But the light of the whole world dies
> With the setting sun.
> The mind has a thousand eyes
> And the heart but one

But the light of the whole life dies
When love is done.[31]

Moving to Europe was not enough. Especially not with the unwillingness of Livy and Mark to live less than the grand life. More money would have to be earned, and Rogers was influential enough to keep Twain from seeking that money with more investments. Instead, Twain suggested, and Rogers agreed, that he would undertake a grand lecture tour. He would tour and lecture in all the English-speaking countries on the earth. Livy, anxious to see the world, easily agreed.

Susy and Jean decided not to make the trip, so Livy, Mark, and Clara left on the round-the-world tour on July 15, 1895, and Twain lectured for 13 months, first going west across the United States and across much of southern Canada, then to the Sandwich Islands, Australia, New Zealand, Ceylon, India, South Africa, and Great Britain. He wrote a book about it, *Following the Equator*, published in 1897, and sent the money from that and from the lecturing to Rogers. Livy and Mark both asked Rogers to pay off the small creditors first, but Rogers said no. He wanted to wait until all the money was in and pay off everyone pro rata. At the end of 1898 or the beginning of 1899, Rogers cabled them in Vienna saying all the creditors had been paid 100 percent. Rogers said there was $18,500 left and asked what he should do with the money. Twain, still addicted to his gambling ways, said, "Put it in Federal Steel," which Rogers did, except for $1,000, and two months later took it out with a profit of 125 percent.[32] The profit was nice, but clearly Twain had not been cured. Rogers, believing his job of getting Twain out of debt was completed, was unwilling to interfere with another man's money.

While on his lecture tour, Twain was frequently interviewed by newspaper reporters and often as not cited Livy's role in his business ventures.

In August of 1895 he told the *San Francisco Examiner* that he owned a two-thirds interest in a publishing firm (Webster) for which he had furnished the capital and that the largest single creditor of the firm was Livy. He added that her investments in the firm from her own money nearly equaled that of all other creditors combined. She now had ownership of his copyrights as payment, he added. "She has helped and intends to help me to satisfy the obligations due to the rest." He said he was able to pay 50 percent of what he owed and would ask creditors to trust that he would eventually pay the other 50 percent.[33]

A week later, the *Examiner* printed another article evidently based on the same interview. In that one, Twain is quoted as saying that he and Livy tried to save the publishing company, but "[w]hen the crash came" they couldn't. He added that Livy wanted to turn their Hartford house over to creditors, but not a single friend would agree. Twain added that he believed not a single creditor would agree, also, but then he quickly revised that comment and said one creditor, to whom he owned $5,000, would not agree and that that creditor had sued him. And he noted that he turned his copyrights over to Livy and that money from the copyrights would be used to pay creditors.[34]

Rogers kept them informed about the progress being made on paying off their debts, and both Livy and Mark came to feel a great burden was being slowly but surely lifted from them. When Rogers informed them that all creditors had been paid, their hearts changed. Clara noted decades later that both of her parents "found comfort in the thought that there were no more creditors in the world to darken their horizon," and both became more patient.[35]

But the trip to that patience was fraught with confusing pain for Livy, far more so than for Mark. He was capable of anger and that relieved much of the stress on him. She wallowed in despair. When they first, with great reluctance, agreed to Rogers's insistence that they declare bankruptcy, Livy wrote to her sister, Sue, "I have a perfect horror and heart-sickness over it. I cannot get away from the feeling that business failure means disgrace."[36] Her husband, as always, could turn his troubles into a joke. When Rogers, as part of the bankruptcy plan, had Twain sign all of his copyrights over to Livy, Twain said, "My wife has two unfinished books, but I am not able to say when they will be completed or where she will elect to publish them when they are done." Rogers in fact told Twain to refer to all of his copyrights as Livy's.[37]

As they approached bankruptcy, Livy became more and more aware of what the pressure was doing to her. She wrote to her sister, "Sue, if you were to see me you would see that I have grown old very fast during this last year. I have wrinkled."[38] The pressure contributed to her poor health. She seriously considered Christian Science as a way of treating her health, but the more she looked into the religion, the less she liked it. In particular she was displeased that the church was selling pictures of the church's founder, Mary Baker Eddy. It "offends one's taste," Livy said, and was too "commericial."[39]

She received electrical treatments in Etretat, on the northern coast of France. Electrical treatments were common in the late 19th century for almost any ailment doctors could not cure. There was little evidence they helped Livy, but she convinced herself that they did. They at least gave her something to think about other than the bankruptcy. She had still one other thing to think about, her husband's writing. He had become interested in the life of Joan of Arc. He considered a biography of the French saint but saw advantages in writing a novel. That would give him more freedom in interpreting her significance in history. Livy wanted him to spend more time writing, so he would spend less time worrying about money. And she wanted to help him. Wanted to edit the Joan book. Wanted a book that she could influence far more than she had influenced anything else he had written.

Livy, in fact, would influence the writing and final editing of the Joan book more than any other book he wrote. And, because of his love for Livy, he would say it was his best book. Almost no one agrees with that judgment.[40]

For the first two decades of their marriage Livy's role in Mark's writings was mostly as an editor making suggestions. She was not a good copy editor. As Twain often pointed out, she was a bad speller. As reading her letters shows, her punctuation and capitalization were often careless. She tried gently to pressure Mark to not use too much profanity and occasionally made suggestions about plot and characterization, although the specifics are elusive because neither one of them ever acknowledged any specific suggestions. We have only Twain's memory that sometimes she made suggestions along those lines and that he never followed them. He did acknowledge allowing her to limit his profanity. But as their financial woes accumulated, she felt a need to say something. But being a good Victorian wife, a woman raised to believe the man made the financial decisions, even if it often was her money, Livy's efforts were directed elsewhere. To his writings.

In December 1889 Twain signed a new agreement with Paige, perpetuating and inflaming the numerous bad decisions he already made. In June and August of 1890 he bought all rights in the Paige composite. In mid–February of 1891 he stopped all payments on the Paige Compositor. On April 26, 1891, Charles L. Webster, the man Twain unfairly blamed for the woes of his publishing company, died. In June and July of 1891 the family was in France, believing somehow that living in luxury in Europe would solve their problems, or at least ease pressures, and that living in luxury in Hartford would not. From June to September of 1891 Livy and Jean visited European health spas to seek relief from their health problems. In August of 1891 the family lived in Germany. In September 1891 in Switzerland. From October 15, 1891, to March 1, 1892, they lived in Berlin. In 1894 Twain finally declared bankruptcy. In January of 1895 Twain bowed to the inevitable and gave up all interest in the Paige Compositor. And on and on. For most of the remainder of the decade.

Where once they had a stable home, they now moved every few months. And not just to another home. Usually to another country. And where once they were wealthy, with multiple substantial incomes, from Livy's inheritance, from Mark's writings, from Mark's lecturing, their debts piled up too fast to manage, and their emotional ability to deal with the stress decreased. Livy had to do something. Had to insist on some change. And since it was not proper for this proper Victorian wife to interfere in business decisions, she sought to influence his writing. Livy's substantial influence on Mark's worst book was a direct result of his addiction to bad business investments.

Personal Recollections of Joan of Arc is purported to be written by the Sieur Louis de Conte, Joan's page and secretary, who grew up with her, served as a general in her army, and testified for her at her trial. The style seems forced, unnaturally flowery, at times awkward, and Joan, one of the most interesting people in world history, seems rather boring. The book was first serialized in *Harper's* in 1895 without Twain's name on it. That was Livy's idea. She didn't want readers to expect a humorous story and be disappointed when they didn't find it. The omission of Twain's name, of course, also allowed Livy to think of herself as co-author.

Twain gave Livy credit for helping to write *Joan of Arc* in every way he could without actually listing her as co-author. He wrote in his autobiography:

In the story of *Joan of Arc* I made six wrong starts and each time that I offered the result to Mrs. Clemens she responded with the same deadly criticism — silence. She didn't say a word but her silence spoke with the voice of thunder. When at last I found the right form I recognized at once that it was the right one and I knew what she would say. She said it, without doubt or hesitation.[41]

And when the book was published in 1896, the dedication page contained a tribute to Livy:

1870, To my wife, 1895, Olivia Langdon Clemens, this book is tendered on our anniversary in grateful recognition of her twenty-five years of valued service as my literary adviser and editor, the Author.[42]

More generally, he gave her credit for helping with everything he wrote, although the evidence of a significant role in editing his other books is less convincing. A reporter once asked if it was true that one of his daughters had never read anything he wrote, and he answered:

My children have edited my manuscript since they were seven years of age; that is, they have had it read to them for criticism. They have always sided with their father, and the sentence which mother would say should be stricken out, they would assert should remain. But we did not stand on these little things. Madam was really the best editor of the lot. Before I used my flock of editors at home I sent my manuscript to Howells, but now we don't.[43]

Twain said he first became interested in Joan of Arc during his childhood in Hannibal when he haphazardly came across a page from a book about her that was blown around by the wind. Many scholars believe the inspiration for the personality of his Joan was his own daughter Susy.[44] Livy sensed the inspiration and that made her attachment to the idea of being a co-creator of *Joan of Arc* all the more powerful.

In addition to influencing Mark's writing of *Joan of Arc*, Livy was kept busy in Europe by the never-ending moving, from one city to another, one country to another, and by visiting various doctors and spas to treat her never-ending list of ailments. When they were in Vienna Mark had taken something called Plasmon and he thought it made him feel stronger. He urged Livy, just after she suffered from an episode of influenza, to also take some.[45] Plasmon was a high-protein powder made from milk that could be mixed with any drink or food. One advertisement for the product said Plasmon "is the nutrition of pure, sweet milk in the form of a cream-colored powder. In its preparation all the nutritive qualities of milk are retained, freed from fat and sugar. One teaspoon is equivalent to an ordinary beefsteak. It will give increased nutritive value to all foods when added to them, without affecting their flavor." In the corner of the ad there was a quote from Mark Twain: "The only needful thing is to get the Plasmon into the stomach — dissolved or in clods or petrified or any way, so it gets there. The stomach will praise God and do the rest." The ad also showed a sketch of a very muscular man from behind standing next to a Greek column.[46]

Twain's introduction to Plasmon came as Rogers was arranging his bankruptcy to make certain the Clemenses would escape financial disaster. Rogers's expertise had resulted in a cash accumulation of almost $60,000. Twain took $25,000 of that and invested it in the English-owned company.[47] Livy as always failed to even attempt to dissuade him from his continuing addiction. Surprisingly, even Rogers did not try to stop him. Twain eventually became "acting president and vice president" of the American branch of the firm. Plasmon Company of America went bankrupt in 1907 and Twain said he had been "swindled" by the firm. He put his losses at $32,000, although he added that most of those losses were due to bad business decisions and only a third of so them to being swindled.[48]

Twain saying he was swindled is not unusual. All of his bad business dealings, it seems, were to be blamed on someone else. Much of the problem with the Webster publishing company, for example, was blamed on Daniel Whitford, an attorney from Dunkirk, New York, about three miles from Fredonia, home of Twain's nephew-in-law, Charles Webster, who ran the company. Webster hired Whitford to represent the firm's business, and when Twain forced Webster out of the company much of the blame was transferred to Whitford. Twain wrote, "He was good-natured, obliging and immensely ignorant, and was endowed with a stupidity which by the least little stretch would go around the globe four times and tie."[49]

Everyone Twain did business with, it seems, was to some degree responsible, through swindling or stupidity, for his bad decisions. Everyone but himself. And Livy. He took Livy's money, invested it unwisely, and lost it. Then he took more of her money and lost that, too. She always acquiesced. Whatever influence for good or bad she may have exerted on his writing—and certainly for *Joan of Arc* the influence was damaging—for business matters she acquiesced. And only she could have had the influence to dissuade him. She never sought to do that. Even after all the losses—rescued only by the sagacity and tough-mindedness of Henry Rogers—she was quiet about Plasmon.

The problem can be seen in her role as head of her household. She once wrote to her sister, Sue, that telling servants to do something bothered her, especially if she knew the servants would not want to do it. "When I was comparatively young I found the burden of that house [in Hartford] very great" largely because the servants, the maids and butlers, the coachman, the cook, sometimes did things in ways she didn't want them to and "I hate the correcting of them."[50] She once canceled a trip she very much wanted to make to visit Elinor Howells, whom she adored. She said Elinor, wife of William Dean Howells, was "exceedingly bright—very intellectual—sensible and nice." But Livy's stayed home because Clara's wet nurse couldn't be trusted while she was away. With Livy home the nurse was "tractable and good," but when Livy was away the nurse "gets drunk." And she was a wet nurse, the main part of her job being to breast-feed baby Clara, something Livy's frailty prevented her from doing. Besides, among the wealthy, wet nurses were standard. Rather than fire an alcoholic wet nurse, Livy cancelled plans to visit a friend she liked and admired.[51] This was not a woman capable of telling her husband his business investments were damaging the family.

But just as her passivity in her husband's ruinous business decisions licensed him to continue his addiction, her moral insistence that the problems be addressed with honor greatly contributed to successfully treating the worst symptom of the disease even if it failed to cure him. She insisted that all debts must be paid, that despite the option of paying only part of each debt, an option available under bankruptcy, it not be exercised. Twain's agreement on this point always followed her lead. And as much as he came to hate lecturing, she reminded him that it was the quickest and easiest way to bring in money. He was the world's most famous American, and fame then as now is convertible to cash. So they toured the world.

On April 23, 1895, Twain while in London signed a contract agreeing to go on a world lecture tour. If everything worked out, he would make enough money from lecturing in at least seven countries to pay off all of his debts. On May 11, the Clemens family sailed from London to New York, arriving on the 20th, then going to Elmira, where they spent the next two months. Susy and Jean did not want to go on the tour. Susy in particular disliked sailing, often becoming seasick. She said she "dreaded the sea." So she and Jean stayed at

Quarry Farm with Sue and Theodore Crane. Katy Leary, meanwhile, had prayed to be invited to join the Clemenses on the tour, and one day she thought her prayers had been answered when she got a letter from Livy saying, "We're making up our minds to go around the world and we are coming to America in July and want you to be ready to join us." But when first Susy and then Jean said they didn't want to go on the trip, Livy decided Katy would live with them and take care of them. Livy would not let Mark make the trip alone and someone had to take care of the two daughters, so the Cranes wouldn't be overburdened.[52]

On July 14, Livy, Mark, and Clara, with James B. Pond, Twain's lecture manager, and Pond's wife, Martha, departed by train for a five-week trip across the continent to Vancouver, British Columbia. Twain lectured in nearly every state and Canadian province they passed through. On August 23 the Clemenses sailed from Vancouver for Honolulu, leaving the Ponds behind, but when they arrived in the harbor on August 30 they were told they could not go ashore because of a cholera quarantine.

During the sailing on the Pacific, they often played cards with the captain and one or two other officers, usually Hearts, one of Twain's favorite games. They played for chips, never for money, but Twain took the game seriously, a problem that had to be addressed by Livy. If Mark lost several times in a row, the muscles under his eyes would twitch, he would throw his cards on the table, and he would say, "By the humping, jumping——who can play with a hand like that? Look at those cards! Just look at them! Products of the devil and his ancestors." Clara wrote, "Mother would then begin cooing out suggestions in an undertone which had a salutary effect, and Father, with a funny little laugh, would gather up his cards again with accompanying remarks: 'I don't care a rap about beating, but I can't stand the sight of such cards. They make me boil—only a saint on ice could keep cool.'"[53]

On September 10 they arrived at Fiji in the South Pacific, and on September 16 they arrived in Australia, where Twain lectured until November 1. Then to New Zealand to lecture from November 6 to December 13. Then back to Australia, where Twain lectured from December 17 to January 5, 1896. For Livy, always frail and not much better at handling the discomforts of 19th-century sailing than Susy, the frantic pace was tiring. Livy was always tired and always feeling unwell during the trip.

Twain in fact had worried even before the trip began that the 13-month world tour would not be good for Livy's frail health, but by the end he decided she held up very well. A decade after the tour he recalled that they left Elmira on July 15, 1895, and that it took 23 days to reach Vancouver, with Twain lecturing every day.[54] There was blistering summer heat plus the heat of forest fires. Because they then traveled south by sea they moved from summer to summer. They went to the Sandwich Islands and then to Sydney, Australia, New Zealand, and Tasmania. Then to Melbourne, where it was summer when they sailed on January 1, 1896. Then to Ceylon, where it was very hot. In January of 1896 they reached Bombay, where the English residents said it was winter, but it seemed to the Clemens family that the weather was the same as in Elmira in mid–July. They traveled around India, and in Jeypore an English physician told them to go to Calcutta and then leave India quickly because the coming hot weather would be unbearable for them. They sailed to South Africa and Livy's health seemed to improve. Twain recalled that Livy and Clara traveled around South Africa with him except for Pretoria. Livy did not have a single day's illness in that time. The tour ended on July 14, 1896, when they sailed for England, arriving on July 31.

When Twain lectured in the United States, Livy seldom attended, but on the world tour she usually did, and that allowed her to extend her editing advice to her husband's use of words beyond the written to the spoken. She and Clara believed they could measure the intelligence of an audience by how it reacted to Twain's pauses. When he read his story "His Grandfather's Old Ram," a bit too long of a pause reduced the laughter, Livy told him. He took her advice and adjusted the length of the pause.[55]

Livy's willingness and ability to influence Mark did not change his habit of teasing her. In fact, they were connected. In the early days of the tour he told a Canadian reporter his "soul chafes under the cast-iron rules and regulations laid down for him by Mrs. and Miss Clemens." He said:

They mean well, but it is a fearful nuisance. Why, I actually have to wear different clothes for different occasions, and just think of the barbarity of making a man shave when he don't feel like it. Why, when I traveled alone on my lecture tour some years ago I had just a single grip with a few collars and a dress coat in it; the trousers and vest of the dress suit I wore while traveling, and when I buttoned the other coat up nobody could tell what kind of a vest I had on; couldn't even tell if I had a shirt on. I didn't mind traveling in those days. There was nothing to bother me or hold me back. Why, I used to go "flying light" and if I didn't shave before the lecture it didn't matter; only the first few rows could notice it, and they couldn't tell for sure whether it was want of a shave or bad soap. Those were good times, but now....[56]

Livy tended to make a good impression as she accompanied Mark around the world. A reporter in Sydney, Australia, called her "a really charming lady."[57]

Another article by the same reporter provided an example of Twain's playfulness when talking about his wife. When they were living in Paris, Jean told her father that her mother would consider him "wicked" for writing on Sundays. Twain told his youngest daughter it was his room and anyone who came in was a trespasser and that Jean must not tell her mother that he was writing on Sunday. He noted also that the doctor who came to see her mother and give her medicine on Sunday was working. Jean said, "Oh, that was different." Her father said, "But I suppose he'll get paid for it. Well, a gentleman with a broken leg told me the other day he laughed over one of my books until he forgot all about his broken leg. So remember, whenever you see me at work on Sundays, that I'm preparing medicine for broken legs, and, like the doctor, I'm going to get paid for it."[58]

While Twain knew and appreciated the advantages of publicity, Livy often tried to protect him from the demands of an inquisitive press. But that wasn't always easy, especially since Twain, a former newspaperman himself, liked reporters. When an interview was about to start with a reporter at their suite in the Hotel Australia in Sydney, Livy entered the room carrying some papers and said, "There's someone waiting to see you." Mark said he would be only ten minutes, and Livy left. The idea was for Livy to give her husband an excuse to cut short the interview if he didn't like it, but Twain immediately told the reporter he could have a half hour, and the interview lasted even longer. At the end, Livy reentered and told Mark he needed to get rest, so the reporter finally left.[59] The next day, while another interview was in progress, Livy entered the room and Mark told her they had just been talking about Bret Harte. Livy, who knew that Mark had come to intensely dislike Harte, said, "Ah, I hope it was nothing critical. That was a great mistake you made. I think it would be better if your wife saw your interviews in print before they were published." The interviewer had asked Twain about published reports that he disliked Harte's writing and Twain had merely said that like anyone he had a right to judge any work of literature.[60]

In still another article, Livy was "entranced" with the wattle bloom (a yellow flower often associated with Australia) and she liked the gum trees because they were "so restful to the eye," and the coloring of the landscape, which "impresses her like music in a minor key." Also, she liked "the soft ethereal blueness of the sky" and said there is "nothing like it in [my] own land."[61]

One of the interviews in Australia shows that Mark's teasing of Livy was sometimes reciprocated. He remarked to a reporter:

> What a queer animal the kangaroo is. I haven't seen one, but I suppose it is. I did see one of your native creatures while I was in New South Wales. That was the laughing jackass. It sat on a tree, and I stood looking at it. But it wouldn't laugh for me. I tried to make it laugh; indeed I did; but it respectfully declined.

Livy, sitting at the opposite side of the carriage they were riding in, said, "Probably it didn't think you were funny."[62]

Next they sailed to New Zealand on a steamer in conditions that Livy was woefully unaccustomed to. It was a "tiny steamer," that Clara said looked like a toy. It was so crowded that no dinner was served in the salon because the tables and floor were used for beds. Overweight people slept on the tables because they were less likely to roll off. Curtains stretching from wall to wall separated men and women. Twain and his manager for that part of the tour, a Mr. Smythe, spent the night in the salon, but Clara and Livy shared a tiny cabin with two other women. It was so small "there was no place to lay down a couple of oranges (our only food for dinner), because the beds as well as the floor were covered with baggage. No towels to wipe with, no pillows to sleep on, and no sheets to protect one from the grimy blankets." The cabin also included very large cockroaches, and Clara only half-jokingly asked Livy if she could go back to America.[63] If all that wasn't bad enough, the ship ran aground as it approached its destination, but no one was hurt. Twain, in fact, slept through the commotion.[64]

Then to India, where they attended the wedding of a 12-year-old Hindu girl to a 20-year-old widower. And visited a rich Moslem man, where the only women present were European and American. And visited a Jain temple where they were required to remove their shoes before entering. They then returned to the home of the rich Moslem, where they met the stepmother, wife, and children of their host, but they couldn't talk to them because of their different languages. As in the Hindu home, they did not sit in chairs but rather squatted around a six-inch-high table. Next the Clemenses visited a maharaja for several days and were given a bungalow of their own. They were required to eat alone because the maharaja and his family would not eat at the same table as whites. However, even though hosts did not eat meat for religious reasons, they did serve the Clemenses bird, meat, and fish.[65]

They also stayed in a hotel in the Himalayas. One morning other guests invited them on a short trip into the mountains to better see the snow. Mark chose to stay in bed, so Livy and Clara made the trip without him. Clara rode on a horse with a man and Livy went in a rickshaw pulled by three men. They marveled at the bluish-white snow.[66]

They visited an Indian museum between 10:00 A.M. and noon because only women could go then, men being banned those hours. The women Livy saw were brightly dressed and wore much colorful jewelry. The Indian women found Livy to be a great curiosity and gathered about her, crowding her. "I fled behind cases and into other rooms to evade them," she wrote to Jean, "but without success. The crowd was always about me. When they tried to talk to me I pointed to my mouth and said I could not speak Hindustani, but one lady knew a little English, pressed her way close to me and then asked most politely, pointing to my veil, 'why do you wear that? It makes black spots on your face.'" The Hindu woman had tattoos on her hands.[67]

The exposure to new cultures, things she had previously only read about, helped alleviate the difficulty of traveling for the frail Livy, but it didn't seem to help Mark much. He was depressed much of time while in India. Livy believed that was because he was tired of giving lectures, having to lecture whether or not he felt like it.[68]

From India they sailed to South Africa, and on the way Livy and Clara slept on the deck because of heat and bugs in their staterooms, but they couldn't sleep well because sailors entertained themselves well into night and got up early to wash the decks.[69] In South Africa, according to Clara, her father and his manager traveled around the country while she and her mother stayed in Durban to rest, but they did manage to go on picnics and for horseback rides near the sea with English people. They were intrigued with the lizards, including chameleons, and unusual birds, wildlife unlike anything they had seen in America.[70]

Finally they sailed to England. They had already made arrangements for Susy and Jean to meet them there. They rented a small house in Guilford, near London, where they planned to spend the summer, the whole family again together. Then they received a letter.

Susy.

CHAPTER SIX

The Wages of Honor

Clara had to tell Livy the terrible news.

The letter had said Susy was ill, so Livy and Clara sailed back to the United States to care for her. Twain stayed in England to make arrangements for the family to live there. Clara, decades later, wrote of what happened on the ship: "On my way to the saloon for letters, I was told the captain wished to speak to me. We met in the companionway. He handed me a newspaper with great headlines." Clara read the headline. "There was much more, but I could not see the letters. The world stood still. All sounds, all movements ceased.... How could I tell Mother? I went to her stateroom. Nothing was said. A deadly pallor spread over her face and then came a bursting cry, 'I don't believe it.'"

The headline said, "Mark Twain's Eldest Daughter Dies of Spinal Meningitis."[1]

Funeral services were held in the Langdon home in Elmira. Twain, knowing he could not arrive in time, remained in England. "Mother spent day and night with the earthly form of her beloved child until even that remaining solace was wrenched from her clinging love and buried in the ground." Livy, trying to ease her own grief, said, "Clara, you look so ill, can't you rest a little while?" And she said to her sister, "Sue, dear, don't worry about me. I shall find strength to bear it some way."[2] Susy was interred in Woodlawn Cemetery in Elmira, in the Langdon family plot. Susy and Clara and Jean had played in the cemetery when they were little girls.

Susy had decided not to go on the world tour mostly because of her tendency to become seasick, but there was an important secondary reason. She was hoping to establish a career as a classical singer, and an Italian singing coach had advised her "to live on a hill ... and gather vigor of body." Both Livy and Mark had encouraged their daughter in her plans for a musical career. Some modest musical talent was common in the family. Clara would later sing professionally and would marry a world-famous composer. Twain always assumed he had more singing talent than he really did and seldom hesitated to sit at a piano and sing loudly for friends and family. When he was a boy and his father died, his older sister, Pamela, helped support the family by giving music lessons. Twain clearly had a good ear, as is evidenced by the various dialects he so accurately captured in *Huckleberry Finn* and other novels and stories. And Susy may have had the most musical talent of any Clemens. She was a soprano, and her parents could afford to send her to the best teachers in cities such as Vienna and Paris.

So much of Olivia Langdon Clemens's identity was as the wife of Mark Twain, something she never for a moment regretted, that she understood that her daughters could benefit immensely from being the children of their father, but she also felt it was important they develop identities of their own. And music could help achieve that.

Twain actually learned of Susy's death before Livy did, because of a cable he received from his brother-in-law Charley. On Wednesday, August 19, 1896, Twain wrote to Livy from England at 6:00 P.M. This was the day after Susy's death. "You always wrote her, over-burdened with labors as you were," he wrote. "You the most faithful, the most loyal wife, mother, friend in the earth."[3]

On Sunday, August 16, 1896, Susy became blind. She told her uncle, "I am blind, Uncle Charlie, and you are blind." But it was the wrong uncle. It was her uncle Theodore Crane who was at her bedside. She reached out with her hands and felt the face of Katy Leary and caressed it and said, "Mama." Then Susy fell into a coma and remained in the coma until Tuesday evening, when she died.[4]

The first letter Livy and Mark received upon returning to England, in early August, said only that Susy was slightly ill, and Clara and Livy packed to be ready to go to America in case things got worse. But they did not immediately plan to make the trip. Then a cable arrived saying, "Wait for cablegram in the morning." Twain cabled back asking for more news and asked that the reply be sent to the post office at Southampton and he waited at the post office all day, but no reply came. He went home and he and Livy and Clara sat in silence until 1:00 A.M. They took the earliest train in the morning and went to Southampton, and a message was waiting. It said recovery was certain but would take a long time. Twain felt relief, but Livy, always prone to worry about her children, did not, so she and Clara boarded a steamer and left for America. Twain, uncertain what to do but not wanting to add to Livy's anxiety, stayed in England to search for a larger house in Guildford.[5]

Livy and Clara were already at sea when Twain received a telegram that said, "Susy was peacefully released to-day." That was on August 18, 1896.

As Twain remembered the sequence of events decades later, Livy and Clara learned of Susy's death only when their ship landed and relatives and friends told only Clara, who then went to the stateroom and did not speak, and Livy said, "Susy is dead." (This, of course, differs from Clara's version, which says the captain on the ship showed her a newspaper headline.[6]) At 10:00 P.M. the same day Livy and Clara arrived by train in Elmira, and Susy's body was already there, "white and fair," in a coffin in the Langdon home, the same home where she had been born. Livy had not seen her oldest daughter since she left on the world tour 13 months earlier. Still attending to Susy was Katy, who had become the family maid when Susy was eight. In her last days Susy, who had moved to Hartford, was surrounded by the Rev. Joseph Twichell, Sue and Theodore Crane, Patrick the coachman, Katy, servants John and Ellen. And Jean. Before Susy died, she found one of Livy's gowns in a closet and kissed it and cried. At noon that day she went blind. Her last word, while blind, spoken while she held Katy's hands, was *Mamma*. She died at 7:07 P.M. on a Tuesday. She was buried on the 23rd, while Livy and Clara and Jean watched.

Twain, feeling helpless, waited and grieved in England. Twain would remember, decades later, that once, at Quarry Farm, when Susy was little, she seemed perplexed about the meaning of life, so she asked Livy, "Mamma, what is it all for?" Livy each night would go to the nursery to listen to Susy pray, but once, because of illness, she could not go for about a week. She told Susy she would definitely come on a particular night and she saw that Susy was having difficulty in saying something she wanted to, so Livy asked her what the matter was and Susy said that the governess, a Miss Foote, had been teaching her about the religions of the Indians and said that while it appeared they had only one God, in reality they had many. As a result, Susy had made changes in the way she prayed.

Livy said, "Tell me about it, dear."

"Well, Mamma, the Indians believed they knew, but now we know they were wrong. By and by it can turn out that we are wrong. So now I only pray that there may be a God and a heaven, or something better."[7]

Katy Leary, who so much wanted to go on the world tour but who was told she had to stay behind to help care for Susy and Jean, and who was one of the last people to see Susy alive, now had to deal with a tragedy that saddened her as much as any other member of the family. Katy had indeed become a member of the family, bound by a mutual love between her and all the Clemenses. William Dean Howells and Joseph Twichell, among the closest friends of Mark Twain and of Livy, went to New York to meet Livy's ship. Twichell told Katy, "Oh, Katy, I don't know how I'm ever going to tell Mrs.

Clemens. I don't know how I can ever talk to her about Susy." But Twichell is the one who told her, according to Katy. Katy also was present when Livy landed. Clara, Katy said, looked "pitiful" and she was worried for her health.[8]

(As noted earlier, there are three mildly conflicting versions of who informed Livy about Susy's death. Clara said she, Clara, was informed on board by the ship's captain and she then informed her mother. Mark Twain wrote that Clara was informed on land after the ship landed by friends and relatives and that Clara then informed Livy. Katy Leary said Twichell informed Livy after the ship landed. Of the three people giving these reports, only Clara was present when Livy was informed, so hers seems the most likely to be accurate.[9])

Livy said to Katy, "Katy, Katy, Susy's gone. Life has killed her."

Katy said, "Oh, Mrs. Clemens, no. No, she just died. God wanted her, and so she died. Everything in the world was done for her and she was talking of you all the time and thinking of you when she died, and the last words she ever said was that she wanted to see her mother." That seemed to comfort Livy, and Katy repeated what she said several times. She told Livy how the final night she lifted Susy in her bed and how Susy put her arms around her neck and rubbed her face with her two hands and laid her cheek against hers, and said, "Mamma, mamma, mamma." When Katy told this to Livy, Livy was sitting in a chair in the Waldorf Hotel in New York and she reached out her hands and held Katy's hands very hard. Katy was then crying too hard to speak.

In the morning they talked a long time as they sat together on the train to Elmira. Livy asked Katy over and over to repeat things Susy said and did, how Katy gave her medicine, how she wouldn't take it from anyone else, how Susy wouldn't let the nurse do anything, that Katy had to do everything, how Katy lay on the couch in front of Susy's bed.

Livy said, "Oh, Katy, oh, Katy, if it could only have been me instead of you. But how glad I am that you were able to do for her when I wasn't there."

When the train reached Elmira, Livy and Katy went together to the drawing room of the Langdon home, where Susy's body lay. Livy stood by the coffin, without speaking, just moaning.

Katy said, "Oh, Mrs. Clemens, come away."

Livy said, "Oh, Katy, can't we stay here just a little longer and look at my Susy? See how beautiful she is."

Two weeks later they returned to Europe, Livy, Clara, and Jean. And Katy.

Now Clara was the oldest daughter and Livy, according to Katy, was drawn closer to her. "Clara is a dear little thing, such a sweet little thing," Livy said to Katy. "She's such a comfort to me now."[10]

Henry Rogers again helped the family. He arranged for Livy, Clara, Jean, and Katy to return to Europe after Susy's funeral. He specifically arranged for Livy to have her own stateroom.

Twain meanwhile had rented a place known at the Hatfield House at No. 23 Tedworth Square in the Chelsea section of London. The family lived in London (and elsewhere) for two years. Livy and Mark seldom went out during that time, so Katy and Jean often went to the theater together. One time there was a mix-up on the tickets and because their seats had mistakenly been given to someone else, and no doubt because Mark Twain's name was involved, they got to sit in the queen's box, and people in the theater mistook Katy for the queen. When they got home, Katy told the story to Livy and Mark and the two of them "roared" with laughter. "Well, Katy," Twain said, "what do you think?"

"Well," Katy said, "I was just feeling all the time like I was the queen."

"Well," Twain said, "well, I'm glad that you was able to do that for once."

Livy and Mark "had spasms about it." It was good to hear them laugh after so much sadness.

There were other small incidents to make them smile. In 1896 in London, Twain received a letter addressed to "Mark Twain, God knows where" from Brander Matthews and Francis Wilson, fellow members of the Players Club in New York. And on the same day Livy received one from friends in New Zealand addressed to "Mrs. Clemens (care Mark Twain), United States of America."[11]

No matter how tragic an event, humans must return to living their lives, and part of Livy and Mark's life was entertaining guests. They invited Poultney Bigelow, a then-famous American journalist based in London, and his wife to dinner, so Livy asked Katy to make cream potatoes. Bigelow said, "Why, why, you've surely got some one from America in your kitchen, because there's no cook in England that could cream potatoes."[12]

The American painter James Whistler lived in a "long rambling old house" near them, in back of them, on Cheyne Walk. Oscar Wilde also lived close by. Rudyard Kipling was a frequent visitor. Livy and Mark actually first met Kipling before he was famous; Kipling had traveled first to Hartford to meet Mark Twain, one of his literary heroes, and — told he was in Elmira — went to Elmira and was told he was at Quarry Farm, so Kipling rented a one-horse shay and went there, but there he was told Twain was at the Langdon home in Elmira, and he went back into the city to meet him. Twain invited him and introduced him to Livy.[13]

Livy had to live with the memory that she was not present in Susy's final hours, when she was most needed. She had to live with the knowledge that Susy had called Katy Leary Mama. And, Livy would later learn, her dear neighbor Susan Warner served as a stand-in mother for Susy. In her last days of life, while in the delirium of fever, Susy would go to the window and when a trolley car passed would say, "Up go the trolley cars for Mark Twain's daughter. Down go the trolley cars for Mark Twain's daughter."[14]

Susy's death darkened Mark's view of life, but Livy tried hard to find comfort in religious thoughts. But she failed. Clara noted that her father's first biographer, Albert Bigelow Paine, said that her father's pessimism in his later years resulted directly from grief over Susy's death. And living with Livy's grief.[15] Clara also noted that the house in Guilford, England, where she, her parents, Jean, and Katy lived after Susy's death was comfortable but gloomy. There was a lot of rain, and fog to obscure the trees and shrubs. At one point Livy reminded Mark of a letter he had written to her a year earlier, before Susy died: "Livy, darling, it broke my heart — what you wrote to Sue about immortality. Let us believe in it! I will believe in it with you. It had been the belief of the wise and thoughtful of many countries for three thousand years; let us accept their verdict; we cannot frame one that is more reasonable or probable. I will try never to doubt it again."[16] But he was trying to comfort his grieving wife, not expressing something he truly believed.

In the autumn they moved to a section of London near the Thames River. The house was less gloomy, but there was still little laughter in the family. Twain was often bitter during these days, and he now walked with quick steps, as if annoyed at any delay, and the drawl in his speech was gone. He no longer spoke slowly enough for it be detectable. Mark said to his wife:

> Do you remember, Livy, the hellish struggle it was to settle on making that lecture trip around the world? How we fought the idea, the horrible idea, the heart-torturing idea. I, almost an old man, with ill health, carbuncles, bronchitis and rheumatism. I, with patience worn to rags, I was to pack my bag and be jolted around the devil's universe for what? To pay debts that were not even of my making. And you were worried at the thought of facing such hardships of travel, and SHE was unhappy to be left alone. But once the idea of that infernal trip struck us we couldn't shake it. Oh, no! for it was packed with sense of honor — honor — honor — no rest, comfort, joy — but plenty of honor, plenty of ethical glory. And as a reward for our self-castigation and faithfulness to ideals of nobility we were robbed of our greatest treasure, our lovely Susy in the midst of her blooming talents and personal graces. You want me to believe it is a judicious, a charitable God that runs this world. Why, I could run it better myself.

Livy replied, "Youth, dear, one does not act honorably for the sake of reward or even approbation."

"I do. I want payment in some coin for everything I do. If I can't get peace and joy in return for propping up my blatherskite of a crumbling soul, then — I'll let her rot and the quicker the better."

"You will not feel so bitterly when time has softened the cruelty of our blow. Susy's death was the kindest gift she ever received from God, for she was utterly unfitted for this terrestrial life. She could never have coped with the many unavoidable trials that fall upon the shoulders of every member of the human race. If only we could have been with her during her illness, it would have been a little easier to endure this sorrow."

"Yes, God would not give us that little solace, not even to you. I should not mention myself—I deserve all I get. But you! What has He done to you? Punished you on the rack for living the life of a ministering angel, a faultless mother. I hate Him for that."

"Oh, Youth, there must be a reason for such tragedies!"

"Well, I would like, just for five minutes, to understand the plan of the Creator, if He has any." Then Mark softened his tone and patted Livy on the head and added, "Don't mind anything I say, Livy. Whatever happens, you know I love you."[17]

Despite the expression of love and caring, this conversation is the closest Livy and Mark are known to have come to an argument. Mark's attack on what he sees as a cruel deity and Livy's struggle to believe in the goodness of that same deity were just too opposed to each other for the tension to not be tangible. And Mark's observation that their sense of honor in paying off their debts somehow caused Susy's death was caustic.

For diversion, and perhaps with a hope that he could actually learn something about his future, Twain visited a famous palmist in London, and was told, "You're a very distinguished man, but there's something in the next year I don't want to tell you." Then she told him. "You're going to be a widower, and going to have a lot of trouble, you're going to lose your wife."

When Twain returned home, he told Clara and Jean, "You mustn't tell your mother. I'll never let her know what that palmist said." And when Livy asked him what the palmist said, he made up stories and said the palmist said they were going to have a wonderful life. He added, "But I'd like you to go to him, Livy." The palmist was from India and he was a handsome man and a large one, and his rooms were decorated with items from his native country. Livy went and the palmist told her she would soon be a widow. Palmistry held no allure for Livy and she was less upset than Mark had been, so when she returned home she had no difficulty telling her husband what the palmist had said.

Now Twain was even more upset. He raged, "Well, now damn that man. I'm going up and knock his head off. He don't know a damn thing. He told me that you were going to die, and I was going to be a widower. Now he tells you that I'm going to die and you're going to be a widow. Why, he's a regular pirate."[18]

As they had done before commencing on the world tour, the family moved around Europe. They lived in London, Switzerland, Vienna, Sweden, and again London until October 1900. Twain sometimes returned alone to the United States to conduct business, usually in connection with a publication of his writing. When he was away, he and Livy wrote to each other nearly every day. Those letters were extremely important to the emotional health of both of them.

In 1893 Twain was on the steamer *New York* returning to Paris, where the family was then living, when he agreed to an interview with William Stead, a reporter for the *Review of Reviews*, a London publication. Twain told Stead that when he traveled during all the years of his marriage Livy wrote to him every day. He wrote to her "with every mail with one exception, which caused him great grief." Someone had told him the quickest steamer sailed on a Thursday, but it really sailed on a Wednesday, and because he wanted to add more to his letter he missed the mail. Livy was "greatly grieved" and he "has been getting letters full of despair ever since." When they were first separated he wrote two or three times a day, but then he learned that the mail went out only once or twice a week. He still wrote daily but saved up what he wrote until mail day. He wrote to her about everything he did every day. He said, "From a literary point of view, these letters to my wife in the last six months satisfy me much better than anything I have ever written. There is a lightness of touch and a vividness of description, and altogether a lightness which I try for in vain when I am writing for magazines or books." He said his letters averaged 25 pages and 4,000 to 5,000 words. He said John Brisben Walker, publisher of *Cosmopolitan* magazine, told him, "What a waste, what a waste to send all those letters to your wife, when you know I would give you a thousand dollars apiece for them," so Twain wrote to Livy and said he may have been "guilty of much waste." He asked her to send back the letters, but Livy replied "she would not give them up for one thousand five hundred dollars apiece." Stead said maybe Walker would indeed pay $1,500 apiece, but then Twain added, "No, she would go up again." And he said he did not want to publish them sometime in the future: "There is nothing that I have written or read compared in value to these letters to my wife."[19]

They moved from Weggis, Switzerland, to Vienna, Austria, allowing Clara to pursue the musical studies they had encouraged since she was a little girl. Because she was Mark Twain's daughter she was able to take lessons from Theodor Leschetitzky, widely considered the greatest piano teacher of the time. Among others he taught Ignacy Jan Paderewski, who would become perhaps the most famous pianist of the day (and who also became prime minister of Poland in 1919). When the Clemenses first arrived in Vienna it was unexpectedly crowded, and because they had not made advance reservations they had to go to nine hotels before finding a room, exhausting the easily tired Livy. They finally found one in the Hotel Muller, on a dirty and dreary street. The next day, however, Twain found more and better space in the Hotel Metropole; it was much more cheerful.

While in Vienna, Livy and Mark received visitors each day after 5:00 P.M., so their hotel drawing room became known as the "second U.S. Embassy." Some aristocratic Vienna ladies smoked pipes or cigars, surprising Clara. Although Twain sometimes skipped the socializing, he did become friendly with one princess who smoked a pipe. Some women's cigars were so large they seemed to Clara to look like flutes. The women were expensively and elaborately dressed. With the princess Twain would sometimes become vehement and contradict her, so Livy would politely urge him to revise what he said by touching his elbow, or his toe with her toe, and say, "You mean, Youth...," and he would say, "Yes, of course, I mean, Princess, I thought it was..." Livy seldom left the hotel in the two years the family spent in Vienna.[20]

By now Twain had developed the habit of often staying in bed late in the morning, even if he had been awake for hours. When an Austrian newspaper reporter arrived for a scheduled interview, Livy went into their bedroom to tell Mark, and he said to show him in. Livy said, "Youth, don't you think it will be a little embarrassing for him to find you in bed?"

Mark said, "Why, if you think so, Livy, we could have the other bed made up for him."[21] Over the years Twain, in fact, would often be interviewed while he was still in bed. As with so much else involving a husband who went out of his way to seem mildly eccentric, Livy learned to accept his habits.

Livy and Mark, both democrats at heart, sometimes found themselves uncomfortable in socially conscious European settings. In Vienna custom called for the highest socially ranking woman to sit on the sofa, so when a baroness sat on the sofa in the Clemens drawing room and a princess then entered and the baroness didn't get up, Livy pointed to an open spot on the same sofa. In America, of course, that would not have been a problem. But the princess in Vienna would have nothing of such equality and tilted her head and said to Livy, "I am so sorry to have intruded. I will return when you are disengaged." Several others in the room had open mouths in surprise as the princess left the room.[22]

Social awkwardness was far more of a problem for Livy than for Mark. He had been born poor and, as his portrayals of Tom Sawyer and Huck Finn showed, saw nothing wrong with that, even took pride in it. Born poor, become rich, that was American. Livy had been born into a family far more financially secure, a family that in fact became rich after she was born, a family that accepted its role as a leader of Elmira society. Protocol was part of her Victorian upbringing, even as she admired her husband's ingrained democratic tendencies.

When she and Mark, after he gave a lecture for a charity, visited the home of Countess Bardi, sister of Archduchess Maria Theresa, etiquette called for them to sign their names in a visitors' book in an anteroom at the countess's home. A servant said he would show them upstairs and the countess would be there shortly. Livy said, "Oh, there is a misunderstanding. We did not come to call, but just to write our names in the book."

The servant, a man dressed in lace and silk, said, "You are Americans, are you not?"

Livy said, "Yes, but we are not expected."

"If you are Americans you are expected and the Countess will be in immediately." Evidently, Clara wrote decades later, another American couple was expected. Livy was very nervous and "her feet seemed to get all tangled." At the door to the drawing room Livy again told the servant she would prefer to just sign the book because they were not expected. Mark enjoyed the misunderstanding. The servant stood militarily erect but didn't speak. Inside the room, Livy and Mark sat and Livy wondered about the correct etiquette, including remembering not to turn her back on the countess. The countess entered, and to Livy's alarm so did the archduchess and "two or three little princes and princesses." The countess spoke excellent English. Livy and Mark soon learned that in fact the servant had been sent to the hotel to invite Livy and Mark to visit at the palace, but the time set was 3:00 P.M. and they arrived at 1:30. They had not been home to receive the invitation. The Clemenses and the Austrian royalty spent an hour talking over tea. When the visit was over Livy remembered to leave backwards, so she wouldn't turn her back on royalty. Mark, although caring less about such formalities, did the same. He cared about offending Livy.[23]

In the same way that their grief eased enough to permit some socializing so, too, did it permit Twain to resume some writing. But he was now far less inclined to be humorous or even just to fashion a well-told story. His bitterness frequently coated his writing with a mixture of sadness and cynicism. And Livy, ever the editor determined to protect and shape her husband's public image, was sometimes alarmed at what he wrote. While in Vienna he wrote a long essay, 65 pages or longer in most editions, titled "What Is Man?" It is the longest essay he ever wrote. It is in the form of a script, a dialogue between Old Man and Young Man. Old Man takes a pessimistic and mechanistic view of human beings, ascertaining they are nothing more than machines designed to carry out the will of an uncaring universe. Young Man objects, offering arguments designed to show Old Man he is wrong, but by the end the reader understands that the author clearly agrees with Old Man. Livy was appalled. No good could come to her husband's reputation with the publication of something so tinged with resentment. She "begged" him not to publish it. She told him that what he wrote was not true. More than that, she said, it would cause harm to people who read it. Mark, obedient in his love for Livy, acquiesced; he would not publish it. He kept the promise as long as she lived. In 1906, two years after she died, he had it published at his own expense.[24]

There was never a shortage of fuel to feed Twain's cynicism. In December of 1897, Livy and Mark learned that Orion had died. He had started to write a novel based on the life of Judas, and one day at age 72 while sitting at his desk and working on his book he died quietly. Livy, who liked Orion but was saddened by the string of failures in his life, said that "although he had been unsuccessful in his life he was most fortunate in his death." Finding something good in death was so typical of Livy and so unlike Mark.[25] Then they learned that their longtime African American butler, George, had also died. Mark had enjoyed kibitzing with George, but Livy was often frustrated by his unwillingness to conform to her ideal of how a butler should behave. Katy said, "Oh, Mrs. Clemens, do you remember the beautiful, elegant parties you used to give [in Hartford] and how George used to stop the gentlemen on the way to the drawing-room to ask what horse he ought to bet on? And once when you told him he should not do that, he had the boldness to say he wasn't asking the gentlemen for help, he was telling them which were the best horses, so the swell gentlemen could make a little more money. Poor Old George, and now he is dead! We could never live in that home again with Miss Susy and George gone."

Livy, in a soft voice, answered, "No, indeed, Katie, we couldn't."[26]

Their grief over the loss of Susy did not blind them to the fact they had two other daughters, and they sought to do what they could for Clara and Jean.

With Livy's permission, Clara invited Leschetitzky to a dinner party at her parents' home, and he brought two former pupils with him, Mark Hambourg and Ossip Gabrilowitsch. Hambourg and Gabrilowitsch were both born in Russia and both were destined to become among the leading pianists of their time, Hambourg in Great Britain and Gabrilowitsch in America. Gabrilowitsch was also destined to become the husband of Clara (in 1909).[27]

Jean, meanwhile, had been diagnosed as an epileptic. The cause was probably a genetic defect, but the family had been given a different reason by a doctor, one of which Clara was skeptical. Clara wrote that her younger sister's epilepsy was "supposedly due to a fall she had at about the age of ten." To Livy, that must have reminded her about her fall on the ice in Elmira decades earlier. Jean's parents took her to doctors in America and Europe in search of a cure, but none of them offered much help or hope. Dr. Jonas Kellgren, a Swedish physician in London, had been reported to have had some success with treating epileptics. So in the summer of 1899 the Clemens family moved from Vienna to Sanna, a Swedish village where Kellgren ran a sanatorium. The town was drab, dull and gray, and the only entertainment was Swedish dance performances, in which Clara and Jean took part, and watching sunsets. But Jean's health did not improve.[28]

And they continued to move, one home to another, one city to another, one country to another. Every move wore down Livy a little more. They started 1898 in Vienna, but on May 25 they moved to Kaltenleutgeben, just outside of the Austrian capital. It was a "water-cure village," and Livy and Jean both received treatments there. From August 16 to 27 they vacationed in the mountain resort of Salzkammegut. Then back to Kaltenleutgeben. In mid–October they moved back to Vienna, to the Hotel Krantz. Beginning March 23, 1899, they visited in Budapest for seven days. Then five days in Prague. Then in June to London. In July to Sweden for Jean to be treated for her epilepsy by Dr. Kellgren. And when they returned to London in the fall, they rented an apartment near the Swedish Institute, where Kellgren had his primary practice. During their stay in London, Livy and Mark spent a great deal of time sitting together under oak trees.[29] And in October they sailed for America.

Among her other health problems, Livy often suffered from dysentery, but Twain claimed it was always cured if she ate a slice of watermelon.[30]

And, as always, Livy was worn down by Christmas. Each holiday season she spent two or three weeks shopping, and that always physically exhausted her. Her typical gift list contained more than 50 names.[31]

In early 1900 they were back in London, living at 30 Wellington Court. In July they moved to Dollis Hill in northwest London. On October 6 they sailed for New York. For the next year they lived at 14 West 10th Street, in Manhattan. Later they moved to Riverdale in the Bronx.

On October 20 their friend Charles Dudley Warner died. He was 71. Mark did not immediately tell Livy about Warner's death. He waited until the next morning so it would not interfere with her sleep. They agreed to tell their children later. Jean and Clara were close friends of Warner's children. But as they were climbing the steps to board the elevated train, someone mentioned to Twain that Warner had died and he said, "Yes, it's a staggering blow to us all," and one of his daughters said, "What is it, papa?"[32] Their daughters called Warner Cousin Charley and called his wife Cousin Susie. The family traveled to Hartford to attend the funeral, and once there Twain told a newspaper reporter, "In the spring I shall return to Hartford, Connecticut, where Mrs. Clemens, my daughters and myself will settle down for some home life, after nine years of wandering up and down on the earth."[33] It was not true. Livy and Mark never again lived in Hartford.

Back in New York a visiting William Dean Howells was told by Livy that she found some compensation in being frequently confined to her room: she did not have to listen to Mark's bitter rantings about "the damned human race."[34]

That summer the Clemenses went to Saranac Lake in the Adirondacks. They stayed in a village called Ampersand. Too small to appear on most maps, it was named for a twisting creek nearby. There were no daily newspapers for Livy, Mark, Clara, and Jean to read, and they let their mail pile up at the post office. As with the palmist and spiritualist and other dealings with the supernatural, they were escaping from a world that had caused them so much pain. And Twain always had his work to retreat into. He sat in a small tent near the lake writing for four to seven hours every day. Inside the tent, the only noises heard were the rippling of the water on the lake and the wind moving through the trees. Mark was more insistent on the escape than Livy. When a newspaper reporter, W.B. Northrop, requested an interview, he was rebuffed. He requested again. And again, and only when his requests were "seconded by the kindly offices of Mrs. Clemens" did Mark agree.[35]

Then they moved again. This time to the Appleton house in Riverdale, on the Hudson River, north of New York City. It was in the country and both Mark and Livy thought it would be better for Livy's health.[36]

As he often did, Mark playfully referred to Livy when talking to others. A writer who used the pen name Pendennis had a photograph of Twain sitting at his desk, and Twain said, "Now, if Mrs. Clemens had come in and seen that desk being photographed in this shape she would have been aghast at its apparent disorder. But that is not disorder. I know exactly where everything is, top and bottom, from a telegraph blank in its hiding place to a manuscript or a letter. What looks like disorder to some people is the best of order to others. My mother had the same disordered sense of order that I have. I might buy her reams and reams of the most magnificent note paper, blue, green, red, pale peacock, anything you like. It was no use. She never would write on anything but odd scraps. Many's the letter I've received from her written on uneven scraps of paper, different colors and qualities all bunched together in an envelope and unpaged. My mother's letters were as hard to understand as any problem book I ever read."[37]

Although neither believed the effort would be successful, Livy and Mark visited a spiritualist in March 1901 in an attempt to communicate with Susy.

There was no contact. It was part of a long series of efforts by Livy and Mark to deal with an unkind world by reaching beyond the dictates of science. They had already visited the palmist in London and would later briefly flirt with Christian Science. When modern technology, things like the Paige Compositor and Plasmon, having done so much damage to their lives, it was inevitable that they should seek comfort in a non-scientific world. Even their joint interest in Joan of Arc fit the new pattern.

Twain told Howells that he, his wife, and daughters had all stopped wearing glasses. They were astigmatic, myopic, and "old-sighted," Howells wrote. "Some sage" had convinced Twain that glasses didn't work. But the next time Howells saw Twain, his friend was wearing glasses again and he said everyone else in his family was also and, in fact, they almost went blind because of the sage's advice.[38]

That autumn the Clemenses put the Hartford house up for sale. It was a financial decision, but it also served to move them away from the home's unpleasant memories. They would live in Riverdale until July of 1903.

Life was different in Riverdale. Howells, who now saw them more frequently than ever before, noted that they lived far less pretentiously than they had in Hartford. He noted also that while Twain did not like to eat out, he often did, especially at the homes of other people, because Livy wanted him to. These changes, Howells believed, were good for both Livy and Mark. They had "two happy, hopeless years" in Riverdale. Then doctors said Livy needed a milder climate.[39] Twain worried constantly about Livy's health. Once he and Howells were on the expansive lawn at Riverdale and they both saw Livy on a balcony waving a handkerchief at them and Twain rose from his seat and ran towards the balcony, calling, "What? What?" He thought Livy needed something, but she didn't; she was only signaling a greeting to Howells.[40]

Not living in Hartford was Livy's choice more than Mark's, but renting a house along the Hudson was more his choice. He grew up near the Mississippi, had a view of the Chemung from Quarry Farm, in London had lived near the Thames, and now saw the Hudson nearby. As much as he was able to, he tried to always be near a river. The Riverdale property contained a huge chestnut tree that held a platform supported by branches large enough to hold a table and chairs. A wooden staircase led up the branches and Twain sometimes sat on the platform and smoked his pipe. He did some writing up there, mostly about Tammany Hall and its then leader Richard Crocker; they were his main topics of conversation that year.[41]

Livy's various ailments meant she had to stay in her bedroom most of each day while at Riverdale. She watched out the window to see changing light and ice storms and snowstorms, all of which she thought were beautiful.

Doctors told Mark and Jean to stay out of the room because they were excitable and would interfere with the rest Livy needed. Clara, however, could go in and act as assistant nurse. Mark usually communicated with Livy by notes and verbal messages through Clara. Two or three times a day Mark gave a note to either the nurse or Clara to give to Livy, and Livy's face always lit up when she received one. One note said, "Don't know the date nor the day. But anyway, it is a soft and pensive foggy morning, Livy darling, and the naked tree branches are tear-beaded, and Nature has the look of trying to keep from breaking down and sobbing, poor old thing. Good morning, dear heart, I love you dearly." It was signed "Y."[42]

The Riverdale house was owned by a Mr. Appleton. One note from Mark to Livy said, "I will write Mr. Appleton what you say, Livy dear. My understanding was — was — oh, well dang it I don't know what it was — I don't reckon I had any. Often I have an understanding that I don't understand and then I come to find out I didn't. Sleep well, Dearest."

Still another note said, "Goodnight, dear heart, Old Brer Howells is coming Saturday night, but John [i.e., Howells's son] can't come, the Count can't come and the Colonel can't come. There are more can't comes than any other guests."

Another note:

Dear heart, how wonderful are old letters in bringing a dead past back to life and filling it with movement and stir of figures clothed in ruddy flesh! It all seems more real and present than it does in a novel, and one feels it more and is more a part of it, with the joy-light in one's eyes, and one's own heart on the skewer. Good morning, sweetheart, it is bright and beautiful and I love you most deeply. This dining-room is a paradise, with the flooding sunshine, the fire of big logs, the white expanse of cushioned snow and the incomparable river. I wish you down here sweetheart.

One more note: "And now the stormy winds do blow, as the sailor ballad says. I believe we have the noblest roaring blasts here I have ever known on land; they sing their hoarse song through the big tree-tops with a splendid energy that thrills me and stirs me and uplifts me and makes me want to live always, a body can have such grand orchestration."

From the same note: "Ship ahoy! Helm alee!— there steady! Let her go off a point!— luff, and bring her to the wind! ... I'm reading sailor-yarns, dearest, and am full of the salt sea and the great winds and the wonders of the deep. Clara and Jean couldn't understand me at dinner, they are land-lubbers and ignorant.... Sleep well, dearest of the dear. I love you."

Twain enjoyed reading a history of the great mutiny in East India and sent Livy a note about it:

I am where the Mutiny is approaching, Livy dear — April 22 — then the 30th —
then May 8th — that awful shadow creeping upon them stage by stage and they
don't know it. May the 9th and they are easy and comfortable, and think it was a
trifling flurry and has blown over. May the 10th and they are junketing — and the
slaughter and the butchery and the burning are raging at Meerut! And they don't
suspect.— By gracious there is something immensely moving and dramatic about
that creeping shadow and those poor self-satisfied people's unconsciousness of it!
... I am loving you, dearest, goodnight, dearheart and sleep well.

Still another note: "Dearest, we've had a grand dispute as to when Clara
was first able to read, either German or English — and of course I was right
and of course I was put down by the strong hand. I will not stay here, I am
going to heaven. There they will not abuse me, but will praise me and pet me
and flatter me and give me a halo, and I am not going to lend it to the children.
Good night, my daring — YOU shall wear it sometimes."

A note from Livy to Mark: "Youth my own precious Darling, I feel
so frightfully banished. Couldn't you write in my boudoir? Then I could
hear you clear your throat and it would be such joy to feel you near. I miss
you sadly, sadly. Your note in the morning gave me support for the day, the
one at night, peace for the night. With the deepest love of my heart, Your
Livy."

Mark did then move his writing to Livy's boudoir, but after a while he
started to talk to Livy from there and the nurse insisted he move to a more
distant room.

Twain watched squirrels playing in trees around the house. He named
one Blennerhasset and two others the Wilkersons. One note he wrote to Livy
said:

> I am lying in bed, working hard when the Wilkersons permit it. But they do love
> to show off and get me all excited watching their hairbreadth escapes from death,
> when they nonchalantly balance their souls and bodies on the tip end of a slender
> branch, flirting their tails, just as a circus-acrobat blows a kiss to the audience
> from a dizzy height at the tip of the tent. I must have jumped half a dozen times
> when it looked as if Mrs. Wilkerson would surely tip off that branch into purga-
> tory and nothing to save her. Blennerhasset sat off at some distance with his paws
> up as if he were praying, so I was not alone in my anxiety. I think I shall have to
> pull down the shades so that I can stick to my work.

Jean caught pneumonia, but Livy was not told. Livy and her nurse shared
a room in one wing of the house; Jean's room was on the other side of the
house, on the third floor. Livy had not seen Jean "for some time," but every
day she asked Clara about Jean's activities, moods, thoughts. Clara had a reputation for truth telling in the family. To help hide Jean's illness, Clara told
lies to Livy, saying Jean went sledding or went shopping in town. Sometimes

Clara forgot exactly what lie she had told Livy. Once Livy said, "Why, Clara, I thought you said Jean was out coasting and now you say you expect her back from town on the five o'clock train."[43]

Clara said, "Oh, Mother, it is really terrible how absent-mindedness is growing on me. Half the time I say something that is entirely different from what is in my mind. And sometimes I can't even tell whether I have dreamed something or whether it has really happened."

Livy said, "That is just because you don't put your entire mind on a thing. Well, which is it? Did Jean go to town or has she been out coasting?"

"Both."

"How could she possibly manage to do both? She must have taken the nine-o'clock train to town if she went to do shopping."

"No. You see, another train has been put on that does not leave until ten-thirty. And Jean got up very early so as to get in some coasting before she went to town."

Once Clara reminded her father to tell Livy in one of his notes that Clara had been lying down and he had visited neighbors. They had actually been consulting with Jean's doctors.

On another occasion, Livy said, "Why, Clara, aren't you going to your lesson?"

"Yes."

"In that costume?"

"Oh no!"

"Well, you can't possibly make the train."

"I know, but I am going to take the other one."

"How can you? You will be late for your lesson."

"No, the lesson-time has been put an hour later."

"But my dear, then that will make you late for Mrs. B——'s luncheon."

"No, the train leaves fifteen minutes earlier than it used to."

When Jean got better, doctors advised her to go to the South for a few months. During that time, Clara had to still invent stories about Jean to tell to Livy as if Jean were still in Riverdale.

Then Clara became ill. She had intercostal neuralgia, a nerve disorder, and black measles. The nerve disorder was painful and the black measles turned her skin dark, so "one looks like the corpse of a drowned woman." She needed an oxygen tank. One night in bed, about 4:00 A.M., something crashed down on her and her room filled with dust. She was pinned in place for four hours.[44] The ceiling in her room had collapsed.

Twain's spirits were subdued while Livy was confined to her bedroom. He occasionally accepted an invitation to dinner and once accepted an invitation from Henry Rogers to join him on his yacht for visits to Havana, western Cuba, Jamaica, Martinique, and other Caribbean islands.[45]

Livy because of her illness wrote few notes to Mark in these years. One she did write was in pencil on both sides of a single piece of paper and is undated. It concerns a letter to the editor Mark had written about Marie van Vorst, a writer whose work he clearly did not like.[46] After reading the letter, Livy left the note to him on his worktable. It said:

> Youth darling, have you forgotten your promise to me? You said that I was con-stantly in your mind and that you knew what I would like & you would not pub-lish what I would disapprove. Did you think I would approve the letter to Marie van Vorst? I am absolutely wretched today on account of your state of mind — your state of intellect. Why don't you let the better side of you work? ... You go too far, much too far in all you say, ... Do darling change your mental attitude, try to change it.... Where is the mind that wrote the Prince & P. Jeanne d'Arc, The Yan-kee &c &c &c. Bring it back! ... Think of the side I know, the sweet dear, tender side — that I love so.... Does it help the world to always rail at it? ... Oh! I love you so & wish you would listen & take heed.
>
> Yours
> Livy.[47]

He read and he obeyed. The letter was never sent to a newspaper.

In January 1902, the family visited Elmira, but in mid–March Twain left Livy behind and took a trip on Rogers's yacht, the *Kanawha*. In mid–April the Clemenses moved again, this time to Tarrytown. From April 24 to August 12 Clara was in Europe while her parents and sister remained in the United States. On May 29 Twain left on a trip to accept an honorary doctorate from the University of Missouri,[48] and along the way he stopped in Hannibal, his boyhood home, to the delight of the town folk, some of whom remembered him as a boy. Livy did not make the trip. She said the heat would be too much for her. She wrote to one of his relatives in St. Louis, "Don't let him stay long for I find life very lonely when he is away."[49] She never visited Hannibal, the town on the Mississippi made world famous by her husband. Her health greatly limited the traveling she could now do. But in the summer she did go with Mark to York Harbor, Maine.

At the end of July they rented a house on the outskirts of York Harbor in the southern corner of the state. Rogers brought his yacht, *Kanawha*, the fastest steam yacht in the United States, to near their Riverdale-on-Hudson home and sent a launch to pick them up along the riverfront. Mark was sur-prised to learn that Livy was not taking a servant on the trip because she thought that would inconvenience Rogers. He knew Rogers would not mind and certainly would not object even if he did. Jean was in bad health at the time, and that meant Livy would have to devote much energy to her care. Livy, without Mark's knowledge, arranged for their furniture to be shipped by rail to York Harbor.[50]

The weather was good and the sailing smooth, but Livy had to stay belowdecks to care for Jean. At nighttime the weather seemed "heavy" and the boat docked in New London, Connecticut. Livy got little sleep because of the attention she was giving to Jean, but the next day they sailed to Fairhaven, Massachusetts, and Livy could have rested on board for two or three hours while the others visited Rogers's family at their country estate, but she went ashore with them and became fatigued.

Twelve years earlier, two Hartford physicians had told her to use the baths of Aix-les-Bains in eastern France; they said with good care she could live two more years. That was the most time they gave her because, they said, she had a weak heart. Other doctors in Rome, Florence, and Berlin also, over the years, gave her two years to live. But a doctor, less famous than all the others, this one in Aix-les-Bains, told her there wasn't really much wrong with her heart and she would probably live a long life. Mark had thought that doctor couldn't be very good, so he paid him and dismissed him, but he was the only doctor who had predicted, more than a decade earlier, that Livy would still be alive at the turn of the century.[51]

But when the Clemenses arrived in York Harbor, Livy was concerned about her heart and sometimes refused to go on carriage rides. She developed a fear of speed and of descending grades and pleaded with coachmen to walk the horses slowly down any grades, no matter how slight. And if the horses went faster than a walk, she would grab Mark with one hand and the side of the carriage with the other, fright on her face.

William Dean Howells was staying at Kittery Point, Maine, that summer and came to visit at least twice. Kittery Point was 45 minutes away by trolley. Howells and Twain sat on the veranda and told stories, while Livy rested upstairs. One story was about a friend of Howells, but it contained details that made Mark think it could be about Livy.

While in York Harbor, Twain told a reporter, "Because of Mrs. Clemens' illness, I am not doing much writing." Several times during the interview he went upstairs "to see about Mrs. Clemens."[52]

Howells described the Clemens home in York Harbor as a "wide, low cottage in a pine grove overlooking York River."[53] The two writers would "sit at a corner of the veranda, farthest away from Mrs. Clemens's window, where we could read our manuscripts to each other, and tell our stories, and laugh our hearts out without disturbing her." Early in the summer Livy sometimes walked around the cottage, and once she made tea for them and served it in the parlor. That was the last time Howells saw and spoke to Livy. She was clearly dying. Howells later said of that last meeting that he did not know if Mark knew, or was willing to admit, that Livy was dying.

Mark and Howells traveled together to Boston to arrange for Livy's return to Riverdale. They inquired about invalid cars on trains, the details of how she might be carried to the train station, how the invalid car would be detached from the train at Boston and attached to another train going to the Hudson River.

Twain told Howells he and Livy would move to Florence, Italy, because doctors thought the mild climate of northern Italy would be good for her. He remembered when they lived there previously, a decade earlier, and how much they liked it. And, he said to Howells, he expected that he and Livy would spend the rest of their lives there.

They had first lived in Florence in 1892, in the Villa Viviana. Not in the city itself, but in the suburb of Settignano, on a hill overlooking Florence. Arrangements for that villa were made with Mrs. Janet Duff Gordon Ross, who made it a habit of befriending writers and artists and who lived in a castle that was a 12-minute walk from the villa.[54]

The Clemens family was passing through Florence on their way to Germany for Livy's treatment at a health spa when they asked friends to arrange for a villa. They returned three to four months later and everything was ready, including servants and even their first dinner. That villa was three miles from Florence. It had a flowery terrace and looked down on olive groves and vineyards. They could see the Ross castle, with its turrets and weather stains. Florence, in the distance, looked pink, gray, and brown. A rusty large dome of a cathedral was its most prominent feature. On one side of the large dome was the small dome of a Medici chapel and on the other side a tower of Palazzo Vecchio, a fortress-like palace that served as Florence's city hall. Dozens of villas could be seen on the surrounding hillsides.

They arrived in Florence for their first stay on September 26, 1892. The *contadino*, or caretaker of the villa, met them and charged them to take their trunks to the villa. Twain on September 27 hired a landau (a four-wheel carriage with a top that can be folded down and a raised seat for the driver), horses, and a coachman for 480 francs per month. As part of the arrangement, Twain furnished housing for both the coachman and the horses. The horses seemed feeble and the landau seemed too heavy for them, and the horses often stopped to turn and look at the wagon. And people living in the area just as often stopped to look at the horses looking at the wagon.

The villa was two stories and was about two centuries old. It was plain and square, painted a light yellow with green shutters, and had a masonry wall around it. The garden included crockery tubs containing lemon bushes, and some pines, fig trees, and other trees. Roses climbed the retaining walls, and there were gravel walks bordered by laurel hedges. Ilex trees in a back terrace stood by a stone table and stone benches. The back terrace was always dark, even in midday. The carriage road extended 800 feet from the inner gate to the public road. A coat of arms was on the east side of the house, and there was a sundial nearby.

The ceilings in the ground-floor rooms were 20 feet high.

There were at least 28 rooms (Twain was uncertain of the exact number). The ceilings in every room had frescoes; all walls were papered, all floors red brick covered with polished, shining cement. Some floors were gray with red borders, some red with gray borders. The many large windows kept the rooms brightly lit during daytime. The ground floor had a chapel large enough to hold a dozen people. An oil painting hung over the altar. In the middle of the house was a salon, two stories high, that extended four feet above the rest of the roof. All the other rooms of the house surrounded it. Five divans were placed against the walls of the salon. Above each of the six doors in the salon were plaster medallions of naked plaster boys and some adult men fully clothed in official-looking garb of centuries past. One was dated 1305. Another 1343. Still another 1463. The salon was 40 feet square and 40 feet high, although it looked even larger.

Water was pumped to the ground floor by hand and then hand-carried to the second. There was no drainage, and cesspools were located directly under windows (allowing water to be dumped out of the windows). The windows opened apart, like doors, and when locked at night they did not rattle. Some rooms had small fireplaces. The salon had a large German stove.

One night a curtain caught on fire, but nothing else burned because the walls, floor, the entire structure, was non-flammable.

In a note he wrote on September 29, 1892, Twain said he had his head shaved when first arriving in Italy but then came to think he made a mistake.

On October 1, 1892, Twain learned that the coachman, Vittorio, was eating his meals in the kitchen, so Twain decided to charge him 30 francs a month for the food.

On October 6, 1892, Twain noted that friends regularly came in the afternoon to have tea. Usually Livy, Clara, and Jean attended these teas.

Clara remembered that her father thought there wasn't enough furniture in the villa and that he called the front hall a "skating rink" because it was large and had a slippery floor. The whole family, she said, would watch the setting sun from the terrace. And she recalled that when her father shaved his head it looked like a billiard ball. The main family entertainment most nights was Twain reading to the family whatever he had written that day. While in Florence he read from *Joan of Arc*.[55]

The family loved the villa and the climate and the people of Florence. That first stay in Florence was a happy time for Livy and Mark.

In November 1902, Twain hired a secretary for Livy, Isabel V. Lyon, but she soon became Twain's secretary instead. That same month the Clemenses visited Elmira again. When they moved to Florence for the second time, Lyon, shortly thereafter, joined them.

They returned to Florence, a city that was sweet and grand and lovely.

CHAPTER SEVEN

Hell and Satan

Florence was hell, and their landlady was Satan.

On October 24, 1903, Livy, Mark, Clara, Jean, and Katy Leary sailed on the *Princess Irene* for what the *New York Evening Journal* called a one-year stay in Florence. Prior arrangements had already been made through an agent for them to stay at the Villa Reale di Quarto, "one of the most beautiful palaces overlooking the Mediterranean." The report is clearly careless. Twain had already said he expected he and Livy would live the rest of their lives in Florence, not stay for just one year. And Florence is an inland city; you cannot see the Mediterranean from there. *The New York Times* of the same date quoted Twain as saying, "I'm peevish today. I have absorbed all my wife's pugnacity and all of my daughters' audacity." *The New York American*: "I shall do some literary work there while Mrs. Clemens tries to recover her health. One of my daughters will act as my amanuensis, while the other makes snapshots of me in the throes of composition for use in the Saturday literary reviews."[1]

They arrived in Genoa on November 6, took a train to Florence, and moved into the Villa di Quarto on November 9. Later that month they were joined by Isabel V. Lyon, who was hired in 1902 as Livy's secretary but had since assumed more general duties. Lyon was accompanied by her mother.[2]

Before making the move to Florence, Twain looked into several possible villas to rent near Florence. It must be a villa, that is, large enough to be roomy, and it must be near Florence, not in it. There was at one point a mix-up involving someone Clara calls Mr. X that prompted a letter from Twain to Jean: "I proposed to send a cable saying: 'Take your Papiniano and go to hell with it.' But Clara and I could not agree. She wanted me to insert 'dam' in front of Papiniano, but I felt that your mother would not approve of that; and so we split that trifle and sent no cable at all. Explain it to your mother, so that she will see that although Clara tried to get me to do wrong, I stood out and done right."[3]

Later, Mark wrote to Livy, "It is good to think of a quiet retreat in a sub-urb of Florence. Yes, I am glad we are going to Italy. You will do well there."

Gregory Smith, a friend of Twain's who lived in Florence, made arrange-ment to rent a villa from a woman Clara calls Mrs. A ——.[4] The landlady orig-inally planned to leave Florence for a while but changed her mind and decided to stay in a room above a stable on her estate. She was an American married to an Italian diplomat who at the time was somewhere in the Far East. Much of the furniture that Smith thought he was renting with the villa was taken by Mrs. A —— to her rooms above the stable. The villa had 50 to 60 rooms. It had been built by one of the Medici and was once occupied by a Russian grand duke. To get to it you had to go up a long garden drive with tall cedars and poplars on either side. There were numerous rosebushes and a fountain. And it was very quiet, which was important for both Livy's health and Mark's writing.

Florence at first seemed good for Livy. She was able to sit up an hour each day in a small parlor off of her bedroom. The parlor opened onto the ter-race. But a week or two after arriving, Livy had a heart attack and the nurse tried to telephone a doctor, but the telephone was dead. After a search it was discovered that someone had cut the wires. A servant walked a "long distance" to find another telephone and near the end of the day finally reached a doctor. The carriage drive from the doctor's office in Florence to the villa was 45 min-utes, so the doctor should have arrived about 7:00 P.M., but at 7:30 he was still not there. Twain went to the front gate and found that it was locked. He said:

> The doctor has been here and gone. Couldn't get in. Outer gate locked. Damn that Medici hellion that built this fortress. Thought he had to protect his soul with a lot of iron gates. Didn't have any soul! The worse a man is the more important he thinks it is to protect himself. Now how are we to get that doctor? No telephone. By the thunder of Zeus, I swear I'll take your mother back to America tomorrow. That's a sane country with sane people in it.

Livy recovered from the heart attack without the doctor, who didn't arrive until the next morning, when he said "he had been at the outer gate and waited nearly an hour, making all the noise he could to attract the attention of some-one, but succeeding only in drawing a small crowd of passers-by."

A few days later, a maid told Clara there was no water for washing or cooking. Just then, Twain knocked on Clara's door and she said, "Come in, Father."

"Just as soon as you are dressed I wish you would drive to town and see Mr. Smith. Tell him I will appreciate it if he will get us a release from this rental contract. And then bring out a list of sailing dates from Thomas Cook. We'll return to America while the weather is still mild."

"Why, Father, what is the matter?"

"The matter? You're not washed are you?"

"No. Is it because of the water you want to leave?"

"Isn't that reason enough? There is a dog-gone devil in this place. Do you want to wait till he has displayed *all* his wares? I've seen enough. The doctors at home never should have advised this trip. An idiotic idea to start with. I always thought so. Look at what your mother has to endure in this place. It's criminal to subject her to such things. What will she have to eat today?"

"We'll manage to get some water to cook with."

And they did. They hired a man to cart water from a nearby spring. That lasted several days, and then they found out what had happened to the regular water. Mrs. A——, the landlady, had cut it off, evidently because Twain had many guests but never invited her. Clara and Jean used to think it funny that the slats in the landlady's window would move when guests arrived. She was watching to see who came.

The landlady had two ugly bulldogs that Jean and Clara befriended, which was hard to do. They wanted to make certain the dogs didn't attack them. One day, some young friends of Jean and Clara visited, both boys and girls, and they stayed for dinner, but as they were leaving, the sudden barking of the dogs frightened them. It was getting dark, and Jean and Clara worried that the dogs would not recognize them. So they spoke to the dogs and they recognized the sisters' voices and wagged their tails and jumped up on them. But the dogs had been covered in kerosene and the girls' dresses were ruined, as were the clothes of the guests.[5]

Twain contacted an Italian lawyer who arranged to have Mrs. A—— "ejected from our vicinity."

With the landlady problem seemingly solved, Livy seemed to improve in the "mild air" and quiet surroundings, but then she became worse and could no longer go on the terrace and was confined to bed. Again Twain and Jean were not allowed to visit her, just as had happened in Riverdale, for fear of exciting her. But Clara could see her.

Mark wrote a note to Livy that said, "Wedding-day Anniversary February 2. It's a long time ago, my darling, but the 33 years have been richly profitable to us, through love — a love which has grown, not diminished, and is worth more each year than it was the year before. And so it will be always, dearest old Sweetheart of my youth. Goodnight, and sleep well."

Another note said, "Goodnight, Livy darling, I am very busy planning the elopement, and I think I shall soon have it all ciphered out. Horseback and closed carriages are not used any more in elopements, they have gone out; but a bicycle is proper, and so is the mobile — this in cases where they used to use the wheelbarrow. I love you very, very dearly, Sweetheart. Goodnight. Y."

One of the notes was a poem:

> Goodnight, Sweetheart, goodnight —
> The stars are shining bright,
> The snow is turning white,
> Dim is the failing light,
> Fast falls the glooming night, -
> All right!
> Sleep tight!
> Goodnight.

Because Twain tended to sleep late and Livy worried that that habit was not healthy, she sent him a note saying he should rise earlier and walk in the fresh air and that would make him healthier. Clara was reading a biography of William Cullen Bryant[6] to Livy and read a passage that Livy said Clara should read to her father. The passage was about how Bryant, although in his eighties, rose early every morning and went for a brisk walk. Twain at the time was 66.

In reply, Mark sent a note to Livy:

Feb. 14 — being St. Valentine's Day.

And so this is to be my Valentine — my especial Valentine and darling and best beloved — with kisses therewith, and many! I have read that half page. Mr. Bryant was wonderful to those early risings, and all that at eighty. If ever I get to be eighty, I mean to do them, too.

Sleep well Livy dear — I shall get up as early as I can, and go out and get fresh air.

Goodnight, Dear heart.

Y.

In still another note, Mark referred to a book written by his cousin Jean Webster, called *Daddy Long Legs*:

There, now, my darling, Clara was here a while ago and says I be'aved 'an'some and was a cherub. Praise from Sir Hubert! I wrote that genterman a nice note, "smoring — the thirty years" deaf one who sent me the card I read to you last night.

I read the most of Jean Webster's book today; and the most of what I read greatly pleased me — the workmanship, I mean. It is limpid, bright, sometimes brilliant; it is easy, flowing, effortless, and brimming with girlish spirits; it is light, very light, but so is its subject. Therefore its lightness is not a fault; its humor is genuine and not often overstrained. There are failures in the book, but that happens with all books. Goodnight my Love, and forget thou me not.

Y.

Another note said, "Livy darling, Clara has been here sassing me — will you attend to it? Now, then, I suppose you and I are exactly in tune; when we sleep, we both sleep; when we don't it's similarly mutual—I didn't break a snore between midnight and 8:30. The top of the morning to you Sweetheart."

Still another note (Clara says she doesn't know what episode this refers to):

Livy darling: Here is the Rev. Dr. X. furnishing some spiritualism of a most unaccountable and interesting character. This is the kind of episode that puzzles a body entirely. It isn't telepathy and it isn't clairvoyance; they can explain many, if not most of the spiritualistic wonders, but they are out of court this time. This is an altogether startling and marvelous case. Love.

Y.

Another note to Livy: "Arouse! The spring is here! There is that subtle and heavenly something in the atmosphere which we recognize as Spring; the buds know it, the grass and the animals know it, all Nature knows it and rejoices. And so shall we, and so do we, my Darling. Y."

A note Livy wrote to Mark:

Youth Darling, I am thankful that you "more believe in the immortality of the soul than disbelieve in it." Why are you "vexed" at this? I should think you would be most pleased, now that you believe, or at least do not disbelieve, there is so much that is interesting to work for. An immortality already begun seems to make it worth while to train oneself. However, you don't need to bother about it. "It" will take care of itself. How your reading did move me Sunday night! How sweet and fine you are! How much of immortality you have in your dear blessed self.

Clara says that at this point her father expected her mother to die soon. Howells would later write:

After they had both ceased to be formal Christians, she was still grieved by his denial of immorality, so grieved that he resolved upon one of those heroic lies, which for love's sake he held above even the truth, and he went to her saying that he had been thinking the whole matter over, and now he was convinced that the soul did live after death. It was too late. Her keen vision pierced through his ruse.[7]

Villa di Quarto was in many ways not that different from Villa Viviana, where they had lived a decade earlier. Both were large and grand in design, both near Florence, and the weather was the same. But the landlady at Villa di Quarto was hellish. And the Clemenses were a different family. Susy's death had drained them. And now everyone knew Livy was dying.

Villa di Quarto was also sometimes called Villa Reale di Quarto, Villa Principessa, Villa Granduchessa. It was owned by Countess Massiglia, whom Twain called Satan.

The house was 200 feet long and 60 feet wide. The basement had stalls for horses, and the horses made noise at night because of the flies. The basement also had feed stores, a carriage house, a kitchen that hadn't been used in years, coal rooms, wood rooms, peat rooms, three furnaces, wine rooms, vacant rooms, a cesspool that has been long uncleaned, and other rooms. It extended under the full house.

The first floor had 23 rooms, plus halls and corridors. The second floor had 18 rooms, including a billiards room and a great drawing room. The third, top, floor had 20 bedrooms, arranged 10 on each side with a wide hallway separating them. There was also a furnace. An elevator allowed passage from one floor to another. The floors were made of unpainted brick, and most of the walls were painted yellow. There were three good bedrooms below the top floor, but Twain believed the top-floor bedrooms were unusable because they lacked furniture and were ugly.

Twain, who had grown tired of the physical act of writing, began dictating his autobiography, working in a ground-level room on the east side of the house. He could step out of the house through a ten-foot-high door into a large garden, which was square and level and surrounded by an ornamental iron rail that had vases with flowers on top of it. The garden had a large lawn, with attractive trees, a large fountain in the middle, and numerous rosebushes of various colorings. Beyond the railing was a private park with a curved road leading to the public road. To get to the public road you had to go through an iron gate, but there was no way to communicate with the mansion from the gate. The custom in Italy was to keep such gates locked throughout the night.

The door leading to the garden was made of glass and had heavy shutters to protect it. Three or four inches inside the glass door were thick wooden doors. Each door had a bolt that locked with a handle. There were several of these doors stretching along the east side of the house. The doors led to a parlor, Twain's bedroom, and the 12-by–20-foot reception room where Twain did his work. The reception room was actually part of a 40-foot-long corridor, which led to a dining room, which in turn attached to two other large rooms, each with glass doors leading to the terrace. Inside was 200 feet of carpeting with numerous colors that had no coordination. On the second floor was a large window directly above each door and the same size as the door, and on the top floor a smaller window was directly above each of those windows, for a total of 33 pieces of glass to let in sunlight. The pattern was duplicated on the west side of the house and in nine similar doors and windows on the north and south sides of the house. Despite all these windows, Twain said, the house did not let in much light, perhaps because of what he called the "dismal upholstering of the walls." Livy's bedroom was an exception; it did receive a good deal of sunlight.

The parlor had an arched, frescoed ceiling. Thick pale blue silk with faint figures covered the doors. A pagoda made of porcelain and banded with brass contained a fireplace. The wallpaper was light gray with gold flowers. Red carpet on the floor was covered with four rugs, each a different color. A sofa had green, blue, and red upholstery. Another sofa and two chairs were upholstered in pale green silk. The chairs were made of cheap walnut. A third sofa was French in design and upholstered in strawberry-colored silk, and it had a matching armchair. There was a plain black walnut table without any covering. Under the table was a large, round ottoman that resembled a mushroom, except that it was pale green. A cheap butternut bookcase stood near the doors. There were nine watercolors on the wall and a portrait of the countess in her bridal veil. There was also a portrait of the count and Twain thought he looked handsome and intelligent.

The bookcase had four shelves. The top one contained good literature, but there was no pattern to them. The next shelf contained books on Christian Science and spiritualism, 40 thin volumes. The other two shelves contained 54 bound volumes of *Blackwood's Magazine*, a British publication; the bound volumes dated from 1870. Twain doubted that the countess read the magazines or books on Christian Science and spiritualism. He called her "the most fiendish character I have ever encountered in any walk of life."[8]

The room with the bookcase was referred to as the library. But when the Clemens family stayed there Livy used it once a day for an hour as a parlor. Otherwise doctors wanted her to stay in bed. The parlor/library was on the south side of the house and it had a view of the terrace and the garden. Blue mountains circled around to the west.

The parlor/library was connected to Livy's bedroom and combined they stretched across the south end of the house. Livy's bedroom received heavy doses of sun most of the day. One of the windows in her room had 12 panes of glass, each two feet square. The bedroom was 31 by 24 feet, and long ago there was no wall between it and the library.

Twain's bedroom was also next to the library, on its north side. It was 30 by 22 feet. The room had a large glass door that led to the terrace. Across the middle of his room were pillars, polished white and about as thick as a man's body. They were Doric in design. There was a white marble fireplace with dainty carvings. The wallpaper was cheap, with what Twain called a "loud" pattern. One wall was painted a dull yellow. The carpeting was red, black, yellow, several shades of each. One door opened to a bathroom and another to a small hallway that led to another bathroom. The interior doors, common in Europe for rich and poor, Twain said, were cheap and thin. All doors had gimlet handles (like a medal loop) rather than doorknobs. Anyone wanting to get to the library needed to pass through Twain's bedroom. The room had a salmon-colored sofa of silk, a matching chair, two plain wooden chairs, a stuffed chair, a thin-legged kitchen table, a wardrobe (i.e., movable closet), a bureau, a chest of drawers (pine painted black, with imitation brass handles, and a brass double bedstead. The two wooden doors were covered by hangings, and the three glass doors had curtains parted in the middle. The curtains were a darker yellow than the walls. A yellow canopy was over the bed, and it was the only yellow in the room that Twain liked. On the wall in front of the bed were two large framed photographs of the countess's parents. On another wall hung framed paintings of female angels escorting the departed to heaven.

Above the library was a large bedroom with a stone balcony that offered a magnificent view. Also on the second floor was a large drawing room, about 40 feet square. That room had wall hangings of brocaded silk and a frescoed ceiling. The room would have been attractive except that it had divans, sofas, and chairs scattered about haphazardly and lemon-colored window hangings.

Twain devoted more than 15,000 words to describing the house, an indication of how much attention he paid to its details, which of course is not unusual for writers, but also of how important the house became. He could not separate it from the strong and negative feelings created in him by the countess who owned it. And he knew that his beloved Livy would die in that house.

After he had spent four and a half months in the Villa di Quarto Twain changed his mind about the house. He might want to live there indefinitely. But still he had some complaints. He still did not like the fact that the horses were stabled in the cellar just beneath Livy's bedroom, for example.

But more than anything else, he hated the countess: He wanted her "to move out of Italy; out of Europe; out of the planet. I should want her bonded to retire to her place in the next world and inform me which of the two it was, so that I could arrange for my own hereafter."[9]

The friends who arranged for Twain to rent the villa knew the countess was mean-spirited, but she told them she was moving to Paris. It was a lie. She was having an affair with her manservant and could not afford to take him to Paris with her. Because the countess continued to live on the grounds, above a stable, Twain hunted for someplace else to live, despite having grown to like the villa itself. During the first three weeks of February, Twain looked at about six villas per week but could not find one that was suitable.

He wrote that Livy lost her good health "nineteen months ago, being smitten helpless by nervous prostration complicated with an affection of the heart of several years' standing, and the times since this collapse that she has been able to stand on her feet five minutes at a time have been exceedingly rare."

Two of the villas he examined were as large as Villa di Quarto, but they wouldn't be comfortable for a family of four (Livy and Mark had both clearly grown accustomed to living well). Four of the villas he looked at were at altitudes that the doctors considered wrong, two too high and two too low. Only after examining the other villas did Twain conclude Villa di Quarto might be the best available choice. It had more furniture, its hideous color schemes were less hideous than the others, and it had more conveniences, like more modern bathrooms. Rooms in his villa had about four paintings each, some painted by the countess, and they showed "moderate" talent. One of her paintings was of a man she had an affair with when married to her first husband. She was divorced by that husband and then had married the Italian count in Philadelphia. Twain noted that because of Italian law in the United States she was legally married, but in Italy she was not. One room on the north side had 25 or 30 drawings that she had done; she had studied art. Twain said the drawings were of nudes, the kind typical of what is done in art classes.

The countess was 42 or 43 years old. Various portraits of her scattered around the villa showed that she was once pretty. But now she dyed her hair and needed to wear a great deal of makeup, but even with those aids her personality wouldn't allow her to be pretty anymore. Twain wrote of the countess: "She is excitable, malicious, malignant, vengeful, unforgiving, selfish, stingy, avaricious, coarse, vulgar, profane, obscene, a furious blusterer on the outside and at heart a coward." She had no friends in Florence and was not invited to visit anyone. No one who worked on the estate and no neighbors liked her. The lone exception was her lover, the steward. She once told Twain that when she first bought the estate she evicted every peasant family on it except one. Many of these families had lived in their homes for generations. She also told Twain that she was no longer American but entirely Italian. Her new title of countess was not enough to get her accepted by European royalty, because she had no money. And she lived with her manservant.

Twain's agent in Italy had paid the countess 2,500 francs for the first three months' rent, and this meant the Clemenses could move in on November 1. On that date, the agent tried to move the servants into the villa, but the countess would not permit that, saying an inventory needed to be completed and signed first. She took a week to complete the inventory and during that time removed much of the furniture to her 12-room apartment above the stables and cattle stalls. Livy and Mark and their daughters arrived in Florence on November 7 and stayed in the city for two days to allow Livy to rest up from the tiring railroad trip from Genoa. They made the long drive to the villa by carriage on November 9, and when they entered the house they found there were no fires going in the furnaces or fireplaces. Jean and Katy had gone ahead by a half hour to make certain everything was in shape. They, in particular, wanted to make certain a bed was ready for Livy, but the countess refused to give them the keys to the bedding closets until the inventory had been reviewed and signed. Nor would she tell them where the trunks, sent ahead, had been stored, so they couldn't take bedding from those, either. When Livy and Mark arrived, however, they quickly found the trunks and had the servants make up a bed for Livy. They selected for Livy's bedroom the room with the silken tapestry. However, the countess said the lease forbade any sick person from staying in the room and produced the lease to prove her point, which Twain's lawyer, who was with him, confirmed. The lease gave the countess control over the reservoir, what time the grounds gates were locked, and details that she had orally promised would be under the control of Twain.

Once, a Professor Grocco, an expensive Florence specialist, and his assistant physician arrived at the gates at 6:00 P.M. They were able to enter the grounds only because Grocco's assistant, Dr. Mesti, found another gate open that led into the *podere* (or farm). From there they had to walk nearly a quarter of a mile to reach the villa.

Part of the problem was malice, but also the countess was trying to pressure Twain into buying food and other supplies through her manservant (and lover),[10] so he could make money. She was very direct on this point, telling Twain he was making a mistake in not buying winter fuel, wine, and oil through the manservant. Also, she said, Twain should have let the manservant furnish a cart and horse each day to the cook to go into the city to buy food and should have let him arrange to have the clothes washing done. And when the manservant cut off the Clemenses' water for more than a week, so they had to pay to have water hauled from outside the estate, the countess said the problem was that they were not friendly with him.

The physicians were three or four miles away, in Florence, but because the countess would not allow Twain to install a telephone the physicians lost more than an hour and a half on three occasions in reaching the Clemenses when Livy was in need of their care. Finally the countess did agree a telephone could be installed, but only if she was present when the telephone people arrived, so she could have final say on its location. But the promise was not in writing. A Mr. Cecchi, manager of the bank, made arrangements with the telephone company, and although Twain should have been 28th on the list, Cecchi moved him to the top because of Livy's condition (and perhaps because of Mark Twain's celebrity). The phone was installed, and by the end of January it began to work and worked fine. An hour later, it was dead. Twain asked Mr. Cecchi to find out what the problem was, and he contacted the telephone company, which informed him that the countess was going to sue them for 18 francs for damage caused by erecting a telephone pole on her *podere*. Also, she ordered the telephone company to remove the telephone no later than noon on February 4. Twain asked Cecchi to threaten to sue the telephone company for 25,000 francs if the phone was not made operable. Within an hour, the phone was working. Twain wrote, "I was losing my belief in hell until I got acquainted with the Countess Massiglia."

Livy sometimes talked to Katy about dying.[11] After first arriving in Florence Livy seemed to get better, but that didn't last long. She had a nurse in the daytime, Clara stayed with her in the afternoon, and Katy stayed with her at night. One night Livy said, "Oh, Katy, how I'd love to be in America and have my sister Sue walk in." Another time Livy said, "Katy, I don't think I can live much longer." Usually she was too weak to talk. Livy told Katy how to dress her when she died: in a lavender dress she had had made in New York, a flowing dress of satin trimmed with lace. Katy slept on a bed next to Livy's. When Livy talked of dying, Katy said, "Oh, Mrs. Clemens, don't talk about death. It's too awful. You're not going to die." Livy did not reply.

Katy added, "I know. I realize everything you're telling me, and what you want done, and I'll make everything just as you'd like it."

That same night owls hooted outside the house. Livy said, "Do you hear those owls, Katy. I know that's a sign of death."

Katy said, "Well, that's what they say, but those owls have been there a long time. The priest says they come every year. They have a nest here, and they come back to visit it."

The priest lived next door. He often visited Livy and always had a candle burning on the altar for her. The church bells rang often because there were so many holy days and feast days in Italy and often they rang in the middle of the night, but when the priest found out the ringing disturbed Livy he had them stopped.

Livy told Katy she knew she was going to die, but she didn't tell Mark or her daughters.

Mark was supposed to see Livy only to say good night, but he often broke the rules and came in during the day. She would put her arms around his neck and he'd give her a tender kiss.

One night when Mark visited Livy, he was so encouraged that he went into another room and played the piano and sang the Negro spirituals that Livy loved.

At times Livy believed, with the belief born of hope, that she would get better. Until mid–May. Then, one day, she looked as earnestly as she could into the face of her beloved and loving husband and asked, "You believe I shall get well?"

For five months Twain had looked for a better place to live. On June 4, a Saturday, he heard about a possible villa, and that Sunday he and Jean drove to it, looked it over, and were satisfied. It would cost $30,000 and they could take possession immediately. They returned home at 5:00 P.M. and then Twain waited two hours without hearing anything about Livy. He was allowed three 15-minute visits a day, and that night he went to her room at 7:00 P.M. and told her about the new villa and said he would buy it on Monday if she agreed. She agreed and her face looked radiant. Twain was immensely pleased. For weeks her face had been pale and white.[12]

On Sunday, June 5, 1904, at 7:15 P.M. Mark sat at Livy's bedside while Clara and Jean were having dinner. Livy was "bright and cheerful." Although she wasn't supposed to talk, she asked about the calls Mark and Jean had made and asked about various people, friends and relatives. She smiled a lot. She talked about the house in the country they were planning to move to. When she had first heard about the house, she liked the idea, but then almost immediately she seemed to feel she would never go there. She said that "we must not mind it if we could not go, but be content here." She said she was "sure the heat would not be unbearable." Mark told her it "would never be any hotter than today and [your] room would always be as cool as now."

Katy, always a practicing Catholic, had gone to church that evening.

Mark was supposed to stay only a few minutes and give Livy a brief kiss, but he stayed a full hour. He told her he had done wrong by staying so long, but she said there was "no harm" and she lavished caresses upon him, as she had done for 34 years, and she said, "You will come back?"

He said, "Yes, to say good-night," meaning at 9:30 P.M. He stood, as he usually did, at the door for a few moments, bending inward and throwing kisses. She threw kisses back. She smiled.

He went to the piano, something he had seldom done in the eight years since Susy died, and played and sang Negro hymns. Only Susy and Livy liked his singing. Susy would come into the room and sit and listen to him play and sing. This time, while he was singing, "My Lord he call me! He call me by the thunder!" Jean came quietly into the room and sat down. Mark was surprised. And embarrassed. He stopped playing, but Jean asked him to continue. He sang several songs he thought he had forgotten. Then a servant came and asked Jean to leave. It was 9:15. Mark stopped playing and went to the head of the stairs, where Isabel Lyon met him. Mark thought of something he wanted to say to his wife: "Livy, Jean has paid me a compliment which I have not had since we last...," but he decided not to say that. Susy's name would break Livy's heart. He entered her room. He saw Livy sitting up in bed, but her head was bent forward. She had not been able to lie down for seven months, so Mark was not surprised. Katy had returned from church and was on one side of the bed, the nurse on the other, supporting Livy. Clara and Jean had entered the room and stood near the foot of the bed. Both looked dazed. Mark went close to Livy, bent over, and looked into her face. He may have said something. He was not certain, but Livy, darling Livy, didn't speak to him.

Clara said, "But is it true? Katy, is it true? It can't be true." Katy started to sob, and Mark then understood that Livy had died. The time was 9:20 P.M.

The nurse later told Mark that five minutes earlier Livy had said, "He is singing a good night carol for me." Livy's final words.

Later, Twain would write, "Five times in the last four months [of her life] she spent an hour and more fighting violently for breath, and she lived in the awful fear of death by strangulation. Mercifully she was granted the gentlest and swiftest of deaths — by heart failure."

Katy Leary had a slightly different version of Livy's final moments: Leary had gone to a local Catholic church for the Forty Hours' Adoration, which involved boys carrying candles from church to church. After the service, Katy returned to Livy and asked the nurse, "How is Mrs. Clemens?"[13]

The nurse said, "She is not so well. She's having a bad spell. I am going to give her some oxygen."

Katy went over to Livy, and Livy said, "Oh, I've been awful sick all the afternoon, Katy."

Katy said, "Well, you'll be all right now." Katy held Livy up in her arms and fanned her, and Livy fell over onto Katy's shoulder. Livy drew a short breath, then nothing. She was dead. She had a smile on her face. Katy laid Livy back on her pillow and left the room. She found Clara in the parlor and Clara looked at her and with neither of them speaking Clara knew her mother was dead. Then Katy found Twain in the dining room and looked at him, and neither spoke and, according to Katy, Twain knew his wife was dead. All three went into Livy's room, and Mark ran up to the bed, took her in his arms, and held her for long seconds. Then he laid her down and said, "How beautiful she is, how young and sweet, and, look, she's smiling." Jean had come into the room, and Clara and Jean put their arms around their father's neck and the three of them cried together. Then Jean took one of her father's hands and Clara took the other and they led him from the room. After a while the doctor came.

Livy was 58 years old.

Later Katy dressed Livy as she had promised she would, in the lavender silk dress and the matching stockings and slippers. Livy was laid in a casket in the parlor, and Mark walked back and forth all that night, a Sunday, from his room to Livy's, back and forth. Clara lay on the floor near the casket and cried, and when Katy put her arms around her Clara said, "Oh, no, let me lie here."

Katy said, "No, Miss Clara, no, you've got to go to bed."

Clara said, "Then I'll lie right here on this bed where mamma was." And she laid herself on her mother's bed.

Livy's coffin was taken to a vault and Katy went with it. Mark and the daughters couldn't go because they were too upset. They remained at the villa two more weeks until a steamer was ready to sail. Livy's body was put on the steamer at Genoa. The coffin was put in the hold of the ship.

President Teddy Roosevelt sent word that Customs was not to delay Mark Twain but just to let him pass through.

The funeral was held in the parlor of the Langdon home in Elmira, the same room Livy had been married in 30 years earlier. The Rev. Joseph Twichell, who had married her and then became her friend and who was among her husband's closest friends, performed the funeral sermon. A Reverend Eastman said the prayers. "Nearer, My God, to Thee" was played. At the end, Clara, Katy said, "gave a great cry and threw up her hands" and Mark caught and held her in his arms. He did not speak. When the carriage came, he put Clara and Jean in it.

Three days after Livy died, still in Florence, Twain wrote to Joseph Twichell. It was June 8, 1904, Clara's 30th birthday. Twain wrote that an hour before Livy died she asked him if he found any other villas for sale and that Livy had said she wanted a home of her own and that she was tired and wanted to rest. For six months she had to sit up in bed and couldn't lie down, he wrote, and got little sleep and could sleep only by resting her forehead against a support. When she died, Twain wrote, she looked sweet and young, girlish, like she did 30 years earlier. When she died, her hair turned from gray to its earlier natural color, a light brown. After she died, he sat and caressed her hand for hours. He stopped only when the embalmers arrived. Five times in the final four months of her life she had choked for more than an hour and when she was done she was white, haggard, exhausted, quivering with fright. The family was all present when she died, he told his friend. Her friend. She was chatting and stopped, and it took a few moments, Twain said, for him to realize Livy had died.[14]

Four days after that, on June 12, 1904, he wrote to Howells, saying, "It was too pitiful, these late weeks, to see the haunting fear in her eyes, fixed wistfully upon mine, & hear her say, as pleading for denial & heartening, 'You don't think I am going to die, do you? Oh, I don't want to die.' For she loved life, & so wanted to keep it."[15]

Twain and his daughters could have sailed back to the United States on the *Princess Irene* but did not want to return home on the same ship that had brought them to Italy, so instead they boarded the *Prince Oscar* on June 28.

Livy's body was in a coffin in the hold of the ship. On a separate ship, a freighter, were two horses, the final gifts Livy had given to her daughters. The *Prince Oscar* landed in New York on July 12, and there was no delay in passing through Customs, because of the directive from President Roosevelt. Then to Elmira. Twain lamented, "[T]his funeral march — how sad & long it is."[16]

Memories were shared. On July 21 Twain wrote to thank a friend, Professor Thomas R. Lounsbury,[17] for his words of condolence. Twain wrote, "I know you are right. I know that my loss will never be made up to me in the slightest.... Our love for her was the ordinary love, but added to it was a reverent & quite conscious workshop. Perhaps it was nearly like a subject's feeling for his sovereign."[18] Twain told the professor how their servants "stayed with her till death or marriage intervened. In particular he noted, "Our black George came, a stranger, to wash a set of windows & stayed 18 years. Mrs. Clemens discharged him every now & then, but she was never able to get him to pack his satchel. He always explained that 'You couldn't get along without me, Mrs. Clemens, and I ain't going to try to get along without you.'" When the Clemenses filed for bankruptcy, George offered to work for free, but Livy insisted he accept pay.

In the same letter, Twain noted that he had received letters of sorrow from "shop-girl, postman, & all ranks in life, down to the humblest." He was particularly moved that Patrick McAleer, who had been their coachman for 20 years but who could not attend the funeral, sent $5 from his meager savings asking that white roses be purchased for Mrs. Clemens.

Clara would later write that her father, and she and Jean, had come to "love" Villa di Quarto, but that they couldn't afford to buy it, and that was why she and her father, or sometimes her father and Jean, shopped for another villa. They planned to live the rest of their lives in Florence, she wrote.

The night her mother died, her father wrote in his notebook, "At a quarter past nine this evening she that was the life of my life passed to the relief and the peace of death after twenty-two months of unjust and unearned suffering."

Clara would write of the day of her mother's death, "The Bestower of Peace entered and set my precious Mother free."[19]

Twain's notebook entry for July 14, 1904, the day of Livy's funeral, says, "Funeral private in the house of Livy's young maidenhood. Where she stood as a bride thirty-four years ago there her coffin rested; and over it the same voice that had made her a wife then, committed her departed spirit to God now." Joseph Twichell presided over both the wedding and the funeral of Livy. Both were held in the same room.

Twichell at the funeral cited Robert Browning, without quoting him

directly. Browning had been a favorite of both Livy and Mark, and Mark often
read from Browning to his wife and daughters. Twichell said:

> Robert Browning, when he was nearing the end of his earthly days, said that death
> was the thing that we did not believe in. Nor do we believe in it. We who jour-
> neyed through the bygone years in companionship with the bright spirit now with-
> drawn are growing old. The way behind is long; the way before is short. The end
> cannot bear off. But what of that? Can we not say, each one:
>
> > So long that power hath blessed me, sure it still
> > Will lead me on;
> > O'er moor and fen; o'er crag and torrent, till
> > The night is gone;
> > And with the morn, their angel faces smile,
> > Which I have loved long since, and lost awhile!
>
> And so good-by. Good-by, dear heart! Strong, tender, and true. Good-by until for
> us the morning break and these shadows fly away.

The poem is by John Henry Cardinal Newman.[20]

All the religiosity that accompanies the honoring of a loved one who has
just died is something that reflected what Livy had once believed, then found
difficult to trust, and, as she approached death, returned to.

And Mark, who loved her so, felt ordered by the dictates of devotion to
pay her a similar tribute.

Within a year following Livy's death, Mark wrote a short story in tribute
to her, "Eve's Diary," which was published in *Harper's Bazaar* in December
1905, in the magazine's Christmas issue. It was published as a book by Harper
and Brothers in June 1906. Today it is most often paired with earlier writings
done by Twain and published as "The Diary of Adam and Eve." The line most
often quoted is the final one: Adam says, "Wheresoever she was, *there* was
Eden." And that clearly was intended as a tribute to Twain's departed wife. It
is a piece of sentimentality untypical of his best writing but typical of how he
spoke about his beloved Livy. An earlier quote, however, is closer to Twain's
better, less sentimental writing. It shows an insight into the relation between
many men and women, one that he understood was involved in Livy's love for
him; Eve writes in her diary:

> "[W]hy is it that I love him? *Merely because he is masculine*, I think.... He is
> strong and handsome, and I love him for that, and I admire him and am proud of
> him, but I could love him without those qualities. If he were plain, I should love
> him; if he were a wreck, I should love him; and I would work for him, and slave
> over him, and pray for him, and watch by his bedside until I died. Yes, I think I
> love him, merely because he is *mine* and is *masculine*. There is no other reason, I
> suppose.... [T]his kind of love is not a product of reasonings and statistics. It just
> comes — none knows whence."[21]

After

After Livy died, Jean again began to have epileptic seizures, and Clara had a nervous breakdown. "My health had completely broken down under the strain of death," Clara would later write. "It was determined that I must resort to a life of rest and inactivity, avoiding all forms of excitement or worry, as I was considered to be seriously ill."[22] In July she entered a sanitarium.

Twain leased a home in New York City, at 21 Fifth Avenue in Manhattan. He spent much of each day thinking about Livy. On February 1, 1906, working on his autobiography, he wrote that she had an "unbroken illness of twenty-two months."[23] That "she was always frail in body"; she always was charitable in judging the character of other people. She chose servants quickly. She was always cheerful. He also said that they spent nine years in poverty and that she was always able to keep him from despairing.

Of course their "poverty" was not true poverty. It was the poverty only of having less money than they had once been accustomed to.

She brought up her children, he said, to be cheerful. She showed her affection in kisses, caresses, and endearing comments. In the Hannibal Clemens family, kissing and caresses were rare. She laughed seldom, but when she did it was a girlish laugh. The first time he heard her laugh she had been in a sickbed more than a year: "She was always cheerful.... During the nine years that we spent in poverty and debt she was always able to reason me out of my despairs and find a bright side to the clouds.... In all that time I never knew her to utter a word of regret concerning our altered circumstances, nor did I know her children to do the like."

In addition to her kisses and caresses, she used "a vocabulary of endearments." Twain said he was born "reserved" and that "I never knew a member of my father's family to kiss another member of it except once, and that at a deathbed. And our village was not a kissing community."

Katy Leary eventually returned to Elmira, to live in the same house where she had been born. Mark Twain once suggested that she write her memoirs, but she didn't do that until the mid–1920s, when Mary Lawton, a close friend of Clara, met with Katy to help her. At first Katy, who with modest incorrectness called herself illiterate, resisted, but finally, with Lawton's persistence, she agreed. Katy spoke and Mary transcribed. The result was *A Lifetime with Mark Twain: The Memories of Katy Leary, for Thirty Years His Faithful and Devoted Servant.*[24] Excerpts were first published in *The Pictorial Review* in 1925, and the full transcript was published as a book that same year.

Katy Leary remembered Livy's ability to calm Mark. She wrote:

It was shortly after the telephone invention that I went to Hartford. They had just put it in about that time and it made Mr. Clemens mad, "just to hear the damned thing ring," he said. Yes, that telephone used to make Mr. Clemens wild, because he would hear all right but he couldn't give his message out good. It wasn't very good service those days, and he used to fight the telephone girls all the time. He'd say, "Are you all asleep down there? If you don't give me better service you can send somebody right up here and pull this thing out. I won't have this old thing in the house, it's a nuisance!" One night Mrs. Taft, the wife of Dr. Taft (lovely people that lived in Hartford) she called him up and George answered the telephone first and then he went and called Mr. Clemens. So Mr. Clemens went out to speak to her, but he didn't know who was at the telephone, so he said, "Hello! Hello!" He thought it was one of them hello girls. Mrs. Taft didn't answer him quick enough, so he says, "What the devil's the matter with you down there? Are you all asleep?" And then she said, "Hello," and then he said, "Hello," and then she says, "Hello," and finally he says, "Dammit, how many times more have I got to say hello?" Why he was so mad by then he didn't even hear Mrs. Taft, and he kept shouting, "If I don't get better service than this I am going to have this old thing pulled right out of my house, if I don't get better service from you hello girls down there!" He was swearing and carrying on something awful.

So Mrs. Clemens heard him and opened the dining-room door and put her finger up to her lips, then he stopped swearing and poor Mrs. Taft had a chance to be heard at last. And she says very polite, "Good evening, Mr. Clemens." "Oh," he says, "is this you, Mrs. Taft? Well," he says, "I just this minute come to the telephone! George has been here trying to talk and he's been having such a bad time with this telephone, I had to come and help him and see what I could do."[25]

Katy, who despite what she said was not illiterate and who had in fact read much of what Twain had written, ended her book by saying she hoped to meet Livy and Mark some day in heaven. And Katy closed with a paraphrase of the final line of "The Diary of Adam and Eve": "...any place would be heaven where they was!"[26]

Howells, too, remembered the gentleness of Livy. Shortly after her death, Twain wrote to his friend saying, "I wish I was with Livy."[27] Howells remembered Livy as "a very beautiful woman, classically regular in features, with black hair smooth over her forehead, and with tenderly peering, myopic eyes, always behind glasses, and a smile of angelic kindness." Later, when the two friends were together Howells told Twain how beautiful everyone thought Livy was, how good and wise, and Twain said, with a "breaking" voice, "Oh, why didn't you ever tell her? She thought you didn't like her."[28]

Returning to Hartford without Livy was too difficult for Twain, but he felt obligated to go back when Patrick McAleer, their longtime coachman, died. Twain attended the funeral on February 27, 1906. Twain told a reporter:

Thirty-five years he said it was, but in reality it was ten years less. In making his calculation Patrick counted in the ten years we spent abroad without him.... In all the time he was with Mrs. Clemens and myself he never ran out. I have had other servants who would say, "Mr. Clemens, I forgot and there isn't a cigar in the house," but that never happened with Patrick McAleer, for he never forgot anything and I never had to give him an order. He was just the age of Mrs. Clemens and he entered my employ the day before I was married.[29]

He was asked if while in Hartford he wanted to see his old house: "I don't want to see it. It is peopled with spirits, not only of my own family, but of the old friends whose faces I used to see so often and who are now gone. Strangers come in with rough shod feet and walk over holy ground. No, I don't want to see inside the old house now."[30]

In a letter dated March 8, 1906, Jock Brown, the son of Dr. John Brown, the Scottish doctor and author and friend of Livy and Mark, said he was planning to publish a book of his father's letters that he inherited in 1902 and wanted to know if he could include letters from Livy and Mark, fifteen typewritten pages, which he included in his letter to Twain. Jock wrote, "Though I did not write as I should to you on the death of Mrs. Clemens, I was very sorry to hear of it through the papers, and as I now read these letters, she rises before me, gentle and loveable as I knew her." Twain notes that Livy saved the letters she received from Dr. Brown, although letters she received from others were lost because of the Clemenses' many moves in Europe.[31]

In 1907, Oxford University said it would give Mark Twain an honorary degree and Twain, delighted, but saddened that Livy could not share the honor with him, quickly accepted. He told Clara, "If only Livy could have known of this triumph."[32] In England, he was invited to a garden party at Windsor Castle, where he met the king and queen consort and they let him keep his hat on during the occasion, the only guest permitted that honor. He was Mark Twain. He met George Bernard Shaw, who confessed to being a "Huckamaniac." Twain wasn't alone in receiving honorary doctorates that year from Oxford. Rudyard Kipling, Auguste Rodin, General William Booth, founder of the Salvation Army, and Camille Saint-Saëns also received the degrees, but when Lord Curzon, chancellor of the university, introduced Twain by saying, "Most amiable and charming and playful sir, you shake the sides of the whole world with your merriment," the applause he received was more enthusiastic and lasted longer than for any of the others.[33] Mark Twain at that time may have been the most loved man in the world, and he knew that, and was saddened that the woman who loved him more than anyone else was not there to help him receive the applause.

Once Livy said to Clara, "Oh, Clara, when are you going to get married? We want a baby in this house."[34] Clara did marry, in 1909. Her husband was Ossip Gabrilowitsch, the Russian-born pianist who had been a fellow pupil with her in Vienna. Her father attended the wedding wearing the same academic gown he had been given when receiving his honorary degree at Oxford. His friend, the family friend, the Reverend Joseph Twichell, officiated, just as he had officiated at Livy and Mark's wedding 39 years earlier. Mrs. John B. Stanchfield, a schoolmate of Livy's, was at both weddings, as was Susan Crane. Mrs. Stanchfield "has grown up children now," Twain told a reporter. "She was a slim young girl then, preparing for Vassar. The bride is named for her." Livy, he said, would be happy that Clara married who she did, because "Mrs. Clemens ... always had a warm affection for Gabrilowitsch."[35] Clara and Ossip had a daughter, Nina, the following year. Clara was the only one of the four children of Livy and Mark to have a child.

Jean's epileptic seizures often resulted in bursts of temper, and Isabel Lyon, whom Twain had hired as a secretary for Livy but who became his secretary instead, conspired to have her institutionalized. After Livy died Lyon wanted to marry Mark Twain, and when he wouldn't do that she took over management of his finances. She and a cohort, Ralph Ashcroft, would have drained Twain's finances, but Clara intervened and convinced him to fire Lyon.[36]

Jean's temper, brought on by her epilepsy, made her the child most distant from her parents. Seeking to be closer to her father, she taught herself how to type so she could help him with his manuscripts. After Livy died, Lyon's influence was more than Twain could resist, and at Lyon's suggestion, or insistence, he agreed to have Jean committed to a sanitarium in Katonah, New York, in October 1906. She remained there until April 1909. Again, Clara's influence was instrumental in getting their father to change his mind. Jean, once free of the sanitarium, did become her father's secretary, taking over those duties from Lyon even before Clara managed to get Lyon fired. Before Jean's time as her father's secretary, the two had never been so close. Their relationship was warm and loving.

But on Christmas Eve, 1909, while taking a bath, Jean suffered an epileptic seizure. Either as a direct result of the seizure or because it caused a heart attack, she drowned in the bathtub. Katy Leary, who had told Mark Twain his wife, Livy, had died, now had to tell him his daughter Jean was dead.

Ossip Gabrilowitsch became a well-known composer and conductor of the Detroit Symphony Orchestra. He died in 1936 at age 58. Eight years later, Clara married Jacques Samossoud, another conductor of Russian descent. They lived in Southern California. Clara died in 1962 at age 88.

Mark Twain famously said in 1909, "I came in with Halley's Comet in 1835. It is coming again next year, and I expect to go out with it. It will be the greatest disappointment of my life if I don't go out with Halley's Comet. The

Almighty has said, no doubt: 'Now here are these two unaccountable freaks; they came in together, they must go out together.'" Twain's prediction was accurate. He died at his final home, Stormfield, in Redding, Connecticut, on April 21, 1910. He was 74.[37]

He was buried in Woodlawn Cemetery in Elmira, next to Livy. Nearby are the graves of Langdon, Susy, Clara, and Jean. And Ossip. Near the graves is a 12-foot-tall monument, paid for by Clara, a tribute to both Mark Twain and Ossip Gabrilowitsch.[38]

Nina never married, and never had children. She became an alcoholic and a drug addict. She died in 1966 at age 56. Drugs and alcohol were found in her room, and her death was officially ruled a suicide. She was the last surviving descendant of Olivia Langdon and Samuel Clemens: of Youth and his Livy.

APPENDIX A

Important Dates in the Life of Olivia Langdon Clemens

1845, November 27
Olivia Langdon born in the parlor at home on Main Street in Elmira, New York. The home was at the corner of either West Second or West Third Street. Father is Jervis Langdon, a wealthy man who made his money selling timber and coal. Mother is Olivia Lewis Langdon. Newborn daughter is called Livy. The family would later move to a larger house on East Union Street and eventually build a mansion, in the early 1860s, across the street from the Park Church in downtown Elmira.

1847–1862
Lives in home at what is now 413 Lake Street, Elmira.

1849, November 15
Charles Jervis Langdon, Livy's brother, born November 15.

1855
Attends Miss Thurston's school for girls in Elmira.

1855
Elmira Female College opens. Livy's father among important financial supporters.

1858
Attends Elmira Female College.

1860
Livy, who suffers from a condition of uncertain diagnosis, receives water cure treatment.

1862
Livy treated for partial paralysis.

1863, November 12
Livy begins keeping a commonplace book.

1864 and 1865
Dr. J.R. Newton, a quack doctor, treats Livy. Twain will later inaccurately claim Newton cured her.

1866
Livy undergoes Swedish Movement Cure in New York City.

1867
Mark Twain, while sailing on the *Quaker City* to the Holy Land, meets Charles Langdon, who tells him about his older sister Livy.

1867, December 27
Livy meets Samuel Clemens (introduced by her brother, Charles). On their first date they attend a reading by Charles Dickens in New York City. Her parents and Charles also attend.

1868, August–September
Mark Twain visits Elmira to see Livy.

1868, September (?)
Twain proposes marriage; Olivia says no.

1868, November 26
Twain proposes for the fourth time; Livy says yes; Twain and Livy become secretly engaged.

1869, February 4
The engagement of Livy Langdon to Sam Clemens is publicly announced.

1869
With financial help from Jervis Langdon, Twain buys a one-third interest in the *Buffalo Express.*

1869, May–June
Twain visits Elmira.

1870, February 2
Livy and Mark married in Elmira. Ceremony performed by two Congregational ministers, Joseph Twichell and Thomas K. Beecher (brother of Harriet Beecher Stowe).

1870, February 3
Livy and Mark move to Buffalo, to live in large house bought as surprise wedding present by Jervis (surprise to Twain, not to Livy).

1870, August 6
Father, Jervis, dies of cancer. Livy inherits about one-quarter of her father's million-dollar estate.

1870, September 29
Livy's friend Emma Nye dies of typhoid fever in the Clemenses' Buffalo home.

1870, October 12
Charles Langdon, brother, marries Ida B. Clark.

1870, November 7
Mark and Livy's son, Langdon, born one month prematurely in Buffalo.

1871, February
Livy contracts typhoid fever.

1871, March 2
Twain puts Buffalo house and his interest in the *Buffalo Express* up for sale.

1871, March 18–September
Mark and Livy stay in Elmira with her sister, Susan, and her husband, Theodore, while looking for a home in Hartford, Connecticut.

1871, October 1
Mark and Livy move to Hartford. They rent a house in the Nook Farm section of the city.

1872, March 19
Daughter, Olivia Susan Clemens (called Susy), born in Elmira (at Quarry Farm).

1872, June 2
Son, Langdon, dies in Hartford.

1873, May 17–November 2
Clemens family visits England, Scotland, and Ireland. They meet many literary luminaries, including Robert Browning, Ivan Turgenev, Herbert Spencer, and Anthony Trollope. In August in Edinburgh they meet Dr. John Brown, who becomes a lifelong friend. When the Clemenses return to the United States, Livy is pregnant.

1873, about November 8–January 1884
Twain returns to England alone for a lecture tour with C.W. Stoddard. Twain throughout his marriage to Livy will frequently go on lecture and business trips without Livy, who, because of her frail health, finds traveling exhausting.

1874, April
Family goes to Elmira to spend summer at Quarry Farm, owned by Livy's older, adopted sister, Susan. The Clemens family will spend 20 summers at Quarry farm. (Susan was born in 1836 and adopted by the Langdons in 1839.)

1874, June 8
Clara Langhorne Clemens born in Elmira (at Quarry Farm).

1874, August
The Clemenses visit Twain's mother and sister, Pamela in Fredonia, New York, where they have moved at Twain's suggestion.

1874, September 19
The Clemenses move into the unfinished mansion they have had built in Hartford. They will live in the home until 1891.

1875
George Griffin, a former slave, becomes the Clemens family butler. He will remain in their employ for 16 years, despite several attempts by Livy to fire him. Twain, who frequently argues with him, enjoys his company.

1877, late November or early December
Telephone line installed in Hartford house. It's a direct line to the *Hartford Courant* and is one of the first telephones in a private home in the country.

1878, February 7
Ossip Gabilowitsch born in Russia; in 1909 he will marry Clara Clemens.

1878, April 11
Family sails for England, later to visit Germany, Switzerland, France, Italy, Belgium, and the Netherlands. In Paris they will meet Henry James, James Whistler, and Charles Darwin.

1879, August 23–September 3
The Clemenses sail back to the United States.

1880, July 26
Youngest daughter, Jane Lampton Clemens, born in Elmira; she is called Jean.

1880, October 19
Katy Leary becomes Clemens family maid, a position she will hold for 30 years.

1881
Livy extensively redecorates Hartford home.

1881, April
Twain makes Charles L. Webster, his niece's husband, his business manager; gives Webster power of attorney in publishing interests. During the same year Twain will begin to invest in the Paige typesetting machine.

1882, June
Jean has scarlet fever; home quarantined.

1884
Early in the year all three children come down with mumps.

1884, May
Twain starts Charles L. Webster & Co., a new publishing firm named after his nephew-in-law, to publish *Huckleberry Finn* and other of his books, plus works by other writers.

1885, February 27
Twain signs contract with Ulysses S. Grant for his memoirs.

1885, March 14
Livy's play adaption of *The Prince and the Pauper* is staged in the Clemenses' Hartford home.

1885, March 20
Twain makes Webster partner in his publishing company.

1885
Susy begins to write a biography of her father; Livy discovers it, tells Twain, who says he is very happy with Susy's efforts; Livy tells Susy her father is pleased.

1885, December 1
Webster & Co. issues first volume of Grant's memoirs.

1890, November
Jean, Livy and Mark's youngest daughter, has the first of many epileptic seizures.

1890, November 28
Olivia L. Langdon, Livy's mother, dies.

1891
Bad decisions at the Webster publishing company and the failure of the Paige typesetting machine have drained the Clemens family resources, including much of Livy's inheritance.

1891, June
The Clemens family moves out of their Hartford home and to Europe, where wealthy people can live more cheaply than in the United States. They will move from country to country, including France, Germany, Switzerland, Italy, and England. From late September 1892 to mid–June 1893 they will live near Florence, Italy, where the weather seems to help Livy's health.

1892–1894
During a business trip back to the United States Twain befriends Henry H. Rogers, a robber baron and one of the richest men in the world. Rogers takes over much of the management of Twain's financial interests. He has Twain transfer his copyrights to Livy to protect them from creditors, talks Mark and Livy into declaring bankruptcy, handles negotiations with creditors, and convinces Twain to stop investing in Paige.

1895, July
Twain begins a world tour to pay off his debts. Livy and Clara will accompany him on the tour. Susy and Jean stay in Elmira with Sue Crane. Tour will take Mark, Livy, and Clara west across the northern United States and southern Canada, then to Australia and New Zealand.

1896
Lecture tour continues in Ceylon, India, and South Africa. *Personal Recollections of Joan of Arc* is published; it is the one book by Twain that most reflects Livy's influence. It is also, perhaps, his one book that is most disparaged by critics and scholars.

1896, July–August
Twain, Livy, and Clara arrive in England, expecting Susy and Jean to shortly join them, but learn that Susy is very ill. Livy and Clara sail for the United States while Twain remains in England to look for a home for the family to live in during the coming months. Before Livy reaches home, Susy dies of spinal meningitis (on August 18).

1897, January–July
Family lives in London. In late July they move to Weggis, Switzerland; from September 29, 1897 to May 1898 they will live in Vienna; in Vienna Clara will study music and meet Ossip Gabrilowitsch, a fellow piano student.

1897–1900
Family continues to move around Europe.

End of 1898 or beginning of 1899
Rogers informs Twain that all creditors are paid off.

1900, October 6–14
Family sails to New York.

1900, October–October 1901
Family lives at 14 West 10th Street, New York; later they will move to Riverdale in the Bronx.

1901, March
Livy and Twain unsuccessfully attempt to communicate with Susy through a spiritualist.

1902
Twain invests in Plasmon Company of America, returning to his habit of making bad investments.

1902, Mid-April–Autumn
Livy and Mark buy a home in Tarrytown, New York, and put their Hartford home up for sale.

1902, June 24–October
They vacation in York Harbor, Maine. While there Livy becomes seriously ill and spends long periods in isolation; doctors won't let Twain see her more than a few minutes each day.

1902, October
They return to Riverdale.

1902, November
Twain hires Isabel Lyon as secretary for Livy, but Lyon quickly becomes his secretary.

1903
Livy's health continues to deteriorate; doctors recommend a milder climate.

1903, May
Hartford house sold.

1903, October 24
The Clemenses leave for Florence, Italy, hoping the climate there will help Livy recover.

1903, November 9–June 1904
They live in a villa near Florence.

1903, January–June 5, 1904
Doctors continue to forbid Twain to see Livy except for short visits of a few minutes. He sends her love notes each day.

1904, June 5
Livy dies in Florence, Italy. She will be buried in Elmira on July 14.

1904, June
Clara has nervous breakdown.

1904, July
Clara enters a sanitarium.

1909, December 24
Jean suffers an epileptic seizure and drowns while taking a bath.

1910, April 21
Mark Twain dies.

1962, November 19
Clara dies.

"A Hint to a Young Person, for His Better Improvement by Reading or Conversation" by John Byrom

Livy Langdon copied the first stanza of this poem in her commonplace book when she was a teenager. Byrom was an English poet who lived from 1692 to 1763. He had more success as the inventor of a type of shorthand that was widely used for more than a century than he did as a poet. This poem reflects Livy's attitude towards literature.

In reading Authors, when you find
Bright Passages that strike your Mind,
And which perhaps you may have Reason
To think on at another Season,
Be not contented with the Sight,
But take them down in *Black* and *White*;
Such a Respect is wisely shown
That makes another's Sense one's own.

When you're asleep upon your Bed
A Thought may come into your Head,
Which may be of good use, if taken
Due Notice of when you're awaken;
Of midnight Thoughts to take no heed,
Betrays a sleepy Soul indeed;
It is but dreaming in the Day
To throw our nightly Hours away.

In Conversation, when you meet
With Persons chearful, and discreet,
That speak, or quote, in Prose, or Rhime,
Things or facetious, or sublime,

Observe what passes, and anon,
When you come Home think thereupon;
Write what occurs, forget it not,
A good Thing sav'd 's a good Thing got.

Let no remarkable Event
Pass with a gaping Wonderment,
A Fool's device —*Lord, who would think!*
Commit it safe to Pen and Ink
Whate'er deserves Attention now;
For when 'tis pass'd, you know not how,
Too late you'll find it, to your Cost,
So much of human Life is lost.

Were it not for the written Letter,
Pray, what were living Men the better
For all the Labours of the Dead,
For all that *Socrates* e'er said?
The Morals brought from Heav'n to Men
He would have carried back again:
'Tis owing to his Short-Hand Youth
That *Socrates* does now speak Truth.

APPENDIX C

"God Is Love"
by John Greenleaf Whittier

Livy heard her father, Jervis Langdon, recite excerpts from this poem several times during the weeks preceding his death. It reflects the religiosity that was part of the household in which Livy was raised. It is not a coincidence that both Whittier, a Quaker, and Langdon, a Congregationalist, were drawn to the anti-slavery movement by their religious beliefs.

O friends! with whom my feet have trod
    The quiet aisles of prayer,
Glad witness to your zeal for God
    And love of man I bear.

I trace your lines of argument;
    Your logic linked and strong
I weigh as one who dreads dissent,
    And fears a doubt as wrong.

But still my human hands are weak
    To hold your iron creeds:
Against the words ye bid me speak
    My heart within me pleads.

Who fathoms the Eternal Thought?
    Who talks of scheme and plan?
The Lord is God! He needeth not
    The poor device of man.

I walk with bare, hushed feet the ground
    Ye tread with boldness shod;
I dare not fix with mete and bound
    The love and power of God.

Ye praise His justice; even such
    His pitying love I deem:
Ye seek a king; I fain would touch
    The robe that hath no seam.

Ye see the curse which overbroods
    A world of pain and loss;
I hear our Lord's beatitudes
    And prayer upon the cross.

More than your schoolmen teach, within
    Myself, alas! I know:
Too dark ye cannot paint the sin,
    Too small the merit show.

I bow my forehead to the dust,
    I veil mine eyes for shame,
And urge, in trembling self-distrust,
    A prayer without a claim.

I see the wrong that round me lies,
    I feel the guilt within;
I hear, with groan and travail-cries,
    The world confess its sin.

Yet, in the maddening maze of things,
    And tossed by storm and flood,
To one fixed trust my spirit clings;
    I know that God is good!

Not mine to look where cherubim
    And seraphs may not see,
But nothing can be good in Him
    Which evil is in me.

The wrong that pains my soul below
  I dare not throne above,
I know not of His hate,— I know
  His goodness and His love.

I dimly guess from blessings known
  Of greater out of sight,
And, with the chastened Psalmist, own
  His judgments too are right.

I long for household voices gone,
  For vanished smiles I long,
But God hath led my dear ones on,
  And He can do no wrong.

I know not what the future hath
  Of marvel or surprise,
Assured alone that life and death
  His mercy underlies.

And if my heart and flesh are weak
  To bear an untried pain,
The bruised reed He will not break,
  But strengthen and sustain.

No offering of my own I have,
  Nor works my faith to prove;
I can but give the gifts He gave,
  And plead His love for love.

And so beside the Silent Sea
  I wait the muffled oar;
No harm from Him can come to me
  On ocean or on shore.

I know not where His islands lift
  Their fronded palms in air;
I only know I cannot drift
  Beyond His love and care.

O brothers! if my faith is vain,
  If hopes like these betray,
Pray for me that my feet may gain
  The sure and safer way.

And Thou, O Lord! by whom are seen
  Thy creatures as they be,
Forgive me if too close I lean
  My human heart on Thee!

APPENDIX D

Selected Love Letters of Livy

All of the letters in this section retain the original spelling, punctuation, and grammar of Livy Clemens, with very few exceptions, which are indicated in brackets.

The oldest surviving love letter[1] written by Livy to Mark Twain is dated November 13, 1869, a Saturday, but an interior date, "Sunday morning," indicates most of it was written the next day. It was written in Elmira and mailed to Twain at Danvers, Massachusetts, one of many stops on a lecture tour. It's reprinted here in its entirety. The Tennessee land referred to was purchased by Twain's father in hopes that it would make him rich; it turned out to be a bad investment. The possibility that there might be coal on the land led the Clemens family to hope Jervis Langdon would develop it. Jervis, Livy's father, had made his fortune in Pennsylvania coal. Twain turned his share of the land, an inheritance after his father died, over to his mother and brother Orion. Both Twain's mother and brother would be financially dependent on Twain for the rest of their lives. The Mrs. Brooks referred to near the end was Mrs. Henry Brooks, at whose home, 675 Fifth Avenue, the Langdon family frequently stayed when visiting New York City. The tone of the letter clearly reflects the strong sense of religiosity that was part of Livy's upbringing.

November 13th, 1869 — Elmira

My dear, I am sorry that there has gone no letter to you today, but it has been a very busy day and I could not find the time to write, and now I must send you only a few lines, as it is rather late —

Sunday morning —

I was too stupid to write last night after I had commenced so I put by the letter and went to bed —

I read Father what you wrote about the Tennessee land, he said, it was too bad for your brother to be such a drag to you, he did not make any remark about his working the land, and I did not like to press the matter because I know that he has a good deal on his hands — more than he ought to have, but if you think that I better bring it before him again, I will do so — I am very sorry that your brother is troubled, and

177

very thankful that you are prospered, glad on your account and glad because you can help others — God gives diversities of gifts, he has not given to your brother money making wisdom, but from what you say, he has given him a beautiful spirit never the less — as God prospers us we will not forget Him and allow ourselves to blame those who seem to use less judgment in getting on in this world, but will help just as many people to live their burdens as we are able — You are a good youth to say what you have to your brother about helping him to the money when he cannot get along longer without it because I know that while you are in debt you do not know very well how to spare money, but it is the gifts that really cost us something that are most valuable in Gods sight — We will be the more economical in our way of living, I will look out that I get our dresses and gloves and the like, and we shall be able to help them on — I am glad that your work is doing so well, for two very obvious reasons —

I am so happy so perfectly at rest in you, so proud of the true nobility of your nature — it makes the whole world look so bright to me that I cannot but have a great desire to do all I can to lift the burdens from those who are carrying a heavy load — I feel that I have no burden, that I am so richly cared for, that I cannot but have a tender yearning for those whose backs seem almost broken with the heavy load under which it is bent — we are happy, my dear, therefore we are the better able and must be the more ready to help others — and I know that you are, I wakened this morning, and looked out on the winter landscape which I so dearly love, with the comfort and beauty of my home, with the love of those here and yours which I know to be true and steady even when separated from me, and I felt like dancing, that seemed the most natural way to express it — I believe dancing and singing is a true way to give praise to God — our whole natures seem to enter in them —

It snowed nearly all night last night and this morning the ground and trees were beautifully arrayed in their white garments —

We are all delighted that you are to be with us on New Year's day, I trust that no adversity may come to you —

I was indeed proud and happy that you succeeded so well in Boston —

Don't let your sister stay away from our wedding because she fancies her clothes are not fine enough — We want her, and her daughter here we don't mind about their clothing.

I had a perfectly delightful letter yesterday from Mrs. Brooks she is as lovely and charming as ever —

I would like to write on but I must close this and get ready for Sunday school —

Now and always lovingly Livy

The next letter,[2] written by Livy to her mother, was included in the same envelope in which Mark sent a longer letter to Jervis and Olivia Langdon. It was sent from Buffalo, probably less than two months after Livy and Mark were married. It reflects the crowded social obligations expected of Victorian women in the second half of 19th-century America. It also displays the Victorian custom of a wife referring to her husband, even when writing or speaking to a close relative, as "Mr." The "Cousin Anna" referred to was actually Anna Crane, Livy's sister-in-law, sister of Theodore Crane, Livy's sister's husband. Olive Logan was a well-known actress and playwright.

[March 26, 1870?]

Mother Dear—Cousin Anna, Mr. Clemens, and I are sitting about the Library table. We have been having a pleasant visit—Now Samuel is speaking of Olive Logan—

Our house is just as prettie and pleasant as ever, perhaps a little more so, we want to see you and father here in it—I am sure you will think it is a restful place—

I was out on two calling expeditions last week—I have rec'd about seventy calls—I had a very pleasant call at Mrs. Wadsworths last week—I thought that I called there two weeks ago, but discovered that I went to the wrong home & left my card—Mrs. George Wadsworth has called too—she is also very attractive—Mr. & Mrs. Gray (he is the editor of the Courier) are attractive people, seem as if they might be friends—

Good night
Lovingly Livy—

అనేం

The following letter,[3] written by Livy to Mark after he made a very brief visit back to their Hartford home while on one of his lecture tours, shows how much she missed him during his frequent absences. The baby she refers to is, of course, their son, Langdon. James Meline, referred to in the second paragraph, was seeking Twain's help in getting a book published. The club referred to in the fourth paragraph is probably a ladies auxiliary to a discussion group that Twain belonged to.

Hartford Monday Eve [November 20, 1871]

My Darling—Last night you were here and how much nicer it was than it is tonight when you are away—didn't we have a good visit together? I do hope that this will be the last season that it will be necessary for you to lecture. It is not the way for a husband and wife to live if they can possibly avoid it, is it? Separation comes soon enough—The Pottier and Stymas bill has come, it is $128, I thought it would probably be 150.00 at least—Then the bill on the insurance of our goods against accident $60—so it is well that you left me the additional $150 if you had not I should have run ashore—

I answered all your letters today except the one from Meline that I could not find, if I do not find it I will get his address in some way and write him. It was a pleasure to be writing letters for you it is a pleasure to do any thing for you—

As soon as I had the baby washed and dressed this forenoon I went up in the guest room lay down and slept until two o'clock.

I am going over to the "the club" now in a few minutes I wish you were going with me I rather dread it—I want you along to protect me.

The baby is so sweet and dear, I know as he grows older you and he will love each other like every thing[.] What a wonderful thing love is. I do trust that we shall be a thoroughly united loving family—it certainly is the heaven here below—

Youth in certain things you must teach me a "don't care" spirit, as regards cooks and the like, and I too will endevour to teach myself—I believe there is nothing that sooner ruins the happiness of a family than a worrying woman—

Cubbie is very anxious to have you get home Sat. he hopes that you not fail us on any account—

I hope it is a pleasant evening in Phila. It is rainy and unpleasant here. I have not been out today, I have slept and visited with the baby most of the day —

Mother sits near me at work on her silk quilt. I will try to add a line to this when I come home from Mr Warners

Send Annie's and Sammy's watches to me, so that I can send them with the other gifts — Am home from Mr Ws, will write about it tomorrow — too sleepy tonight

With never ending love

Your Livy

∾⊗⫐∾

The following note[4] was written by Livy to Mark on the back of a letter their ten-year-old daughter, Susy, wrote to her father. It was written more than a decade after the preceding one but still reflects Livy's sadness on being married to a man who is so often gone from home.

[April 23 or April 27, 1882]

Dear Youth — I hoped for a dispatch or letter today. I wonder if you have reached New Orleans safely — I surely hope so.

We are all well. The house seems pretty dull & quiet with no one in it, particularly after the children go to bed, but it is a pleasant change after the rush that we have been in — however I should like you to enjoy it with me.

Good night I love you and am so glad that you are having such a good time.

With deepest love yours

Olivia L. Clemens

∾⊗⫐∾

This next letter[5] shows Livy's determination that she and Mark pay all their debts, her sense that not doing so would be dishonorable and that honor is more important than money. While not inconsistent with views expressed by Mark, it shows none of the hostility towards creditors that was frequently present in his comments. The letter was written from Paris, while Mark was once again away from his family, in New York on a business trip. Etretat is a town on the north coast of France. Mr. Rogers is, of course, Henry Rogers, the robber baron who guided the Clemenses through bankruptcy. Harriet Shelley was the first wife of poet Percy Bysshe Shelley, whom he abandoned to be with Mary Wollstonecraft Godwin; Harriet died a suicide. Twain published an essay about her, "In Defence of Harriet Shelley," in the *North American Review*. *The Golden House* is a novel written by their friend and Hartford neighbor Charles Dudley Warner. The poem in her postscript is "Light" by Francis W. Bourdilon.

Hotel Brighton, 218 Rue de Rivoli, Paris.
July 31st, 1894

Youth darling: We came back from Fontainbleau today. We did hate to leave that lovely spot. It was simply charming there. Susy enjoyed it very much. She has rather dreaded having our travels end, and so have I, for that matter still I believe I shall be glad to get settled in Etretat.

We arrived here a little before one today. We went out this afternoon to get our cup of tea and while we were taking it Miss Dater came into the Café where we were. She had just returned from Etretat, and she told Susy it was perfectly lovely down there. I have been careful not to say one single encouraging thing about the place, but have put forward every-thing that could strike one unpleasantly. The loneliness of the situation of the cottage &c. Thinking it better to let all that was agreeable to be unexpected to her.

Oh darling, I hope you will be able to come soon. Is this going to be an unadvantageous time for you to do business? I do pray not. Is the weather so hot that every one is out of town. I feel that I can not wait while you are waiting for other people. Couldn't you put the work in Mr. Geo. Warner's hands. That is if you find that now is not a good time for you to do it.

In a letter which I rec'd today Sue [Crane] says that they do not yet know whether you are in America or not.

You say that Mr Rogers wanted to ask the creditors 25 cents and that you felt that .20 was enough for Puddin' head Wilson. In that case if I were over there I should probably ask them .10 or .15[.] What we want is to have those creditors get all their money out of Webster & Co. and surely we want to aid them all that is possible. Oh my darling we want those debts paid and we want to treat them all not only honestly, but we want to help them in every possible way. It is money honestly owed and I cannot quite understand the tone which both you & Mr Rogers seem to take — in fact I cannot understand it at all. You say Mr Rogers has said some caustic and telling things to the creditors (I do not know what your wording was) I should think it was the creditors place to say caustic things to us.

My darling I cannot have any thing done in my name that I should not approve. I feel that we owe those creditors not only the money but our most sincere apologies that we are not able to pay their bills when they fall due. When these bills are all paid, as they of course will be, I do not want the creditors to feel that we have in any way acted sharply or unjustly or ungenerously with them. I want them to realize & know, that we had their interest at heart, more, much more than we had our own. You know my darling, *now* is the time for you to add to or mar the good name that you have made. Do not for one moment [let] your sense of our need of money get advantage of your sense of justice & generosity. Dear sweet darling heart! You will not throw this aside thinking that I do not understand will you? You will always consider at every proposition whether it is one that I would approve will you not?

How fine the mention is of your defense of Har[r]iet Shelly. I am delighted that it has rec'd its merited praise. I like it so very much. The Magazine has come to Susy & now tonight I am going to reread the article.

Mr Warner's Golden House I like very much. It will and tellingly I think. We bought a cope of the magazine as ours did not come. I hope the Eng. Number will soon be here. Will you not make inquiries about it? Come back soon my own darling: you are unspeakably dear to me — So is your honor above every thing else. Don't fail to write me freely about everything, machine & all.

We start for Etretat at noon tomorrow.

Good night yours in the deepest love of my heart.

Livy L. C.

P.S. This poem which was in the "Critic" the other day expresses exactly what I feel for you and more finely & truly than I can ever hope to do it.

The night has a thousand eyes
And the day but one
But the light of the whole world dies
With the setting sun.

The mind has a thousand eyes
And the heart but one
But the light of the whole life dies
When love is done.

One letter[6] of uncertain date has provided fuel for scholars who charge that Livy had a censoring impact on Mark's writing. It concerns a letter that Twain wrote, probably in 1902 or a year earlier or later, critical of a writer named Marie Van Vorst. The letter Twain wrote does not survive, but he seems to have intended to send it to a newspaper. Livy read it before he could mail it and wrote the following letter in pencil on both sides of a single sheet of paper. Wecter in *Love Letters* speculates that Livy left it on a table for Mark to find. Van Vorst, interestingly, dedicated a book that she co-wrote with Mrs. John Van Vorst, *Woman Who Toils*, to Twain when it was published in 1903.

Youth darling, have you forgotten your promise to me? You said that I was constantly in your mind and that you knew what I would like & you would not publish what I would disapprove. Did you think I would approve the letter to Marie van Vorst?

I am absolutely wretched today on account of your state of mind — your state of intellect. Why don't you let the better side of you work? Your present attitude will do more harm than good. You go too far, much too far in all you say, & if you write in the same way as you have in this letter people forget the cause for it & remember only the hateful manner in which it was said. Do darling change your mental attitude, try to change it. The trouble is you don't want to. When you asked me to try mental science I tried it & I keep trying it. Where is the mind that wrote the Prince & P. Jeanne d'Arc, The Yankee &c &c &c. Bring it back! You can if you will — if you wish to. Think of the side I know, the sweet dear, tender side — that I love so. Why not show this more to the world? Does it help the world to always rail at it? There is great & noble work being done, why not sometimes recognize that? Why always dwell on the evil until those who live beside you are crushed to the earth & you seem almost like a monomaniac. Oh! I love you so & wish you would listen & take heed. Yours

Livy

Chapter Notes

Preface

1. Willis, *Mark and Livy: The Love Story of Mark Twain and the Woman Who Almost Tamed Him* (New York: Atheneum, 1992).
2. See Lorraine Welling Lanmon, "Quarry Farm: A Study of the 'Picturesque,'" *Quarry Farm Papers*, Elmira College Center for Mark Twain Studies, Elmira, New York, 1991.

Introduction

1. Twain, *Autobiography of Mark Twain*, edited by Harriet Elinor Smith and other editors of the Mark Twain Project (Berkeley: University of California Press, 2010), pp. 346–348; *The Autobiography of Mark Twain*, edited by Charles Neider (New York: Washington Square Press, 1962), pp. 229–232.
2. Mark Twain wrote about his short-lived experiences in the militia, lasting about two weeks, in "The Private History of a Campaign That Failed," a fictionalized version of the events, and his trip out west in *Roughing It*.
3. For Livy's attempt to fire George Griffin, see Willis, *Mark and Livy*, p. 109. Willis notes that when Livy did fire George, the butler simply served the family breakfast the next morning, telling a surprised Livy, "I knew you couldn't get along without me, so I thought I'd better stay a while." Clearly he could not have gotten away with that without Mark's approval. Willis notes: "For the very reasons Clemens liked [George], Livy disliked him — he gambled, he lent money at extortion rates, he lied for his employer by telling callers that Clemens wasn't at home when he was."
4. Susy Clemens, *Papa: An Intimate Biography of Mark Twain, with a Foreword and Copious Comments by Her Father*, edited and with an introduction by Charles Neider (Garden City, NY: Doubleday, 1985), p. 114. Susy died 11 years after Livy told her about the letters, and it's not known if she was ever given permission to read them.
5. See Twain, *Love Letters*.

Chapter One

1. Details about the fall on the ice incident and its aftermath can be found in Twain, *Autobiography* (California), p. 356; Twain, *Autobiography* (Neider), pp. 200–201; Wecter, in Twain, *Love Letters*, p. 6n; and Willis, *Mark and Livy*, pp. 22, 24, 27, 159.
2. The marriage and early years together of Jervis and Olivia Langdon are detailed in Willis, *Mark and Livy*, pp. 13–16.
3. Gretchen Ehle Sharlow, "Love to All the Jolly Household,' A Study of the Cranes of Quarry Farm, Their Lives and Their Relationship with Mark Twain," unpublished masters thesis, Elmira College, Elmira, New York, 1991, pp. 7–8 (the original letter is with the Mark Twain papers in Berkeley).
4. Since the 25th Amendment to the Constitution, which provides in section 2 that if the office of the vice president becomes vacant the president may appoint, with the approval of two-thirds of both houses of Congress, a new vice president, was not ratified until 1967, Madison's plan to appoint a successor to George Clinton to be vice president stood on unclear constitutional grounds.
5. For details of the lives of Jervis and Olivia Langdon, see Willis, *Mark and Livy*, pp. 13–15.
6. For the Panic of 1837, see MacGrane, *The Panic of 1837: Some Financial Problems of the Jacksonian Era*; Aladair Roberts, *America's First Great Depression*; and Brands, *Andrew Jackson*, pp. 332–33, 343, 415, 455–471.
7. For details of the career of Jervis Langdon, see Willis, *Mark and Livy*, pp. 14–15. Willis and most biographies of Mark Twain note that Twain's father, John Marshall Clemens, was particularly damaged by the Panic of 1837. He had

invested much of what little money he had in 100,000 acres of land in Tennessee. With the panic, land prices plummeted and John Marshall Clemens became a very poor man.

8. See Heather A. Wade, "Elmira," *The Encyclopedia of New York State* (Syracuse, NY: New York University Press, 2005).

9. For the Battle of Newtown and Sullivan's March, see Joseph F. Fischer, "Newtown," *The Encyclopedia of New York State*; Fischer, "Sullivan-Clinton Campaign," *The Encyclopedia of New York State;* Christine Sternberg Patrick, "Cherry Valley Raid," *The Encyclopedia of New York State*; and Graymont, *The Iroquois in the American Revolution.*

10. For the Elmira prisoner-of-war camp, see Horigan, *Elmira, Death Camp of the North,* and Meyer, "Elmira Prison Camp."

11. For a history of coal, including the differences in types of coal, see Barbara Freese, *Coal: A Human History* (Cambridge, MA: Perseus, 2003) and Grace Palladino, *Another Civil War: Labor, Capital, and the State in the Anthracite Regions of Pennsylvania, 1840–1868* (New York: Fordham University Press, 2004.

12. For the history of American churches and slavery, see Molly Oshatz, *Slavery and Sin: The Fight Against Slavery and the Rise of Liberal Protestantism* (New York: Oxford University Press, 2011); and Randall Miller, Harry S. Stout, and Charles Wilson, *Religion and the American Civil War* (New York: Oxford University Press, 1998).

13. The quote, of course, is from Lincoln's Second Inaugural Address, delivered on March 4, 1865, in Washington, D.C.

14. See previous note.

15. See Willis, *Mark and Livy,* p. 16.

16. For William Lloyd Garrison, see Henry Mayer, *All on Fire,* and Fredrickson, *William Lloyd Garrison.*

17. For Gerrit Smith, see Harlow, *Gerrit Smith, Philanthropist and Reformer,* and Frothingham, *Gerrit Smith.*

18. For Frederick Douglass, see William S. McFeely, *Frederick Douglass* (New York: Norton, 1991), and Frederick Douglass, *Narrative of the Life of Frederick Douglass, an American Slave* (New York: Barnes and Noble Classics, 2003.

19. For Thomas K. Beecher, see Glenn, *Thomas K. Beecher*; for the Beecher family, see Rugoff, *The Beechers.*

20. For the history of slavery in New York, see Hodges, "Slavery."

21. For the Jerry Rescue, see Eisenstadt, "Jerry Rescue."

22. For John W. Jones, see Reynolds, "Jones, John W(alter)."

23. See Eastman, "Mark Twain in Elmira," pp. 126–147.

24. See Emerson, *The American Scholar,* and Whitman, *Leaves of Grass.*

25. For a history of women's colleges in the United States, see Solomon, *In the Company of Educated Women.*

26. For Livy as a student at Elmira Ladies' Seminary and Elmira College, see Willis, *Mark and Livy,* pp. 18–22.

27. Ibid.

28. Ibid.

29. Barbara Wiggins Taylor, "Education in the Life of Olivia Langdon Clemens," pp. 32–33.

30. The quote is from the Library of Congress Prints and Photographs Online Catalog, Historical American Buildings Survey, Engineering Record, Landscape Survey, and can be found at http://www.loc.gov/pictures/item/NY0556/.

31. For Fowler, see Deitrick, "Fowler."

32. Barbara Wiggins Taylor, "Education in the Life of Olivia Langdon Clemens," p. 38. A perusal of these texts at libraries and online shows they tended to be dictatorial in tone and stressed rules over intellectual engagement.

33. See Byrom, *Miscellaneous Poems.* The full poem, titled "A Hint to a Young Person, for His Better Improvement by Reading or Conversation," appears as appendix B.

34. Barbara Wiggins Taylor, "Education in the Life of Olivia Langdon Clemens," pp. 39–41.

35. Ibid., p. 20.

36. See the Gunnery School Web site, http://portal.gunnery.org/netcommunity.

37. Barbara Wiggins Taylor, "Education in the Life of Olivia Langdon Clemens," pp. 24–25.

38. Ibid., p. 22 (the original letter, dated Nov. 1, 1869, is in the Stowe-Day Library in Hartford).

39. Ibid., pp. 24–25 (the original letter, dated June 7, 1867, is in the Stowe-Day Library in Hartford).

40. Willis, *Mark and Livy,* p. 24.

41. Willis, *Mark and Livy,* pp. 24–25 (the internal quote—"among the well-to-do and the intellectual"—is from Beard, *American Nervousness,* p. 204).

42. See Cayleff, *Wash and Be Healed,* p. 92.

43. Willis, *Mark and Livy,* p. 25 (the internal quotes—"the fast ways..." and "anxiety as to dress..."—are from Gleason, *Talks to My Patients,* pp. 14–17).

44. Gleason, *Talks to My Patients,* pp. 14–17.

45. Willis, *Mark and Livy,* p. 26.

46. See ibid., pp. 26–27, and Cayleff, *Wash and Be Healed,* pp. 67, 72, 76–78, 80–82, 86, 87, 92–94, 102–105, 107, 126, 132, 142, 165–166, 171, 205n, 215n.

47. Willis, *Mark and Livy,* p. 27.

48. Ibid.

49. Barbara Wiggans Taylor, "Education in the Life of Olivia Langdon Clemens," p. 2 (original letter is in the Stowe-Day Library in Hartford).

50. Twain, *Autobiography* (Neider), p. 200, and Twain, *Autobiography* (California), p. 356.

51. Ibid.

52. For a brief biography of Newton, see the editors' note in Twain, *Autobiography*, California, p. 591n. See also World Research Foundation, "Dr. James Rogers Newton and His Gift of Healing," http://www.wrf.org/men-women-medicine/dr-james-newton-healing-gift.php. The World Research Foundation, headquartered in Sedona, Arizona, maintains a Web site dedicated to extolling the virtues of "allopathic medicine alongside complementary and alternative medicine ... ancient and traditional techniques and healing therapies as well as the latest medical technology." Mostly it seems to praise medical techniques used by people whom much of the rest of the world views as quacks. It does provide a 2,150-word biography of Newton, which notes in its opening paragraph that he "was a lineal descendant of John Rogers, who was burned at the stake." (Rogers was burned at the stake in England in 1555, the first Protestant martyr after the Catholic queen Mary I, known as Bloody Mary, ascended to the throne.) Most of the rest of the biography comes unquestioningly from the autobiographical collection, Newton, editor, *The Modern Bethesda*.

53. See the editors' note in Twain, *Autobiography* (California), p. 591n.

54. Andrew Langdon (1835–1919) was Livy's first cousin. See the editors' note in Twain, *Autobiography* (California), p. 591n.

55. See Twain, *Autobiography* (Neider), pp. 200–201, and Twain, *Autobiography* (California), p. 356. Andrew Langdon's use of the word *temporaries,* of course, refers to the common practice of fake healers in all centuries employing people to fake being crippled or blind or possessing some other ailment that could easily be miraculously healed.

56. Ibid.

57. Ibid.

58. Ibid.

59. Willis, *Mark and Livy*, p. 27; Willis, "Clemens, Olivia," pp. 155–158.

60. Ibid.

61. Wecter, in Twain, *Love Letters*, p. 5.

62. Willis, *Mark and Livy*, p. 268.

63. See the editors' note in Twain, *Autobiography* (California), p. 590n.

64. Barbara Wiggans Taylor, "Education in the Life of Olivia Langdon Clemens," p. 38; Taylor's information comes from telephone conversations she had with Skandera on February 7 and April 8, 1991. See also Skandera-Trombley, *Mark Twain in the Company of Women*.

65. Barbara Wiggans Taylor, "Education in the Life of Olivia Langdon Clemens," p. 38 (original letter is in the Stowe-Day Library in Hartford).

66. See the editors' note in Twain, *Autobiography* (California), p. 590n. Also see Newton, *The Modern Bethesda*, p. 294.

67. See the editors' note in Twain, *Autobiography* (California), p. 591n.

68. See note 66 earlier.

69. See the editors' note in Twain, *Autobiography* (California), p. 591n. Their source for this information was Skandera-Trombley, *Mark Twain in the Company of Women*.

70. Barbara Wiggans Taylor, "Education in the Life of Olivia Langdon Clemens," p. 6.

71. Ibid.

72. *Story of a Bad Boy* by Thomas Bailey Aldrich was published in 1870, so Twain, writing in late 1869, probably had an advance copy, since he refers to the "volume." However, the novel was first serialized in *Our Young Folks*, a magazine for teenagers, in 1869, so it's possible that's where he read it. The novel is semi-autobiographical and concerns the adventures and misadventures of a Thomas Bailey, who as a teenager joins a gang of boys in Rivermouth, New Hampshire, where, among other antics, they push a wagon into a bonfire and shoot off a cannon. The novel is often credited with initiating a string of "bad boy" novels in the second half of the 19th century. Although Twain, in his letter, clearly doesn't like Aldrich's semi-autobiographical novel, several of his own works, notably *Tom Sawyer* and *Huckleberry Finn*, fit into the same category.

73. *Gil Blas* was a picaresque novel written by the Frenchman Alain-René Lesage in the early 18th century (it was published in portions and varying versions between 1715 and 1735). It's about a boy born into poverty who as a young man is forced to help a gang of thieves but who eventually works himself up to be secretary to the prime minister and develops a friendship with the king. Mark Twain clearly found much fault with the book but would later acknowledge (in a letter to William Dean Howells) that it had some influence on his writing of both *Tom Sawyer* (he avoided what he saw as Lesage's mistake of taking the protagonist into adulthood and success) and *Huckleberry Finn* (partly copying the essential picaresque structure of the novel).

74. Twain, *Love Letters*, p. 132.

Chapter Two

1. See the editors' note in Twain, *Autobiography* (California), pp. 577n–578n.

2. Susy Clemens, *Papa*, pp. 112–113. *Papa* was first published in 1988; it had been edited

by her father, who retained all of her idiosyncratic spellings and grammatical usages. Twain wrote in his introduction to his daughter's biography of him, "I never had any large respect for good spelling. That is my feeling yet. Before the spelling-book came with its arbitrary forms, men unconsciously revealed shades of their characters and also added enlightening shades of expression to what they wrote by their spelling, and so it is possible that the spelling-book has been a doubtful benevolence to us" (*Papa*, p. 83).

3. Twain, *Autobiography* (California), p. 355. Mrs. Berry is not further identified.

4. Twain, *Autobiography* (Neider), p. 190.

5. Ibid., pp. 190–191.

6. Ibid., p. 190.

7. Mark Twain's height and weight are noted on a sign in the Mark Twain Exhibit in Hamilton Hall on the Elmira College campus in Elmira, New York.

8. See Twain, *Autobiography* (Neider), pp. 200–201, and Twain, *Autobiography* (California), p. 356.

9. The depictions of her by others include writings by Mark Twain, their oldest daughter, Susy, and their second-oldest daughter, Clara.

10. See Plazak, *A Hole in the Ground*.

11. Wecter, in Twain, *Love Letters*, p. 6.

12. For Twain's eventual unpleasant experiences working with Bliss and the American Publishing Company, see Hill, *Mark Twain and Elisha Bliss*.

13. Wecter, in Twain, *Love Letters*, p. 16.

14. Twain's first book, *The Celebrated Jumping Frog of Calaveras County, and Other Sketches*, a collection of 27 short stories, was published in 1867 and gained the author his first national attention.

15. Wecter, in Twain, *Love Letters*, pp. 17–18.

16. For Twain's unusual attire and the Langdons' reaction, see Wecter, in Twain, *Love Letters*, p. 7.

17. Twain, *Love Letters*, pp. 19–21.

18. Ibid., pp. 28–29.

19. Wecter, in Twain, *Love Letters*, p. 35.

20. See Twain, *Autobiography* (California), vol. 1, pp. 357–359, and Twain, *Autobiography* (Neider), pp. 204–207.

21. Editors' note, *Autobiography* (California), vol. 1, p. 591.

22. Twain, *Love Letters*, pp. 22–23.

23. Clara Clemens, *My Father, Mark Twain*, pp. 15–16. Clara puts the quote "(to save her sacred name from the tongues of the gossips)" in parenthesis, while Wecter does not (see Wecter, in Twain, *Love Letters*, p. 23).

24. In a letter dated Dec. 1, 1868, to his older sister, Pamela, Twain wrote that after two recent rejections "I had just been *refused* by my idol a few days before — was refused again afterward — was warned to *quit* after that —& have

won the right at last & am the happiest man alive" (Twain, *Love Letters*, p. 29).

25. Twain, *Autobiography* (California), vol. 1, pp. 358–359; Twain, *Autobiography* (Neider), pp. 206–207.

26. Ibid.

27. Twain, *Autobiography* (California), vol. 1, pp. 357–359; Twain, *Autobiography* (Neider), pp. 204–207.

28. Twain, *Love Letters*, p. 26. Wecter, in a footnote, indicates that he believes the Ed referred to was Ed Bement, an Elmira neighbor of the Langdons. Bement was evidently visiting New York at the time.

29. Twain, *Autobiography* (California), vol. 1, pp. 357–359; Twain, *Autobiography* (Neider), pp. 204–207. Twain wrote in his autobiography: "She was my faithful, judicious and painstaking editor from that day forth until within three or four months of her death — a stretch of more than a third of a century" (California, p. 359; Neider, p. 207).

30. Twain, *Love Letters*, pp. 29–31.

31. Ibid., p. 32.

32. Ibid., pp. 33–34. The bracketed insert, "[English]," was added by Wecter.

33. For Twain's disdain for Cooper's writing, see "Fenimore Cooper's Literary Offenses" in Twain, *The Complete Humorous Sketches and Tales of Mark Twain*, and "Cooper's Prose Style" in *Letters from the Earth*. For his disdain of Scott's writing, see *Life on the Mississippi*, pp. 208–210 (in chapter 46).

34. Wecter, in Twain, *Love Letters*, p. 34.

35. One other thing they had in common was that they came from families that were very concerned with the mistreatment of blacks. Elizabeth Barrett's family's wealth came from plantations in Jamaica that were worked by black slaves. Elizabeth, in fact, came to believe that she had black ancestors, although later genealogists usually disagree. (Other members of her family did, they say, but she did not.) The title of her most famous work derives from her dark complexion and the fact that the Portuguese are often darker skinned than the English. (See Leighton, *Elizabeth Barrett Browning*.)

36. Twain, *Love Letters*, p. 41. Wecter, editor of the love letters, believes Twain simply didn't like the stories in the volume anymore, although he acknowledges that Twain later changed his mind.

37. Ibid.

38. Wecter, in Twain, *Love Letters*, p. 14.

39. Twain, *Love Letters*, pp. 41–42.

40. Wecter, in Twain, *Love Letters*, p. 50n.

41. Twain, *Love Letters*, pp. 42–43.

42. Wecter, in Twain, *Love Letters*, p. 48.

43. Twain, *Love Letters*, p. 52.

44. Ibid., p. 53; *critise* is not a misspelling by

Twain, either deliberate or unintentional; it was a common 19th-century spelling.

45. Twain, *Autobiography* (California), vol. 1, pp. 333–334. (See note 2, this chapter.)

46. Ibid.

47. Wecter, in Twain, *Love Letters*, p. 62.

48. Twain, *Love Letters*, p. 60. The letter in which Livy informed Twain that her parents called him a wanderer does not survive, but he refers to the remark in a letter he wrote to her from Cleveland dated Jan. 24, 1869.

49. Ibid.

50. Ibid., p. 66.

51. Ibid., pp. 67–72.

52. Ibid., p. 76.

53. Ibid., pp. 9, 53. Henry Ward Beecher's sermons were distributed throughout the country as leaflets, with a readership that extended far beyond his Congregationalist denomination.

54. Wecter, in Twain, *Love Letters*, pp. 78–79, 101.

55. Twain, *Love Letters*, pp. 80–82.

56. Wecter, in Twain, *Love Letters*, p. 84. Livy's letter containing the revelation has not survived.

57. Twain, *Love Letters*, p. 84.

58. Ibid., pp. 85–86.

59. Ibid., p. 89.

60. Wecter, in Twain, *Love Letters*, p. 97.

61. Twain, *Love Letters*, p. 93.

62. Wecter, in Twain, *Love Letters*, p. 102.

63. Twain, *Love Letters*, p. 103.

64. Ibid., p. 109.

65. Wecter, in Twain, *Love Letters*, p. 109.

66. Twain, *Love Letters*, pp. 106–109.

67. Ibid., pp. 110–111. Charlie Langdon began his around-the-world trip on September 30, 1869, accompanied by Professor D. R. Ford of Elmira College, who years earlier had tutored Livy in natural philosophy while she was bedridden. Charlie married Ida Clark on October 12, 1870.

68. Wecter, in Twain, *Love Letters*, p. 119. The full text of the letter excerpted appears in appendix D.

69. Twain, *Love Letters*, pp. 119–121.

70. Ibid., p. 126.

71. Ibid., pp. 124–125.

72. Wecter, in Twain, *Love Letters*, p. 127.

73. Twain, *Love Letters*, p. 131.

74. Ibid., p. 132.

Chapter Three

1. Details of the wedding come, mostly, from Willis, *Mark and Livy*, pp. 54–56. Willis's sources include letters Livy sent to Alice Hooker Day dated Nov. 1, 1869, to Joseph Twichell dated Oct. 3, 1869, and to her parents dated Feb. 6, 1870; Twain, *Autobiography* (Neider); and Twain, *Autobiography* (Paine). Additional details come from Varble, *Jane Clemens*, pp. 284–285; Twain, *Autobiography* (California), pp. 320–322, 355, 357–359, 508, 577–578, 591–592; and Wecter, in Twain, *Love Letters*, pp. 4, 142.

2. Varble, *Jane Clemens*, pp. 284–285.

3. Twain, *Love Letters*, pp. 134–137.

4. Varble, *Jane Clemens*, p. 285.

5. For Jane Clemens's move to Fredonia, see ibid., pp. 285–286.

6. Twain, *Autobiography* (California), p. 359.

7. Wecter, in Twain, *Love Letters*, p. 4, citing Twain's Victorian attitudes towards women, concludes that Twain was indeed a virgin at his wedding, despite being 34 years old at the time.

8. Information on Livy and Mark's trip from Elmira to Buffalo and on their arrival in Buffalo comes primarily from Twain, *Autobiography* (California), pp. 321–322, and Twain, *Autobiography* (Neider), p. 203, but also from Wecter, in Twain, *Love Letters*, p. 142; Willis, *Mark and Livy*, pp. 55–57; McCullough and McIntire-Strasburg, *Mark Twain at the* Buffalo Express, p. xxv; Ward, Duncan, and Burns, *Mark Twain: An Illustrated Biography*, pp. 78–82; and Susy Clemens, *Papa*, pp. 114–116.

9. Twain, *Autobiography* (California), p. 322; Twain, *Autobiography* (Neider), p. 203. Twain says in his autobiography that he in fact did scold Slee at the scene, but this was dictated four decades after the fact and seems unlikely, since he would have had to do so within hearing of Jervis Langdon and others.

10. Twain, *Mark Twain at the* Buffalo Express, p. 153. The article appeared in the *Express* on February 19, 1870. Nasby was the pen name of David Ross Locke, a strong supporter of the Union cause in the Civil War and of rights for blacks and women. His fictional creation Petroleum Nasby supported the Confederacy and opposed rights for nearly everyone not like him, but his logic was so flawed he inevitably proved himself obviously wrong. Among Nasby's biggest fans were Mark Twain and Abraham Lincoln, who often quoted him.

11. Ibid., pp. 153–157. Burlingame was also one of the original founders of the Republican Party. He is best remembered, however, for his role in taking a strong stand against one of the most shameful moments in the history of Congress. On May 22, 1856, three days after Senator Charles Sumner of Massachusetts delivered a speech criticizing violence by pro-slavery forces in Kansas and South Carolina senator Andrew Butler for his support of the violence, Sumner was viciously attacked on the floor of the Senate by Preston Brooks, a member of the U.S. House from South Carolina and nephew of Butler. Brooks repeatedly beat Sumner with his part-metal cane, even when the senator fell to the

floor blinded by his own blood. Brooks stopped the beating only when Sumner became unconscious. The House, shamefully, refrained from condemning Brooks, and he was widely praised in Southern newspapers. Burlingame, nearly alone among his colleagues, spoke on the floor of the House to denounce Brooks's cowardly act, and Brooks responded by challenging Burlingame to a duel, saying Burlingame could set the terms of the confrontation. Brooks was surprised when Burlingame called his bluff, selecting rifles as their weapons and Niagara Falls, Canada, as the location (since dueling was illegal everywhere in the United States). Brooks, knowing that Burlingame was an expert shot, failed to show up.

12. Twain, *Love Letters*, pp. 143–144.

13. Wecter, in Twain, *Love Letters*, p. 13.

14. Twain, *Love Letters*, pp. 144–146.

15. Ibid.

16. Ibid., p. 146.

17. McCullough and McIntire-Strasburg, *Mark Twain at the* Buffalo Express, p. 300n.

18. Twain, *Love Letters*, p. 150. McCullough and McIntire-Strasburg, *Mark Twain at the* Buffalo Express, p. 300n., say the number of sales of *Innocents Abroad* had reached 55,000 at the time, suggesting the *Tribune* figure was inaccurate. Twain completed the form that had been left and paid the tax.

19. Twain, *Mark Twain at the* Buffalo Express, "The Mysterious Visit," pp. 166–170.

20. Twain, *Love Letters*. The Mark Twain letters to the Langdons of February 26, 1870, and of March 2, 1870, and excerpts from Livy's letter to her parents (of February 14, 1870) and Jervis Langdon's letter to Twain (of late February or early March 1870) appear on pp. 144–148.

21. Willis, *Mark and Livy*, p. 61. The letter is dated Feb. 6, 1870.

22. Ibid.; Twain, *Autobiography* (California), vol. 1, pp. 360–361.

23. Willis, *Mark and Livy*, p. 62, identifies this poem as "God Is Love," which was in fact one of several titles it obtained. First published in 1867, it is sometimes called "The Eternal Goodness," which is the title Whittier first gave it. It sometimes appears in anthologies with its first line used as the title: "O Friends! With Whom My Feet Have Trod." And parts of it have been adapted as lyrics in hymnals, with music by such composers as Ernst Bacon, Uzziah Christopher Burnap, Charles Hawley, Sidney Homer, W. Imer, Herbert Johnson, W. A. F. Schulthes, and Luigi Zaninelli. It was in fact used as a Congregational hymn in the late 1860s, and it's possible Jervis first heard it at the Park Church. Whittier, a devout Quaker, was, like the Langdons, active in the anti-slavery movement. Excerpts from the poem often appear in anthologies. The full poem appears in appendix C.

24. Ibid., p. 62.

25. Ibid.

26. Ibid.

27. Ibid.

28. Susy Clemens, *Papa*, pp. 118–120; Twain, *Autobiography* (California), p. 373. There are slight differences between the versions of the letter as copied by Susy and as recorded by her father. For example, Susy indicates that the letter was addressed from "The Farm, April 16th/85," while Twain reports it as being addressed from "Quarry Farm. April 16, '85." The version included in this book comes from Susy's *Papa*. Susan Crane was evidently mistaken in describing Judge (H. Boardman) Smith as an executor of the estate; rather he was a witness to the will; also, at the time he was an attorney and not yet a judge (editors, *Autobiography* [California], p. 598). The reference to Grant was no doubt sparked by the fact that their father was at the time helping the general and ex-president write his memoirs, the first ex-president to do so.

29. The song "I Want a Girl Just Like the Girl That Married Dear Old Dad" was written in 1911, with music by Harry Van Tilzer and lyrics by William Dillon, and sold more than 5,000,000 copies in sheet music, at a time when recordings were expensive. It has often been seen as reflecting an Oedipal complex. The title alone, perhaps, makes such speculation inevitable.

30. Twain, *Love Letters*, p. 139. He started writing *Roughing It* in 1870, the year of his marriage, and he had known Livy only two years before the marriage, and much of that time she urged him to quit smoking, something she of course would not have done if he had actually quit. Thus, his claim that he actually quit for her for a year and a half seems unlikely.

31. It's often carelessly reported that Twain served briefly in the Confederate Army and then deserted. Rather, when the war started 25-year-old Sam Clemens, still living in Hannibal, Missouri, and some friends formed an informal militia, some of its members saying they would eventually join the Confederate Army. But Missouri, a slave state, did not secede from the Union (nor did the slave states of Kentucky, Maryland, and Delaware). The "militia" had no contact with the Confederate Army or any Confederate officeholders; it had no guns, and its weapons consisted largely of broomsticks posing as rifles. The militia was together less than two weeks when a rumor reached town that a detachment of the Union Army was coming to Hannibal, causing the militia members to panic and flee into nearby hills. Most came back within a few hours, some a day or two later. The Union Army never showed up, but the militia was dead. Some members of the militia did eventually fight for the Confederacy. Clemens often in later years jokingly said he deserted. More

accurately, he chose not to serve either side, although his older brother, Orion, edited a pro-Lincoln newspaper, which earned him a political appointment as secretary to the governor of the Territory of Nevada. Orion traveled to Nevada in the summer of 1861, shortly after the Civil War started, taking Samuel with him. That trip to the West became the subject of Twain's *Roughing It* (1872). For details of Clemens's time in the "militia," see any book-length biography of Mark Twain; for a concise summary, see Ward, Duncan, and Burns, *Mark Twain*, pp. 26–27. Also, see note 2 to introduction, earlier.

32. Twain, *Love Letters,* pp. 152–153.

33. For details on typhoid fever, see Emmeluth, *Typhoid Fever*. The disease was common in the United States throughout the 18th and 19th centuries and was often spread by contaminated water. Today, according to the Centers for Disease Control, the incidence of typhoid fever in the United States is very low because of the chlorination of public water supplies.

34. Details of Livy nursing Emma come from Wecter, *Love Letters*, p. 155; Twain, *Autobiography* (California), vol. 1, p. 362; and Susy Clemens, *Papa*, pp. 117–118.

35. Twain, *Autobiography* (California), p. 362. Twain refers to a "visitor whose desire Mrs. Clemens regarded as law" and does not name Mrs. Fairbanks, but the editors of the California edition of the autobiography identify the visitor as "apparently Mary Mason Fairbanks" (p. 592). Mrs. Fairbanks had probably stopped in Buffalo on her way back from Charlie's wedding. See, also, Willis, *Mark and Livy*, p. 63.

36. Susy Clemens, *Papa*, pp. 116–117.

37. Clara Clemens, *My Father, Mark Twain*, pp. 209–210. Clara Clemens says this letter is "undated," but it clearly says Jan. 10 on top; she is no doubt referring to the uncertainty of the year. She says (p. 209) that it "was written soon after they were married, judging from the paper and envelope used." Wecter does not include the letter in *Love Letters*, but his checklist in the back of the book places it in 1870. That, however, would place it before Mark and Livy were married. Wecter probably assumed 1870 because Twain lectured in Albany in January of that year. He may or may not have been in Albany in January of 1871. Regardless of the date, the point is that the sentiment — Mark Twain praising Livy for helping him with his writing — was ever present throughout their relationship.

38. Twain, *Autobiography* (California), p. 362. Twain places the Gleason incident at a time when Emma Nye was still alive, but, as the editors of the California edition of the autobiography note, he clearly confused his dates (p. 592). See, also, Willis, *Mark and Livy*, p. 64.

39. Twain, *Love Letters*, pp. 155–157.

40. Ibid., p. 161.

41. Ibid., p. 158.

42. Ibid., p. 159.

43. Willis, *Mark and Livy*, p. 66.

44. Twain, *Love Letters*, p. 162.

45. Ibid., pp. 163–164.

46. Ibid., pp. 164–165. The mother referred to is probably Jane Clemens, who had moved to Hartford, although Livy's mother might also have been visiting Hartford at the time. The full text of the letter excerpted appears in appendix D.

47. Ibid., p. 166.

48. Ibid.

49. Ibid., pp. 167–169.

50. Wecter, in Twain, *Love Letters*, pp. 10–11.

51. Twain, *Love Letters*, pp. 168–169.

52. Ibid., pp. 172–173, 173n.

53. Ibid., pp. 173–174.

54. Ibid, p. 173.

55. Ibid., pp. 174–175. See, also, Willis, *Mark and Livy*, p. 72.

56. Twain, *Autobiography* (California), vol. 1, p. 433; Twain, *Autobiography* (Neider), p. 208.

57. Langdon was a victim of one of the most common causes of death in world history. Millions of people throughout history have died from diphtheria. In the United States, as late as the 1920s, up to 200,000 cases of and 15,000 deaths per year from diphtheria were reported. In 1943, with the Second World War significantly interfering with effective treatment, 50,000 people died from the disease in Europe. In 1925, an outbreak of diphtheria in Nome, Alaska, led to a frantic and largely successful effort to rush serum to inflected patients by dogsled. That event is commemorated every year by the famous Iditarod Trail Sled Dog Race. Children are far more likely to die from diphtheria than adults. Today, because of vaccinations, it is almost non-existent in industrialized countries. In the 21st century in the United States, only two cases were reported in the first 12 years.

58. Susy Clemens, *Papa*, p. 133.

59. Wecter, in Twain, *Love Letters*, p. 175

Chapter Four

1. Wecter, in Twain, *Love Letters*, p. 176.

2. Twain, *Love Letters*, p. 177.

3. Ibid., p. 181.

4. See Wecter, *Love Letters*, p.182, and Willis, *Mark and Livy*, p. 80.

5. Ibid.

6. Sadly for Warner, his best-known saying is often mistakenly attributed to Twain: "Everybody complains about the weather, but nobody ever does anything about it." Twain sometimes used the quote in his lectures but was always careful to credit Warner.

7. Wecter, in Twain, *Love Letters*, p. 184. Miller's birth name was Cincinnatus Heine Miller.

8. Twain, in Susy Clemens, *Papa*, pp. 69–70.

9. Editors, Twain's *Autobiography* (California), vol. 1, p. 581. The only reference to Livy's illness during her trip to Scotland is in her husband's autobiography, written three decades later, and it provides no details of the ailment or the treatment.

10. Twain, *Autobiography* (California) vol. 1, p. 328; Twain, *Autobiography* (Neider), pp. 212–213.

11. Twain, *Love Letters*, pp. 188–189.

12. The house is now a museum. For information about the design of the house, see the museum's Web site at http://www.marktwain house.org/.

13. Willis, *Mark and Livy*, p. 90, places Clara's birth at Quarry Farm, as does Ward, Duncan, and Burns, *Mark Twain: An Illustrated Biography*, p. 96, and most other sources. For reasons that are not explained, the usually authoritative editors of the University of California edition of Twain's *Autobiography* place her birth at Hartford (see vol. 1, p. 656). At another point, however, the editors place her birth at Quarry Farm (p. 480).

14. Salsbury, *Susy and Mark Twain*, p. 31.

15. Information on Quarry Farm and the picturesque movement in the 19th century comes from "Quarry Farm: A Study of the 'Picturesque'" by Lorraine Welling Lanmon, pp. 1–12. Livy Clemens and Susan Crane may also have been familiar with two books by Andrew Jackson Downing that were highly influential in promoting the picturesque aesthetic in the United States: *A Treatise on the Theory and Practice of Landscape Gardening, Adapted to North America*, first published in 1841, and *Cottage Residencies*, first published in 1842. Even if the two Langdon sisters had not read these books, Quarry Farm, as Lanmon points out, clearly reflects the ideas presented in them.

16. The study still exists but has been moved to the campus of Elmira College. It is often open to the public, and even when it's closed visitors can look in through its windows. Quarry Farm is owned by Elmira College but is generally not open to the public. It is made available to scholars doing research on Mark Twain, however. (Our research for this book included a weekend stay at Quarry Farm.) Trees have grown up on the edges of the property and the Chemung River is no longer visible from the front porch or the original site of the study, although much of Elmira and the Pennsylvania hills can still be seen.

17. Howells, *My Mark Twain*, p. 5.

18. Ibid., p. 19.

19. Ibid., p. 48.

20. Wecter, in Twain, *Love Letters*, p. 190.

21. Twain, *Love Letters*, p. 193.

22. Wecter, in Twain, *Love Letters*, p. 194.

23. Twain, *Autobiography* (Neider), pp. 325–326.

24. Ibid., p. 326.

25. Ibid., p. 203.

26. Ibid., pp. 203–204.

27. Twain, *Love Letters*, p. 196.

28. Howells, *My Mark Twain*, p. 12.

29. Information on letters written by Livy to Dr. John Brown and the Clemenses' discussion of death come from Twain, *Autobiography* (California), vol. 1, pp. 434–435 and 635. Jock Brown later asked for and received permission from the Clemenses to reprint parts of their letters in a book he wrote about his father.

30. Twain, *Autobiography* (Neider), p. 218.

31. Twain, *Papa*, p. 75.

32. Twain, *Autobiography* (California), vol. 1, pp. 327, 581.

33. For details of Twain's speech at the John Greenleaf Whittier dinner, see Twain, *Autobiography* (California), pp. 261–264. For details of the letter from Ellen Emerson, see editors' note, Twain, *Autobiography* (California), p. 554.

34. Twain, *Autobiography* (California), vol. 1, pp. 387–396.

35. Twain, *Papa*, pp. 64–67.

36. The story of Katy Leary first meeting Livy comes from Leary, *A Lifetime with Mark Twain*, pp. 3–7. This book was dictated by Leary to Mary Lawton, a friend of Mark Twain. (Lawton believed the Mr. Langdon referred to was Livy's father but is clearly wrong, since Jervis Langdon had died a decade earlier. Livy might have been referring to her brother, Charlie, but more likely Lawton recorded what Leary said incorrectly and Livy said Mr. Clemens would give her the money she needed.)

37. For Livy's support of women's suffrage and Twain's conversion on the issue, see Willis, *Mark and Livy*, pp. 76–78.

38. Leary, *A Lifetime with Mark Twain*, p. 50.

39. Details on Katy's work as a maid with the Clemens family come from ibid., pp. 8–9.

40. Lawton, "Foreword," in ibid., pp. xi–xv.

41. Leary, *A Lifetime with Mark Twain*, pp. 10–11.

42. Details of Susy's suggested punishment, her comment to the nicely dressed lady, and the incidents involving the Japanese fan, Jean's crying, and the gift sled come from Twain, *Autobiography* (California), vol. 1, pp. 329–333. The story of the sled can also be found at Twain, *Papa*, pp. 79–80.

43. Clara Clemens, *My Father, Mark Twain*, p.30.

44. Ibid., p. 32.

45. Ibid., p. 33.
46. The Christmas stories come from ibid., pp. 36–38, 42.
47. Ibid., pp. 42–43.
48. Ibid., pp. 67–68.
49. Ibid., pp. 68–70. In one letter quoted by Clara he writes, "I have long wanted to meet you, get acquainted with you and kill you." Clara does not say who the letter was addressed to or provide a date. It is, of course, likely that Twain was facetious in writing the letter.
50. Ibid., pp. 71–73, 75, 78, 83, 267. Details of Twain seldom eating lunch are quoted by Clara Clemens from a letter he wrote to Livy. Clara doesn't provide a date for the letter, but it was probably written before they were married. But Twain seldom ate lunch throughout his life.
51. Susy Clemens, *Papa*, pp. 90–91; Twain, *Autobiography* (California), vol. 1, pp. 342–344; Twain, *Autobiography* (Neider), pp. 224–225.
52. Twain, in Susy Clemens, *Papa*, pp. 92–93.
53. Ibid., pp. 95–99; Twain, *Autobiography* (California), vol. 1, pp. 343–345. Twain's version of the break-in at his home is no doubt exaggerated for comic effect, but it does illustrate, since a break-in actually occurred and he did resist Livy's efforts to have him take some action, the frustration she sometimes felt with him.
54. Twain, *Autobiography* (California), pp. 346–348; Twain, *Autobiography* (Neider), pp. 229–232. Twain in reporting what his daughters said about him swearing uses the words "they said," but of course it's highly unlikely that all three would use the exact same words.
55. Susy Clemens, *Papa*, pp. 99–100.
56. Twain, in Susy Clemens, *Papa*, pp. 109–110.
57. Susy Clemens, *Papa*, pp. 140–141.
58. Ibid., 194–200.
59. Clara Clemens, *My Father, Mark Twain*, p. 2.

Chapter Five

1. Twain, "The Machine Episode," in *Autobiography* (California), vol. 1, p. 101. Twain wrote this as a separate article and it's not clear that he originally intended to include it in his autobiography, but it is clearly autobiographical in tone and the editors of the California edition did include it; Neider did not include it in his edition.
2. Twain, *Autobiography* (California), vol. 1, p. 455.
3. Twain, "The Machine Episode," in *Autobiography* (California), vol. 1, p. 102.
4. Resa Willis in *Mark and Livy* puts the amount at "over one hundred thousand dollars" (p. 169). Twain in "The Machine Episode" (p. 106; see note 1 earlier, this chapter) refers to "a

full cost of about $150,000." Part of the reason for the inconsistency is that there were multiple contracts signed between Twain and Paige, some of which replaced older ones, some of which were additions. Also, Twain himself seems to have lost track of exactly how much he gave to Paige. And at least some of the money Twain was to give to Paige was to come from future sales of books. The $300,000 figure can be reached only if royalties from future Twain books are counted, but there's no evidence these were ever actually paid to Paige. A figure somewhere around $150,000 is the one most often cited by Twain scholars.
5. Leary, *A Lifetime with Mark Twain*, p. 109.
6. Twain, *Love Letters*, pp. 263–264. Note the sentence "I should greatly prefer appearing in the Century or Harpers." By the early 1890s Livy often referred to his writing in a manner that could be interpreted as her taking joint credit for the authorship, although she never specifically made such a claim.
7. Twain, "The Machine Episode," in *Autobiography* (California), vol. 1, p. 103.
8. Twain, *Autobiography* (California), p. 455.
9. For Twain's dissatisfaction with the Blisses, see Twain, *Autobiography* (California), pp. 300–301, and the editors' note in the same volume on pp. 596–597.
10. Twain, *Autobiography* (California), p. 372.
11. Pope Leo XIII was born in 1810 and died at age 93 in 1903, making him the oldest pope ever. He became pope in 1878, and his 25-year reign was the third longest papacy ever.
12. For Twain's enthusiasm about the biography of Pope Leo XIII, see Willis, *Mark and Livy*, pp. 168–170, 175.
13. For Twain's inventions and smaller investments, see Ward, Duncan, and Burns, *Mark Twain: An Illustrated Biography*, p. 137.
14. *The Kansas City Star*, "The Publisher of Grant's Book."
15. *Columbus* (Georgia) *Enquirer-Sun*, "Grant's Publisher Dead."
16. For the Clemens family trip to Iowa in the summer of 1886, see Willis, *Mark and Livy*, pp. 170–171, and Varble, *Jane Clemens*, pp. 349–350.
17. For the Clemens family stay in Keokuk in the summer of 1886, see Varble, *Jane Clemens*, pp. 349–350. For Mark Twain's view of Mollie, his sister-in-law, see Twain, *Autobiography* (Neider), p. 102.
18. Twain, *Autobiography* (Neider), p. 102.
19. Clara Clemens, *My Father, Mark Twain*, p. 34.
20. Ibid., pp. 35–36.
21. Editor's note, Twain, *Autobiography* (California), vol. 1, p. 632.

22. Olivia Clemens, in Twain, *Love Letters*, p. 284.

23. Leary, *A Lifetime with Mark Twain*, p. 110.

24. Wecter, in Twain, *Love Letters*, p. 249.

25. Dehler, "Blizzard of 1888."

26. Olivia Clemens, in Twain, *Love Letters*, pp. 255–256.

27. For biographical information on Rogers and for his relationship with Twain, see Messent, *Mark Twain and Male Friendship*.

28. For details of Rogers's business advice to Mark Twain, see ibid.; the editors' note in Twain, *Autobiography* (California), vol. 1, p. 192; and the editor's note in Twain, *Autobiography* (Neider), pp. 281–286. Neider says the amount Webster owed to Twain was $65,000. See, also, Willis, *Mark and Livy*, pp. 211–13, 216–220, 223–224, 238, 248–250, 253–254, 261, 264–266, 274, 277.

29. Willis, *Mark and Livy*, p. 212.

30. Olivia Clemens, in Twain, *Love Letters*, pp. 308–309.

31. Ibid., pp. 309–310. The full text of the letter excerpted is included in appendix D.

32. Twain, *Autobiography* (Neider), pp. 287–288.

33. *San Francisco Examiner*, "Mark Twain to Pay All," p. 2. See Twain, *The Complete Interviews*, pp. 185–186.

34. "Twain Programme," *San Francisco Examiner*, August 24, 1895, p. 6. See Twain, *The Complete Interviews*, pp. 190–192.

35. Clara Clemens, *My Father, Mark Twain*, p. 216.

36. Willis, *Mark and Livy*, p. 217.

37. Ibid.

38. Ibid., p. 218.

39. Ibid., p. 215.

40. George Bernard Shaw said Twain's book distorted history because the author was "infatuated" with Joan, and Bernard DeVoto called it "mawkish."

41. Twain, *Autobiography* (Neider), p. 291.

42. Twain, *Personal Recollections of Joan of Arc*, dedication page.

43. *Minneapolis Penny Press*, "Twain," p. 1.

44. For Twain using Susy as his inspiration or model for Joan of Arc, see Hoffman, *Inventing Mark Twain*, p. 396, and Powers, *Mark Twain: A Life*, p. 553. Some critics have also seen traces of Livy in Twain's Joan portrait. And many years later, when Twain befriended Helen Keller, he compared Keller to Joan (see Twain, *Autobiography* [California], p. 466), suggesting that for Twain Joan symbolically represented any admirable woman.

45. *Minneapolis Penny Press*, "Twain," p. 1.

46. The advertisement appeared in *The New York Times* on February 9, 1903, p. 14.

47. Willis, *Mark and Livy*, p. 254.

48. *The New York Times*, "Mark Twain Concern Gives Up the Ghost," page number unknown.

49. Twain, *Autobiography* (Neider), pp. 256–257.

50. Willis, *Mark and Livy*, p. 255.

51. Ibid., p. 97.

52. Leary, *A Lifetime with Mark Twain*, pp. 129–130.

53. Clara Clemens, *My Father, Mark Twain*, pp. 141–142.

54. For Twain's recollections of the tour, see Twain, *Autobiography* (Neider), pp. 354–357. Some of the details of Twain's memory do not match details from other sources, such as newspaper interviews along the way. This is especially true of dates, but the differences in these details do not affect the overall accuracy of his account. However, Twain's memory that Livy and Clara traveled around South Africa with him is not consistent with Clara's memory; see note 70 later, this chapter.

55. Twain, *Autobiography* (Neider), p. 199.

56. *Globe* (Toronto), "Mark Twain Interviewed," p. 1.

57. Low, "Mark Twain: The Humorist's Arrival," p. 4.

58. Low, "A Ramble with Mark Twain: His Views of Men and Things."

59. Becke, "Mark Twain: A Talk About His Books," p. 3. The editor of Twain, *The Complete Interviews*, is not positive Becke was the author of the interview.

60. *Sunday Times* (Sydney, Australia), "A Chat with Mark Twain," p. 4.

61. Low, "Mark Twain," p. 2.

62. *Herald Standard* (Melbourne, Australia), "The Tramp in Melbourne: A Morning with Mark Twain."

63. Clara Clemens, *My Father, Mark Twain*, pp. 150–152.

64. Ibid., p. 152.

65. For details of the trip to India, see ibid., pp. 156–165.

66. Ibid.

67. Ibid.

68. Ibid.

69. Ibid., p. 165.

70. Ibid., p. 166. However, see note 54 earlier, this chapter.

Chapter Six

1. Clara Clemens, *My Father, Mark Twain*, pp. 170–172. As will be noted later, Twain's remembrance of how Livy learned of Susy's death is slightly different from Clara's.

2. Ibid.

3. Twain, in Susy Clemens, *Papa*, pp. 47–48.

4. Ibid.

5. Twain's remembrances of learning of Susy's death can be found in his autobiography; see Twain, *Autobiography* (California), vol. 1, pp. 323–328,and Twain, *Autobiography* (Neider), pp. 351–353.

6. See note 1 earlier, this chapter.

7. See Twain, *Autobiography* (California), pp. 323–328,and Twain, *Autobiography* (Neider), pp. 351–353.

8. For Katy Leary's version of the events following Susy's death, see Leary, *A Lifetime with Mark Twain*, pp. 136–140.

9. There is in fact even a fourth version. *The New York Times* on Sunday, August 23, 1896, carried the following headline: "Learns of Her Daughter's Death / Mrs. Clemens Faints When the News Is Broken to Her." The accompanying story: "Among the passengers who arrived yesterday on the American Line Steamship Paris were the wife and daughter of Samuel L. Clemens (Mark Twain), whose oldest daughter, Olivia Susy Clemens, died on Tuesday night last, at the home in Hartford, Conn. Mr. Clemens, who was expected also, had started, with his wife and Miss Clara, the second daughter, when the news of their eldest daughter's illness reached them, but was detained on business at the last moment in Southampton. He, therefore, was advised of the death by cable while Mrs. Clemens and the sister were on the ocean. They were notified by Dr. [Clarence C.] Rice [a New York physician], a friend of the family, who boarded the Paris at Quarantine. The mother was prostrated and swooned when the news was conveyed to her. A carriage awaited the party at the pier, and they went directly to the grand Central Station. Mr. Clemens sailed from Southampton yesterday for New York." This is the only version that says Livy fainted upon hearing the news. The report that Twain sailed to New York is inaccurate.

10. For Katy Leary's version of events immediately before and after Livy returned to England, see Leary, *A Lifetime with Mark Twain*, pp. 141–145.

11. Editors' note, Mark Twain, *Autobiography* (California), vol. 1, p. 637.

12. Leary, *A Lifetime with Mark Twain*, pp. 148–149.

13. For the famous neighbors of the Clemens family in London, see ibid., pp. 157–160. For additional details of the first time Livy and Samuel Clemens met Kipling, see Twain, *Autobiography* (Neider), pp. 312–314. Kipling eventually became a frequent visitor to upstate New York, because he married an American woman from Rochester, 125 miles to the northwest of Elmira.

14. Twain, in Susy Clemens, *Papa*, pp. 50–56.

15. Clara Clemens, *My Father, Mark Twain*, p. 176.

16. Ibid., p. 177.

17. This conversation is recorded in ibid., pp. 178–180. A blatherskite is a foolish person who bladders a lot.

18. The story of the palmist comes from Leary, *A Lifetime with Mark Twain*, pp. 182–183.

19. Stead, "Character Sketch/Mark Twain," pp. 123–133.

20. For Livy and Mark socializing in Vienna, see Clara Clemens, *My Father, Mark Twain*, pp. 188–195.

21. Ibid., p. 203.

22. Ibid., pp. 204–205.

23. For Livy and Mark's visit with the archduchess, see ibid., pp. 206–208.

24. For Livy's reaction to "What Is Man?" see ibid., pp. 208–209. Clara, oddly, does not mention that the essay was published after her mother died. The essay can be found in Twain, *The Complete Essays of Mark Twain*, pp. 335–399. The title comes from the King James version of the Bible, Psalms, chapter 8, verse 4: "What is man, that thou are mindful of him?"

25. For Livy's reaction to Orion's death, see Willis, *Mark and Livy*, p. 248.

26. For Katy Leary's comment on George the butler, see Clara Clemens, *My Father, Mark Twain*, pp. 211–212.

27. Ibid., pp. 212–213. Clara, in her memoirs, spelled *Hambourg* as *Hamburg*. Gabrilowitsch and Twain would have a close relationship, and the son-in-law requested that when he died he be buried next to his famous father-in-law. Both are interred in Woodland Cemetery in Elmira in the Langdon family plot.

28. Ibid., p. 214.

29. See Leary, *A Lifetime with Mark Twain*, pp. 190–191.

30. Wecter, in Twain, *Love Letters*, pp. 402–403.

31. Twain, *Autobiography* (Neider), p. 409.

32. *Hartford Courant*, "What Mr. Clemens Said," p. 10. The newspaper report does not indicate which daughter asked the question.

33. *New York Herald*, "Mark Twain Home, an Anti-Imperialist," p. 4.

34. Howells, *My Mark Twain*, p. 76.

35. Northrop, "Mark Twain in the Woods," pp. 1–2.

36. Leary, *A Lifetime with Mark Twain*, pp. 214–215.

37. Pendennis (pen name of W. de Wagstaffe), "Mark Twain Bearded in his New York Den by a Camera Fiend," p. 3.

38. Howells, *My Mark Twain*, p. 81.

39. Ibid., pp. 83, 86–87.

40. Ibid., p. 87.

41. For Twain's activities while at Riverdale, see Clara Clemens, *My Father, Mark Twain*, p. 223.

42. For Livy and Mark communicating while at Riverdale, see ibid., pp. 227–231.

43. For keeping Jean's illness a secret from Livy, see ibid., pp. 231–236. A longer and slightly different version of the conversations between Livy and Clara appears in Twain, *Autobiography* (Neider), pp. 362–366.

44. Ibid.

45. Ibid., pp. 237–238.

46. Wecter, in Twain, *Love Letters*, p. 332. Van Vorst (1869–1936) was the daughter of a New York City judge who had instilled in her a desire to reform society. She became a novelist and often championed unions to improve life for working women. Three of her novels were made into silent films: *The Girl from His Town*, 1915; *Big Tremaine*, 1916; and *Mary Moreland*, 1917. The full text of the letter excerpted is included in appendix D.

47. Ibid., p. 333. The Van Vorst letter no longer exists, and it's not known which newspaper Twain intended to send it to.

48. The Missouri degree was one of three honorary doctorates he received. Yale had earlier given him one and Oxford, in England, would later bestow upon him the same honor. In accepting the Missouri degree he said, "I take the same childlike delight in a new degree that an Indian takes in a fresh scalp and I take no more pains to conceal my joy than the Indian does." (See Twain, *Autobiography* [Neider], p. 378.)

49. Willis, *Mark and Livy*, p. 265.

50. For Livy and Mark's trip to Maine, see Twain, *Autobiography* (Neider), pp. 354–357.

51. Ibid.

52. *New York World Magazine*, "My First Vacation and My Last," p. 3.

53. For Howells's comments on his visits to see Livy and Mark in York Harbor, see Howells, *My Mark Twain*, pp. 90–92.

54. For details of Livy and Mark's 1892–1893 stay in Florence, see Twain, *Autobiography* (California), vol. 1, pp. 244–248.

55. For Clara's recollections of the family's first stay in Florence, see Clara Clemens, *My Father, Mark Twain*, pp. 119–120, 126.

Chapter Seven

1. *New York Evening Journal*, "Twain Off Shooting Shafts of Humor," p. 3. Authors and page numbers for *The New York Times* and *The New York American* are unknown; dates for both are October 25, 1903. See Twain, *The Complete Interviews*, p. 487. An amanuensis is a secretary. At this point, Isabel Lyon was still expected to be Livy's secretary. Margaret Sherry, a trained nurse, also made the trip on the *Irene* (see Twain, *Autobiography* [California], p. 540).

2. Twain, *Autobiography* (California), vol. 1, p. 540.

3. For Clara's recollections of the move to Florence, see Clara Clemens, *My Father, Mark Twain*, pp. 240–251. Twain, of course, must have meant *damn*, not *dam*.

4. Mrs. A——was Frances Lloyd Paxton, who became Countess Massiglia when she married Count Annibale Raybaudi Massiglia. It's unclear why Clara did not use the countess's name, since it had appeared in print on numerous occasions in connection with Mark Twain renting the villa from her.

5. Katy Leary provides a slightly different account of the dog story. Leary's version has one dog, not two, and the countess covers it with grease, not kerosene. And the girls are having a tea party, not dinner. Also, Leary does not mention visiting friends. See Leary, *A Lifetime with Mark Twain*, pp. 220–234.

6. Clara Clemens, *My Father, Mark Twain*, pp. 240–251. It's probable that Clara was reading *William Cullen Bryant: A Biographical Sketch, with Selections from His Poems and Other Writings*, by Andrew James Symington, published by Harper and Brothers in New York in 1880. Bryant died in 1878 at age 83.

7. Howells's comments are quoted in Twain, *Love Letters*, p. 345.

8. The description of the Villa di Quarto comes from Twain, *Autobiography* (California), vol. 1, pp. 230–238. The "most fiendish" quote appears on p. 235.

9. For Twain's hatred of Countess Massiglia, see Twain, *Autobiography* (California), vol. 1, pp. 238–244.

10. The exact identity of the manservant is uncertain, but his name may have been Ugo Piemontini. (See editors' caption on photograph of the staff at Villa di Quarto on pages following p. 204 in Twain, *Autobiography* [California].)

11. For Leary's account of her conversations with Livy in Florence, see Leary, *A Lifetime with Mark Twain*, pp. 220–234.

12. Mark Twain's recollections of the events of May and June 1904 can be found in his *Autobiography* (Neider), pp. 372–375.

13. Katy Leary's account of Livy's death can be found in Leary, *A Lifetime with Mark Twain*, pp. 220–234.

14. Twain, *Love Letters*, pp. 348–349.

15. Ibid., p. 349.

16. Willis, *Mark and Livy*, p. 278.

17. Lounsbury (1838–1915) wrote scholarly books about Shakespeare, Chaucer, and others. He was the editor of the *Complete Works of Charles Dudley Warner*, Twain's friend, but Lounsbury's most famous connection to Twain was as the subject of one of one of Twain's jokes. Twain opened his famous essay "Fenimore Cooper's Literary Offenses" with quotes of praise about Cooper from Lounsbury, a Professor Matthews from Columbia University, and

Wilkie Collins. He quotes Lounsbury as saying of *The Pathfinder* and *The Deerslayer*, two of Cooper's most famous books, "The defects of these tales are comparatively slight. They were pure works of art." Twain wrote, "It seems to me far from right for [Lounsbury, Matthews, and Collins] ... to deliver opinions on Cooper's literature without having read some of it. It would have been much more decorous to keep silent and let persons talk who have read Cooper." See Twain, *The Complete Humorous Sketches and Tales of Mark Twain*.

18. For Twain's letter to Lounsbury, see Twain, *Love Letters*, pp. 349–350.

19. Clara's comment on her mother's death, Twain's comment, and Clara's statement that the family had come to love Villa di Quarto can be found in Clara Clemens, *My Father, Mark Twain*, pp. 253–254.

20. Twichell's full quote, including the Cardinal Newman poem, is found in Paine, *Mark Twain: A Biography*, p. 1223. Willis in *Mark and Livy* (p. 273) mistakenly attributes the poem to Browning, probably because Paine, her source, did not clearly indicate that Cardinal Newman wrote it. The excerpt is the final stanza in a three-stanza poem, "The Pillar of the Cloud."

21. Twain, "The Diary of Adam and Eve," in *The Complete Short Stories of Mark Twain*, pp. 273–295. The cited excerpts appear on pp. 294–295.

22. Clara Clemens, *My Father, Mark Twain*, pp. 254–256.

23. Twain's 1906 remembrances of Livy can be found in Twain, *Autobiography* (California), vol. 1, pp. 320–322, and Twain, *Autobiography* (Neider), pp. 200, 202–203.

24. For the background to Mary Lawton helping Katy Leary write *A Lifetime with Mark Twain*, see Lawton, "Foreword," in that book. See also *The New York Times*, "Mark Twain as Seen by His Housemaid."

25. Leary, *A Lifetime with Mark Twain*, pp. 98–99.

26. Ibid., p. 352.

27. Howells, *My Mark Twain*, p. 13.

28. Ibid., p. 87.

29. *Hartford Courant*, "Mark Twain Pays Tribute to Servant," p. 3.

30. Graham, "Mark Twain — Dean of Our Humorists."

31. For Jock Brown's letter to Twain, see Twain, *Autobiography* (California), vol. 1, pp. 429–430. Twain agreed the letters could be published. Jock's actual first name was John, the same as his father's.

32. Clara Clemens, *My Father, Mark Twain*, p. 270.

33. Ward, Duncan, and Burns, *Mark Twain: An Illustrated Biography*, pp. 240, 244. The king of the United Kingdom was then Edward VII, and the queen consort was his wife, Alexandra of Denmark.

34. Leary, *A Lifetime with Mark Twain*, p. 334.

35. *New York Tribune*, "Miss Clemens Weds," p. 7; *New York World*, "Twain's in Oxford Gown at Daughter's Bridal," p. 5.

36. For the story of Isabel Lyon, see Skandera-Trombley, *Mark Twain in the Company of Women*; Skandera-Trombley, *Mark Twain's Other Woman*; Lystra, *Dangerous Intimacy*; and the film *Dangerous Intimacy*, which is based on the Lystra book.

37. The Halley's Comet quote is from Paine, *Mark Twain: A Biography*, p. 1511.

38. *Mark Twain* is a riverboat term meaning the depth of water has been measured at two fathoms, or 12 feet. A statue of Twain on the campus of Elmira College is also 12 feet tall from the base of the podium to the top of his head. So is a nearby statue of Olivia Langdon Clemens.

Appendix D

1. The letters written by Livy to Mark Twain can be found in Twain, *Love Letters*. The first one, the oldest existing letter she wrote to him, appears on pp. 118–121.

2. Ibid., p. 151.

3. Ibid., pp. 164–165.

4. Ibid., pp. 209–210.

5. Ibid., pp. 308–310.

6. Ibid., p. 333.

Bibliography

Aldrich, Thomas Bailey. *Story of a Bad Boy*. Ticknor and Fields, New York, 1870. Available on Project Gutenberg at http://www.gutenberg.org/files/1948/1948-h/1948-h.htm.

Baetzhold, Howard G. *Mark Twain and John Bull: The British Connection*. Indiana University Press, Bloomington, 1970.

Barber, W. Charles. "Mark Twain's Last Visit to Elmira." *Chemung Historical Journal*, October 1987, pp. unnumbered.

Beard, George Miller. *American Nervousness: Its Causes and Consequences: A Supplement to Nervous Exhaustion (Neurasthenia)*. G. P. Putnam's Sons, New York, 1881.

Becke, Louis. "Mark Twain: A Talk About His Books." *Evening News* (Sydney, Australia), September 21, 1895, p. 3. In Mark Twain, *The Complete Interviews*, pp. 213–215. Edited by Gary Scharnhorst. University of Alabama Press, Tuscaloosa, 2006. The editor of the *Interviews* is not positive Becke was the author of the article.

Beecher, Henry Ward. *Notes from Plymouth Pulpit: A Collection of Memorable Passages from the Discourses of Henry Ward Beecher, with a Sketch of Mr. Beecher and the Lecture-Room*. Cornell University Press, Ithaca, NY, 2009. First published in 1895.

Beecher, Thomas K. *Thomas K. Beecher, Teacher of the Park Church at Elmira, New York, 1854–1900*. Park Church, Elmira, NY, 1900. This book, published by Beecher's church shortly after he died, contains tributes to him and some of his sermons.

Bellavance-Johnson, Marsha. *Mark Twain in the U.S.A.* The Computer Lab, Ketchum, ID, 1991.

Benson, Ivan. *Mark Twain's Western Years*. Russell & Russell, New York, 1996.

Brands, H. W. *Andrew Jackson: His Life and Times*. Doubleday, New York, 2005.

Browning, Elizabeth Barrett. *Aurora Leigh*. Ohio University Press, Athens, 1992. First published in 1856.

_____. *Sonnets from the Portuguese and Other Poems*. Hanover House, Garden City, NY, 1954. *Sonnets* was first published in 1850; the other poems in this volume were published at varying dates in the mid–19th century.

Byrom, John. *Miscellaneous Poems*. J. Harrop, Manchester, UK, 1773.

Camfield, Gregg. *The Oxford Companion to Mark Twain*. Oxford University Press, Oxford and New York, 2003.

Cardwell, Guy. *The Man Who Was Mark Twain*. Yale University Press, New Haven, 1991.

Cayleff, Susan E. *Wash and Be Healed: The Water-Cure Movement and Women's Health*. Temple University Press, Philadelphia, 1987.

Clemens, Clara. *My Father, Mark Twain*. Harper & Brothers, New York, 1931.

Clemens, Susy. *Papa: An Intimate Biography of Mark Twain, with a Foreword and Copious Comments by Her Father*. Edited and with an introduction by Charles Neider. Doubleday, Garden City, NY, 1985.

Columbus (Georgia) *Enquirer-Sun, The*. "Grant's Publisher Dead." April 29, 1891. Obituary of Charles L. Webster.

Cooper, Robert. *Around the World with Mark Twain*. Arcade, New York, 2000.

Cotton, Michelle L. *Mark Twain's Elmira, 1870–1910*. Chemung County Historical Society, Elmira, NY, 1985.

Courtney, Steve. *Joseph Hopkins Twichell: The Life and Times of Mark Twain's Closest*

Friend. University of Georgia Press, Athens, 2008.

Cox, Clinton. *Mark Twain, America's Humorist, Dreamer, Prophet: A Biography.* Scholastic, New York, 1995.

Dehler, Gregory. "Blizzard of 1888." In *The Encyclopedia of New York State.* Syracuse University Press, Syracuse, NY, 2005.

Deitrick, John R. "Orson Squire Fowler." In *The Encyclopedia of New York State.* Syracuse University Press, Syracuse, NY, 2005.

De Koster, Katie, editor. *Readings on Mark Twain.* Greenhaven Press, San Diego, 1996.

DeVoto, Bernard. *Mark Twain in Eruption.* Harper & Brothers, New York and London, 1940.

Douglass, Frederick. *Narrative of the Life of Frederick Douglass, an American Slave.* Barnes and Noble Classics, New York, 2003. First published in 1845.

Dworkin, Rachel, Michael Kiskis, Casey Lewis, Kerry Lippincott, Barbara Snedecor, and Amy Wilson. "Mark Twain in Elmira." *Chemung Historical Journal,* December 2010, pp. 6261–6267.

Eastman, Max. "Mark Twain in Elmira." In Robert D. Jerome and Herbert A. Wisbey, *Mark Twain in Elmira.* Mark Twain Society, Elmira, NY, 1977.

Eisenstadt, Peter. "Jerry Rescue." In *The Encyclopedia of New York State.* Syracuse University Press, Syracuse, NY, 2005.

Emerson, Everett. *The Authentic Mark Twain.* University of Pennsylvania Press, Philadelphia, 1984.

_____. *Mark Twain, a Literary Life.* University of Pennsylvania Press, Philadelphia, 1999.

Emerson, Ralph Waldo. *The American Scholar,* Cornell University Press, Ithaca, NY, 1955. First published in 1837.

Emmeluth, Donald. *Typhoid Fever.* Chelsea House Publishers, Philadelphia, 2004.

Fischer, Joseph R. "Newtown, Battle of." In *The Encyclopedia of New York State.* Syracuse University Press, Syracuse, NY, 2005.

_____. "Sullivan-Clinton Campaign." In *The Encyclopedia of New York State.* Syracuse University Press, Syracuse, NY, 2005.

Fishkin, Shelley Fisher. *Lighting Out for the Territory: Reflections on Mark Twain and American Culture.* Oxford University Press, New York, 1997.

Foner, Philip S. *Mark Twain, Social Critic.* International Publishers, New York, 1958.

Fredrickson, George M. *William Lloyd Garrison.* Prentice-Hall, Englewood Cliffs, NJ, 1969.

Freese, Barbara. *Coal: A Human History.* Perseus, Cambridge, MA, 2003.

Frothingham, Octavius Brooks. *Gerrit Smith.* G. P. Putnam's Sons, New York, 1878.

Gaskell, Elizabeth. *The Life of Charlotte Brontë.* E. P. Dutton, New York, 1908. First published in 1857.

Geismar, Maxwell. *Mark Twain: An American Prophet.* Houghton Mifflin, Boston, 1970.

Gleason, Rachel B. *Talks to My Patients; Hints on Getting Well and Keeping Well.* Wood & Holbrook, New York, 1870.

Glenn, Myra C. *Thomas K. Beecher, Minister to a Changing America, 1824–1900.* Greenwood Press, Westport, CT, 1996.

Globe (Toronto). "Mark Twain Interviewed." August 10, 1895, p. 1. In Mark Twain, *The Complete Interviews,* p. 170. Edited by Gary Scharnhorst. University of Alabama Press, Tuscaloosa, 2006.

Goldsmith, Oliver. *The Vicar of Wakefield.* Oxford University Press, New York, 1974. First published in 1766.

Graham, William A. "Mark Twain — Dean of Our Humorists." *Human Life* 3, May 1906.

Graymont, Barbara. *The Iroquois in the American Revolution.* Syracuse University Press, Syracuse, NY, 1972.

Harlow, Ralph Volney. *Gerrit Smith, Philanthropist and Reformer.* Holt, New York, 1939.

Harnsberger, Caroline Thomas. *Mark Twain, Family Man.* Citadel Press, New York, 1960.

Harris, Susan K. *The Courtship of Olivia Langdon and Mark Twain.* Cambridge University Press, New York, 1996.

Hartford Courant. "What Mr. Clemens Said." October 26, 1900, p. 10. In Mark Twain, *The Complete Interviews,* pp. 368–369. Edited by Gary Scharnhorst. University of Alabama Press, Tuscaloosa, 2006.

Herald Standard (Melbourne, Australia). "The Tramp in Melbourne: A Morning with Mark Twain." September 27, 1895, p. 4. In Mark Twain, *The Complete Interviews,* p. 227. Edited by Gary Scharnhorst. University of Alabama Press, Tuscaloosa, 2006.

Hill, Hamlin Lewis. *Mark Twain and Elisha Bliss.* University of Missouri Press, Columbia, 1964.

Hodges, Graham Russell. "Slavery." In *The Encyclopedia of New York State.* Syracuse University Press, Syracuse, NY, 2005.

Hoffman, Andrew. *Inventing Mark Twain.* William Morrow, New York, 1997.

Holmes, Clary W. *The Elmira Prison Camp: A History of the Military Prison at Elmira, N.Y., July 6, 1864 to July 10, 1865.* G. P. Putnam's Sons, New York, 1912.

Horigan, Michael. *Elmira, Death Camp of the North.* Stackpole Books, Mechanicsburg, PA, 2002.

Howells, William Dean. *Mark Twain–Howells Letters.* See Twain, *Mark Twain–Howells Letters.*

_____. *My Mark Twain: Reminiscences.* Harper & Brothers, New York, 1910.

Irving, Washington. *The Life of George Washington.* Twayne Publishers, Boston, 1982. First published 1855–1859.

Jerome, Robert D., and Herbert A. Wisbey. *Mark Twain in Elmira.* Mark Twain Society, Elmira, NY, 1977.

The Kansas City Star. "The Publisher of Grant's Book: He Tells How the General Was Induced to Write—Some New Books—Mark Twain's Cyclopedia of Wit and Humor." June 25, 1887.

Kaplan, Justin. *Mr. Clemens and Mark Twain.* Simon and Schuster, New York, 1966.

_____. *The Singular Mark Twain: A Biography.* Anchor Books, New York, 2005.

Kirk, Connie Ann. *Mark Twain: A Biography.* Greenwood Press, Westport, CT, 2004.

Kiskis, Michael J. "Samuel Clemens' Unmentionable Wound: Langdon Clemens' Death and a Close Reading of Mark Twain's Literary Biography, Part One." *Chemung Historical Journal,* March 2010, pp. 6178–6187.

_____. "Samuel Clemens' Unmentionable Wound: Langdon Clemens' Death and a Close Reading of Mark Twain's Literary Biography, Part Two." *Chemung Historical Journal,* June 2010, pp. 6210–6217.

Langdon, Ida. "My Uncle Mark Twain." *Chemung Historical Journal,* October 1987, pp. unnumbered.

_____. "Three Generations of the Langdon Family." *Chemung Historical Journal,* October 1987, pp. unnumbered. Also published in the same journal in 1958.

Langdon, Jervis. "Mark Twain in Elmira." *Chemung Historical Journal,* October 1987, pp. unnumbered.

Lanmom, Lorraine Welling. "Quarry Farm: A Study of the 'Picturesque.'" *Quarry Farm Papers.* Elmira College Center for Mark Twain Studies, Elmira, NY, 1991.

Lauber, John. *The Inventions of Mark Twain.* Hill and Wang, New York, 1990.

Lawton, Mary. *A Lifetime with Mark Twain: The Memories of Katy Leary, for Thirty Years His Faithful and Devoted Servant.* Harcourt, Brace, 1925.

Leary, Katy *see* Lawton, Mary.

Leighton, Angela. *Elizabeth Barrett Browning.* Indiana University Press, Bloomington, 1986.

LeMaster, J. R., and James D. Wilson, editors. *The Mark Twain Encyclopedia.* Garland Publishing, New York and London, 1993.

Lesage, Alain René. *Gil Blas.* H. Holt, New York, 1938. Originally published in France in portions in the early 18th century.

Lienhard, John H. *Engines of Our Ingenuity.* Oxford University Press, New York, 2000.

Loving, Jerome. *Mark Twain: The Adventures of Samuel L. Clemens.* University of California Press, Berkeley, 2010.

Low, Herbert. "Mark Twain." *Evening News* (Melbourne, Australia), September 26, 1895, p. 2. In Mark Twain, *The Complete Interviews,* pp. 223–224. Edited by Gary Scharnhorst. University of Alabama Press, Tuscaloosa, 2006.

_____. "Mark Twain: The Humorist's Arrival." *Evening News* (Sydney, Australia), September 16, 1895, p. 4. In Mark Twain, *The Complete Interviews,* pp. 199–200. Edited by Gary Scharnhorst. University of Alabama Press, Tuscaloosa, 2006.

_____. "A Ramble with Mark Twain: His Views of Men and Things." *Daily Telegraph* (Sydney, Australia), p. 5. In Mark Twain, *The Complete Interviews,* pp. 209–210. Edited by Gary Scharnhorst. University of Alabama Press, Tuscaloosa, 2006.

Lystra, Karen. *Dangerous Intimacy: The Untold Story of Mark Twain's Final Years.* University of California Press, Berkeley, 2006. See Filmography.

Lyttle, Richard B. *Mark Twain: The Man and His Adventures.* Atheneum, New York, 1994.

MacGrane, Reginald C. *The Panic of 1837: Some Financial Problems of the Jacksonian Era.* University of Chicago, Press, Chicago, 1924.

Mayer, Henry. *All on Fire: William Lloyd Garrison and the Abolition of Slavery.* St. Martin's Press, New York, 1998.

McCullough, Joseph B., and Janice McIntire-Strasburg. See Twain, *Mark Twain at the Buffalo Express.*

McFeely, William S. *Frederick Douglass.* Norton, New York, 1991.

Messent, Peter B. *Mark Twain and Male Friendship: The Twichell, Howells, and Rogers Friendships.* Oxford University Press, New York, 2009.

Meyer, Nathan R. "Elmira Prison Camp." In *The Encyclopedia of New York State.* Syracuse University Press, Syracuse, NY, 2005.

Miller, Randall M., Harry S. Stout, and Charles Reagan Wilson, editors. *Religion and the American Civil War.* Oxford University Press, New York, 1998.

Minneapolis Penny Press. "Twain." July 23, 1895, p. 1.

Neider, Charles. *The Outrageous Mark Twain, and His Rare Controversial Writings.* Doubleday, New York, 1989.

Newton, Alonzo Eliot, editor. *The Modern Bethesda, or, The gift of healing restored. Being some account of the life and labors of Dr. J. R. Newton, healer, with observations on the nature and source of the healing power, and the conditions of its exercise, notes of valuable auxiliary remedies, health maxims, etc.* Newton Publishing Company, New York, 1879.

New York Evening Journal. "Twain Off Shooting Shafts of Humor." October 24, 1903, p. 3.

New York Herald. "Mark Twain Home, an Anti-Imperialist." October 16, 1900, p. 4. In Mark Twain, *The Complete Interviews,* p. 356. Edited by Gary Scharnhorst. University of Alabama Press, Tuscaloosa, 2006.

The New York Times. "Learns of Her Daughter's Death / Mrs. Clemens Faints When the News Is Broken to Her." Sunday, August 23, 1896.

_____. "Mark Twain as Seen by His Housemaid." March 15, 1925.

_____. "Mark Twain Concern Gives Up the Ghost." December 21, 1907, page number unknown.

_____. Plasmon advertisement. February 9, 1903, p. 14.

New York Tribune. "Miss Clemens Weds." October 7, 1909, p. 7.

New York World. "Twain's in Oxford Gown at Daughter's Bridal." October 7, 1909, p. 5.

New York World Magazine. "My First Vacation and My Last." September 7, 1902, p. 3. In Mark Twain, *The Complete Interviews,* pp. 469, 472–473. Edited by Gary Scharnhorst. University of Alabama Press, Tuscaloosa, 2006.

Northrop, W. B. "Mark Twain in the Woods." *New York World Sunday Magazine,* July 21, 1901, pp. 1–2. In Mark Twain, *The Complete*

Interviews, pp. 394–396. Edited by Gary Scharnhorst. University of Alabama Press, Tuscaloosa, 2006.

Oshatz, Molly. *Slavery and Sin: The Fight Against Slavery and the Rise of Liberal Protestantism.* Oxford University Press, New York, 2011.

Paine, Albert Bigelow. *Mark Twain: A Biography.* Harper & Brothers, New York, 1912.

Palladino, Grace. *Another Civil War: Labor, Capital, and the State in the Anthracite Regions of Pennsylvania, 1840–1868.* Fordham University Press, New York, 2006.

Patrick, Christine Sternberg. "Cherry Valley Raid." In *The Encyclopedia of New York State.* Syracuse University Press, Syracuse, NY, 2005.

Pendennis (pen name of W. de Wagstaffe). "Mark Twain Bearded in His New York Den by a Camera Fiend." *New York Herald,* January 20, 1901, section 5, p. 3. In Mark Twain, *The Complete Interviews,* p. 390. Edited by Gary Scharnhorst. University of Alabama Press, Tuscaloosa, 2006.

Plazak, Dan. *A Hole in the Ground with a Liar at the Top: Fraud and Deceit in the Golden Age of American Mining.* University of Utah Press, Salt Lake City, 2006.

Pond, James B. *Overland with Mark Twain: James B. Pond's Photographs and Journal of the North American Lecture Tour of 1895.* Edited by Alan Gribben and Nick Karanovich. Center for Mark Twain Studies, Elmira, NY, 1992.

Powers, Ron. *Mark Twain: A Life.* Free Press, New York, 2005.

Rasmussen, R. Kent. *Mark Twain A to Z.* Facts on File, New York, 1995.

Reigstad, Thomas J. *Scribblin' for a Livin': Mark Twain's Pivotal Period in Buffalo.* Prometheus Books, Amherst, NY, 2013.

Reynolds, Glenn. "Jones, John W(alter)." In *The Encyclopedia of New York State.* Syracuse University Press, Syracuse, NY, 2005.

Roberts, Aladair. *America's First Great Depression: Economic Crisis and Political Disorder After the Panic of 1839.* Cornell University Press, Ithaca, NY, 2012.

Rugoff, Milton. *The Beechers: An American Family in the Nineteenth Century.* Harper & Row, New York, 1981.

Salsbury, Edith Colgate. *Susy and Mark Twain: Family Dialogues: The Intimate Story of a Famous Victorian Family During the Lifetime of Mark Twain's Eldest Daughter.* Harper & Row, New York, 1955.

San Francisco Examiner. "Mark Twain to Pay All." Printed as "Mark Twain's Plan of Settlement," New York Times, August 17, 1895, p. 8. In Mark Twain, The Complete Interviews, pp. 185–186. Edited by Gary Scharnhorst. University of Alabama Press, Tuscaloosa, 2006.

_____. "Twain Programme." August 24, 1895, p. 6.

Shapiro, James. Contested Will: Who Wrote Shakespeare? Simon and Schuster, New York, 2010.

Sharlow, Gretchen Ehle. "'Love to All the Jolly Household': A Study of the Cranes of Quarry Farm, Their Lives and Their Relationship with Mark Twain." Unpublished master's thesis, Elmira College, Elmira, NY, 1991.

Shelden, Michael. Mark Twain: Man in White: The Grand Adventure of His Final Years. Random House, New York, 2010.

Skandera-Trombley, Laura E. Mark Twain in the Company of Women. University of Pennsylvania Press, Philadelphia, 1994.

_____. Mark Twain's Other Woman: The Hidden Story of His Final Years. Alfred A. Knopf, New York, 2010.

Solomon, Barbara Miller. In the Company of Educated Women: A History of Women in Higher Education in America. Yale University Press, New Haven, 1985.

Stead, William T. "Character Sketch/Mark Twain." Review of Reviews (London), August 16, 1897, pp. 123–133. In Mark Twain, The Complete Interviews, pp. 320, 328–329. Edited by Gary Scharnhorst. University of Alabama Press, Tuscaloosa, 2006.

Stowe, Harriet Beecher. "The True Story of Lady Byron's Life, Lady Byron Has Not Spoken at All; Her Story Has Never Been Told." The Atlantic, September 1869.

_____. Uncle Tom's Cabin, or Life Among the Lowly. Many editions, first published as a book in 1852 (it was first serialized in National Era in 1851).

Sunday Times (Sydney, Australia). "A Chat with Mark Twain." September 22, 1895, p. 4. In Mark Twain, The Complete Interviews, p. 218. Edited by Gary Scharnhorst. University of Alabama Press, Tuscaloosa, 2006.

Taylor, Barbara Wiggans. "Education in the Life of Olivia Langdon Clemens." Unpublished master's thesis, Elmira College, Elmira, NY, 1991.

Taylor, Eva. "Langdon-Clemens Plot in Wood-lawn." Chemung Historical Journal, June 1973, pp. 2273–2281.

_____. "Mark Twain's Grave." Chemung Historical Journal, October 1987, pp. unnumbered.

Twain, Mark. The Adventures of Huckleberry Finn. Harper Brothers, New York, 1896.

_____. The Adventures of Tom Sawyer. American Publishing Company, Syracuse, NY, 1892.

_____. The Autobiography of Mark Twain. Edited by Charles Neider. Washington Square Press, New York, 1962.

_____. Autobiography of Mark Twain. Edited by Harriet Elinor Smith and other editors of the Mark Twain Project. University of California Press, Berkeley, 2010.

_____. The Bible According to Mark Twain: Irreverent Writings on Heaven, Eden, and the Flood. Edited by Howard G. Baetzhold and Joseph B. McCullough. University of Georgia Press, Athens, 1995.

_____. The Complete Essays of Mark Twain. Edited by Charles Neider. Doubleday, Garden City, NY, 1963.

_____. The Complete Humorous Sketches and Tales of Mark Twain. Edited by Charles Neider. Doubleday, Garden City, NY, 1961.

_____. The Complete Interviews. Edited by Gary Scharnhorst. University of Alabama Press, Tuscaloosa, 2006. Individual interviews cited in the text are listed separately in the bibliography.

_____. The Complete Short Stories of Mark Twain. Edited by Charles Neider. Bantam, New York, 1971.

_____. A Connecticut Yankee in King Arthur's Court. Bantam, New York, 2005.

_____. Letters from the Earth. Fawcett Publications, Greenwich, CT, 1962.

_____. "Lewis and the Runaway." Chemung Historical Journal, October 1987, pp. unnumbered.

_____. Life as I Find It. Edited by Charles Neider. Perennial Library, New York, 1977.

_____. Life on the Mississippi. Dover, Mineola, NY, 2000.

_____. The Love Letters of Mark Twain. Edited by Dixon Wecter. Harper Brothers, New York, 1949. In the text, when a letter written by Twain or someone else is quoted, Twain is cited. See also Wecter, Dixon, below.

_____. Mainly the Truth, Interviews with Mark Twain. Edited by Gary Scharnhorst. University of Alabama Press, Tuscaloosa, 2009.

_____. Mark Twain at the Buffalo Express:

Articles and Sketches by America's Favorite Humorist. Edited by Joseph B. McCullough and Janice McIntire-Strasburg. Northern Illinois University Press, DeKalb, 1999. See also McCullough, Joseph B., and Janice McIntire-Strasburg.

_____, *Mark Twain-Howells Letters.* Edited by Henry Nash Smith and William M. Gibson, with the assistance of Frederick Anderson. 3 vols. Belknap Press of Harvard University Press, Cambridge, MA, 1960.

_____. *Mark Twain's Autobiography,* vols. 1 and 2. With an introduction by Albert Bigelow Paine. Harper & Brothers, New York, 1924.

_____. *Mark Twain's Letters,* vols. 1 and 2. Edited by Albert Bigelow Paine. Harper & Brothers, New York, 1919.

_____. *Mark Twain's Letters.* Vol. 1, *1853–1866.* Edited by Edgar Marquess Branch, Michael B. Frank, and Kenneth M. Sanderson. University of California Press, Berkeley, 1988.

_____. *Mark Twain's Letters.* Vol. 2, *1867–1868.* Edited by Harriet Elinor Smith and Richard Bucci. University of California Press, Berkeley, 1990.

_____. *Mark Twain's Letters.* Vol. 3, *1869.* Edited by Victor Fischer and Michael B. Frank. University of California Press, Berkeley, 1992.

_____. *Mark Twain's Letters.* Vol. 4, *1870–1871.* Edited by Victor Fischer and Michael B. Frank. University of California Press, Berkeley, 1995.

_____. *Mark Twain's Letters to Mary.* Edited with commentary by Lewis Leary. Columbia University Press, New York, 1961.

_____. *Mark Twain's Notebook.* Prepared for publication with comments by Albert Bigelow Paine. Harper & Brothers, New York and London, 1935.

_____. *Mark Twain's Notebooks & Journals.* Vol. 1, *1855–1873.* Edited by Frederick Anderson, Michael B. Frank, and Kenneth M. Sanderson. University of California Press, Berkeley, 1975.

_____. *Mark Twain's Notebooks & Journals.* Vol. 2, *1877–1883.* Edited by Frederick Anderson, Lin Salamo, and Bernard L. Stein. University of California Press, Berkeley, 1975.

_____. *Mark Twain's Notebooks & Journals.* Vol. 3, *1883–1891.* Edited by Robert Pack Browning, Michael B. Frank, and Lin Salamo. University of California Press, Berkeley, 1979.

_____. *Mark Twain's Own Autobiography, the*

Chapters from The North American Review. With an introduction and notes by Michael J. Kiskis. University of Wisconsin Press, Madison, 1990.

_____. *Mark Twain Speaks for Himself.* Edited by Paul Fatout. Purdue University Press, West Lafayette, 1978.

_____. *Papa: An Intimate Biography of Mark Twain, with a Foreword and Copious Comments by Her Father.* See Clemens, Susy.

_____. *Personal Recollections of Joan of Arc.* Oxford University Press, New York, 1996.

_____. *The Prince and the Pauper.* Barnes & Noble Classics, New York, 2004.

_____. *Pudd'nhead Wilson.* Penguin, London, 1986.

_____. *Roughing It.* Signet Classics, New York, 1962.

_____. *The Selected Letters of Mark Twain.* Edited by Charles Neider. Harper & Row, New York, 1982.

_____. *Tom Sawyer Abroad* and *Tom Sawyer Detective.* Magnum, New York, 1968.

_____. *A Tramp Abroad.* Edited by Charles Neider. Perennial Library, New York, 1977.

_____, and Lee Nelson. *Huck Finn & Tom Sawyer Among the Indians.* Council Press, Springville, UT, 2003.

Varble, Rachel M. *Jane Clemens: The Story of Mark Twain's Mother.* Doubleday, Garden City, NY, 1964.

Wade, Heather A. "Elmira." In *The Encyclopedia of New York State.* Syracuse University Press, Syracuse, NY, 2005.

Ward, Geoffrey C., Dayton Duncan, and Ken Burns. *Mark Twain: An Illustrated Biography.* Knopf, New York, 2001.

Wecter, Dixon, editor. *The Love Letters of Mark Twain.* Harper Brothers, New York, 1949. In the text, when an editor's comment is cited, reference is made to Wecter; if a letter is quoted, its author (Livy Langdon Clemens or Mark Twain) is cited.

Whitman, Walt. *Leaves of Grass.* Barnes & Noble Classics, New York, 2004. The earliest edition of *Leaves of Grass* was published in 1855; it was issued in expanded and revised editions many times while Whitman was alive; the Barnes & Noble Classics edition contains all the poems from all of those editions.

Willis, Resa. "Clemens, Olivia Langdon (1845–1904)." in J. R. LeMaster and James D. Wilson, eds., *The Mark Twain Encyclopedia,* pp. 155–158. Garland Publishing, New York and London, 1993.

_____. *Mark and Livy: The Love Story of Mark Twain and the Woman Who Almost Tamed Him*. Atheneum, New York, 1992.

Filmography

Dangerous Intimacy, The Untold Story of Mark Twain's Final Years," directed and written by *Richard Altomonte*, Entertainment Programs, Inc., 2011, 56 minutes, based on the book of the same title by Karen Lystra.

Mark Twain, directed by Ken Burns, written by Geoffrey C. Warn and Dayton Duncan, PBS, 2001, 212 minutes.

The Thomas Edison film of Mark Twain, the only known film of Mark Twain, shot by Thomas Edison in 1909 in Connecticut, 1 minute, 47 seconds, no sound, http://io9.com/5931709/the-only-existing-video-footage-of-mark-twain-as-filmed-by-thomas-edison.

Websites

Center for Mark Twain Studies, Elmira College, Elmira, New York, http://www.elmira.edu/academics/distinctive_programs/twain_center.

Library of Congress Prints and Photographs Online Catalog, Historical American Buildings Survey, Engineering Record, Landscape Survey, http://www.loc.gov/pictures/item/NY0556/.

The Mark Twain House and Museum, Hartford, Connecticut, http://www.marktwainhouse.org/.

Mark Twain Project Online, Authoritative Texts, Documents, and Historical Research, University of California, http://www.marktwainproject.org/

Mark Twain Quotations, Newspaper Collections, & Related Resources, http://www.twainquotes.com/.

The Official Website of Mark Twain, http://www.cmgww.com/historic/twain/community/tribute.htm.

World Research Foundation, "Dr. James Rogers Newton and His Gift of Healing," http://www.wrf.org/men-women-medicine/dr-james-newton-healing-gift.php.

Index

Whitmore, F.G. 96
Whittier, John Greenleaf 67–68, 87, 175,
    188*n*23
Wilde, Oscar 129
Wilkersons (squirrels) 140
Willis, Resa 25–28, 30–33, 183*Intro*3, 191*n*4
Wilson, Francis 129
Windsor Castle 165

Woman Who Toils 182
Woodlawn Cemetery 19, 68, 77, 125, 167,
    193*n*27
Wooster, Ohio 75
Worcester, Massachusetts 106

York Harbor, Maine 142–143, 173
York River 143